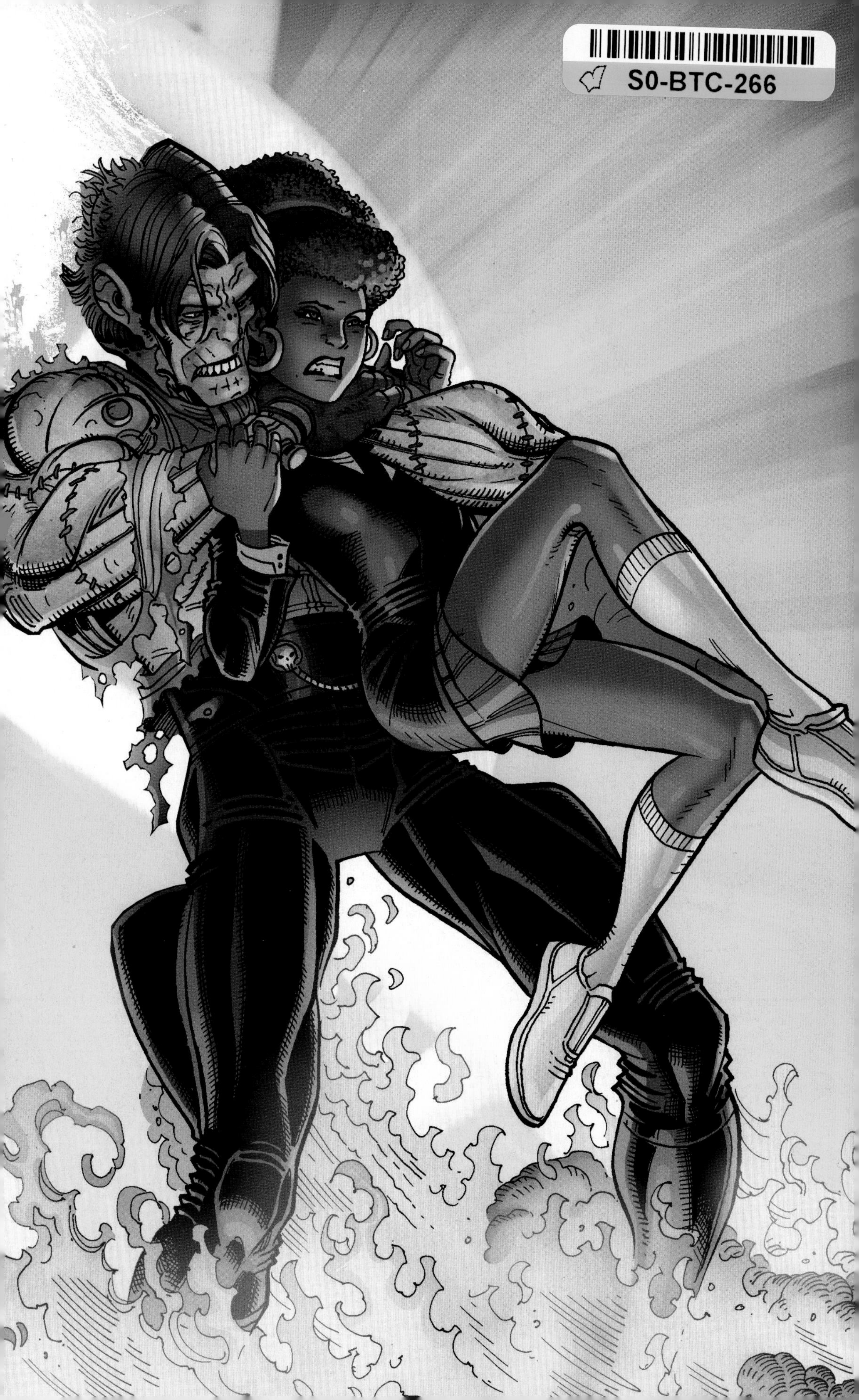

19 "MORE PENCILS, MORE BOOKS, MORE TEACHERS' DIRTY LOOKS"

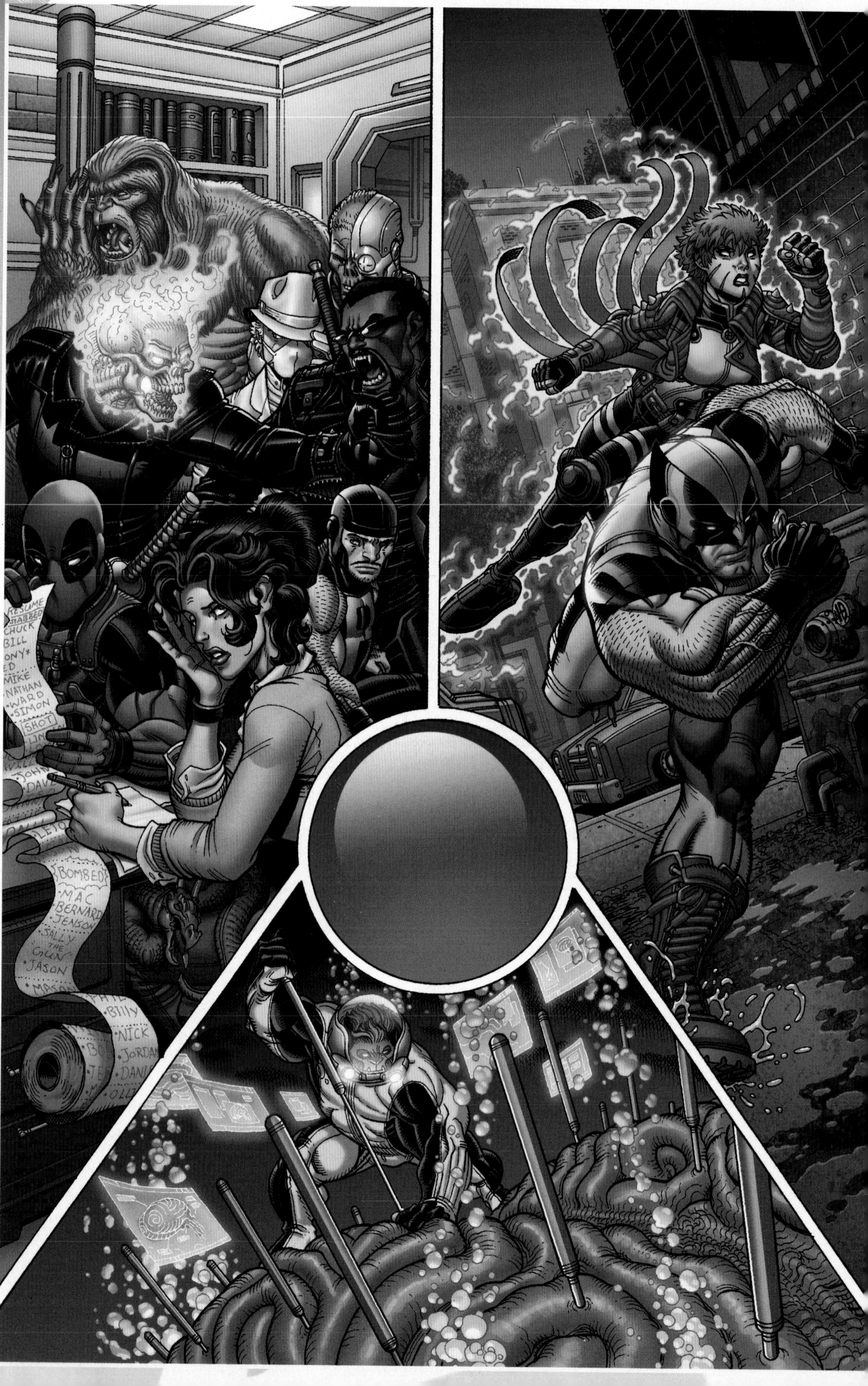

RESUME
STABBED
CHUCK
BILL
MIKE
NATHAN
WARD
SIMON
SHOT
JOHN
BOMBED
MAC
BERNARD
JENSON
SALLY "THE GUN"
JASON
MASON
Billy
NICK
JORDAN

WOLVERINE and the X-MEN

If you were born different with mutant super-powers, the Jean Grey School for Higher Learning is the school for you. Founded by Wolverine and staffed by experienced X-Men, you will learn everything you need to know to survive in a world that hates and fears you.

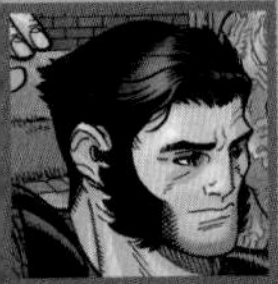

WOLVERINE
Clawed Headmaster

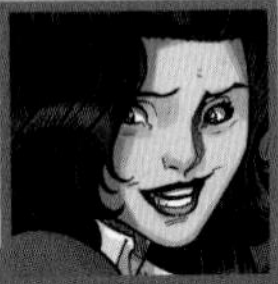

KITTY PRYDE
Phasing Headmistress

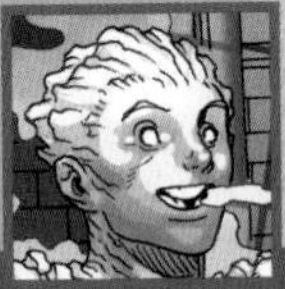

ICEMAN
Ice-Controlling Teacher

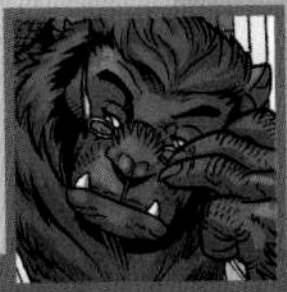

BEAST
Animalistic, Intellectual Vice-Principal

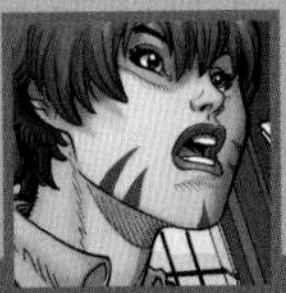

RACHEL GREY
Telekinetic, Telepathic Teacher

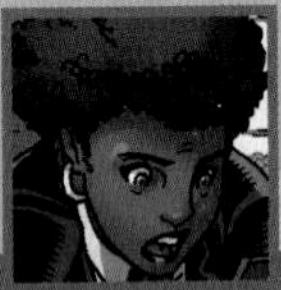

IDIE OKONKWO
Temperature-Controlling Student

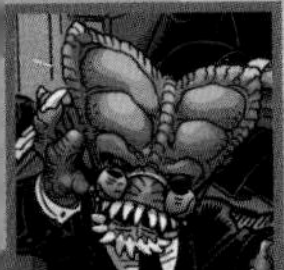

BROO
Alien Student

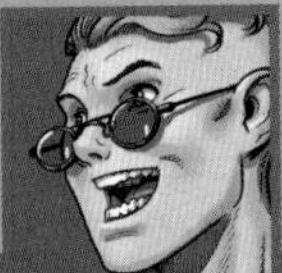

QUENTIN QUIRE
Telepathic Student

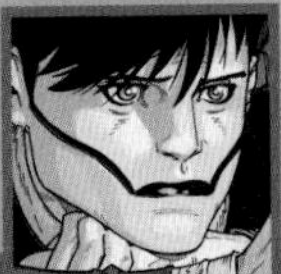

GENESIS
Flying, Eye-Blasting Student

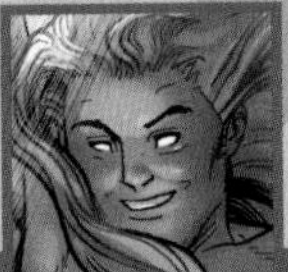

ANGEL
Metal-Winged Student

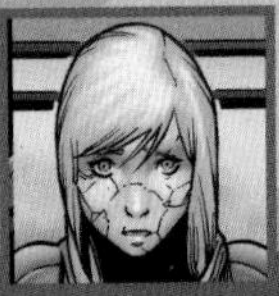

HUSK
Tear-Away Power-Shifter Teacher

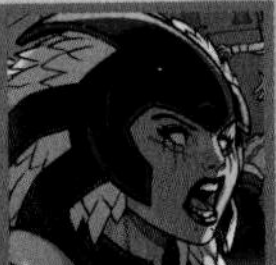

WARBIRD
Shi'ar Warrior Teacher

PREVIOUSLY

AS THE X-MEN AND THE AVENGERS CONTAINED THE CATASTROPHIC WRATH OF THE PHOENIX-POSSESSED CYCLOPS, THE JEAN GREY SCHOOL FOR HIGHER LEARNING FACED ITS OWN CALAMITIES. PROFESSOR PAIGE GUTHRIE, A.K.A. HUSK, HAS BEEN BEHAVING OUT OF SORTS – PROFESSIONALLY ERRATIC AND PERSONALLY ENGAGING IN A ROMANTIC RELATIONSHIP WITH THE HEAD JANITOR AND FORMER MUTANT BROTHERHOOD MEMBER TOAD. WHEN HEADMISTRESS KITTY PRYDE ASKED HER TO SEEK PSYCHIATRIC EVALUATION, HUSK INSTEAD OPTED TO QUIT.

STUDENT IDIE OKONKWO WAS ALSO ACTING UNUSUALLY SPIRITED AFTER SNEAKING OFF TO A LOCAL CHURCH. AND AT THE SCHOOL DANCE, IDIE TOOK THE HAND OF QUENTIN QUIRE INSTEAD OF HER ADORABLE ALIEN ADMIRER BROO. UPON INVESTIGATING, BROO DISCOVERED THAT THE CHURCH WAS A FAKE, ESTABLISHED FOR THE SOLE PURPOSE OF MANIPULATING IDIE BY KADE KILGORE AND THE HELLFIRE CLUB. EVEN AS MUTANTKIND WAS RESTORED BY HOPE DISPERSING THE PHOENIX FORCE, BROO LAY ON THE FLOOR OF THE CHURCH, DYING FROM THE BULLET THAT KILGORE FIRED INTO HIS SKULL.

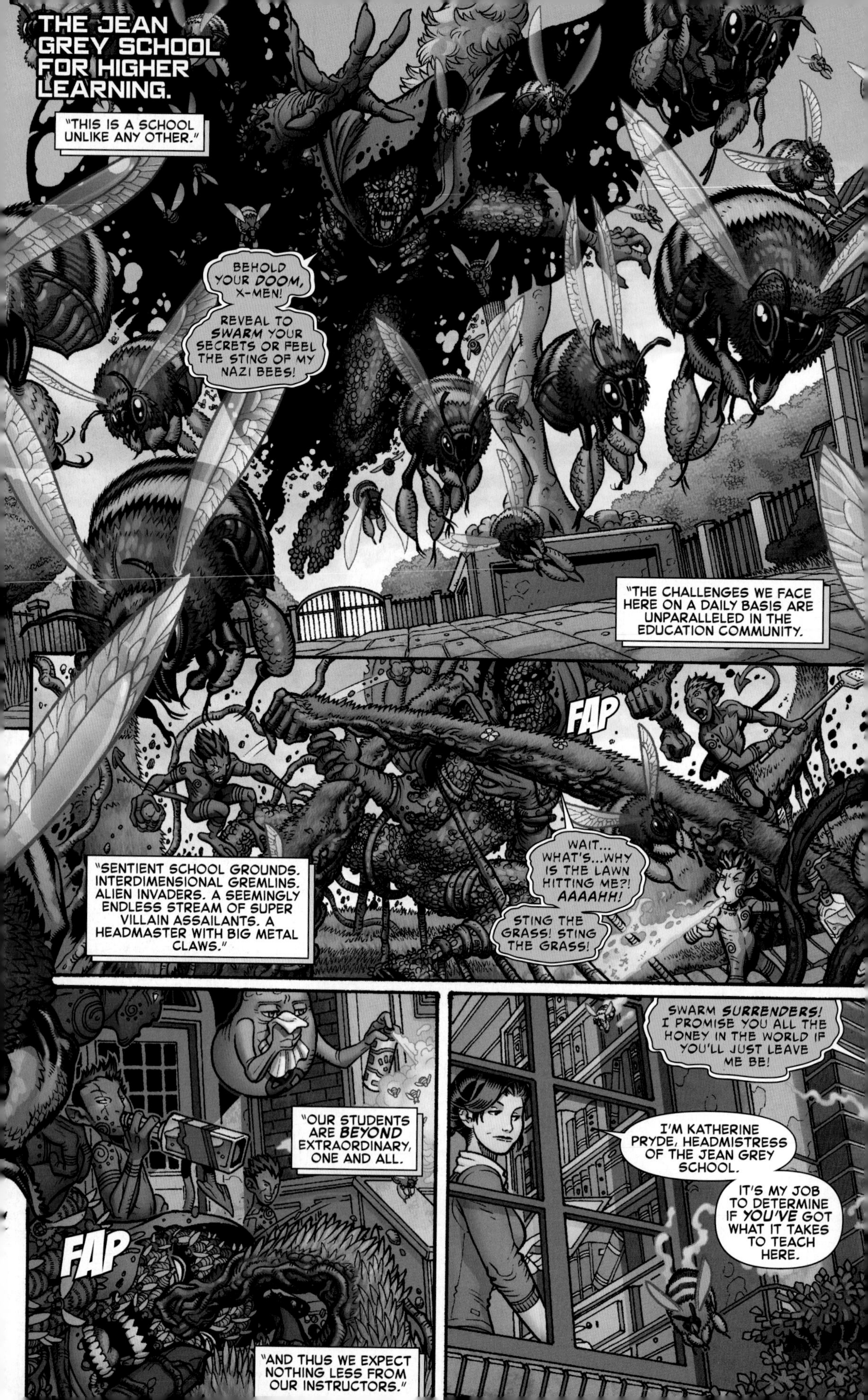
THE JEAN GREY SCHOOL FOR HIGHER LEARNING.
"THIS IS A SCHOOL UNLIKE ANY OTHER."
BEHOLD YOUR DOOM, X-MEN!
REVEAL TO SWARM YOUR SECRETS OR FEEL THE STING OF MY NAZI BEES!
"THE CHALLENGES WE FACE HERE ON A DAILY BASIS ARE UNPARALLELED IN THE EDUCATION COMMUNITY.
FAP
"SENTIENT SCHOOL GROUNDS. INTERDIMENSIONAL GREMLINS. ALIEN INVADERS. A SEEMINGLY ENDLESS STREAM OF SUPER VILLAIN ASSAILANTS. A HEADMASTER WITH BIG METAL CLAWS."
WAIT... WHAT'S...WHY IS THE LAWN HITTING ME?! AAAAHH!
STING THE GRASS! STING THE GRASS!
"OUR STUDENTS ARE BEYOND EXTRAORDINARY, ONE AND ALL.
FAP
"AND THUS WE EXPECT NOTHING LESS FROM OUR INSTRUCTORS."
SWARM SURRENDERS! I PROMISE YOU ALL THE HONEY IN THE WORLD IF YOU'LL JUST LEAVE ME BE!
I'M KATHERINE PRYDE, HEADMISTRESS OF THE JEAN GREY SCHOOL.
IT'S MY JOB TO DETERMINE IF YOU'VE GOT WHAT IT TAKES TO TEACH HERE.

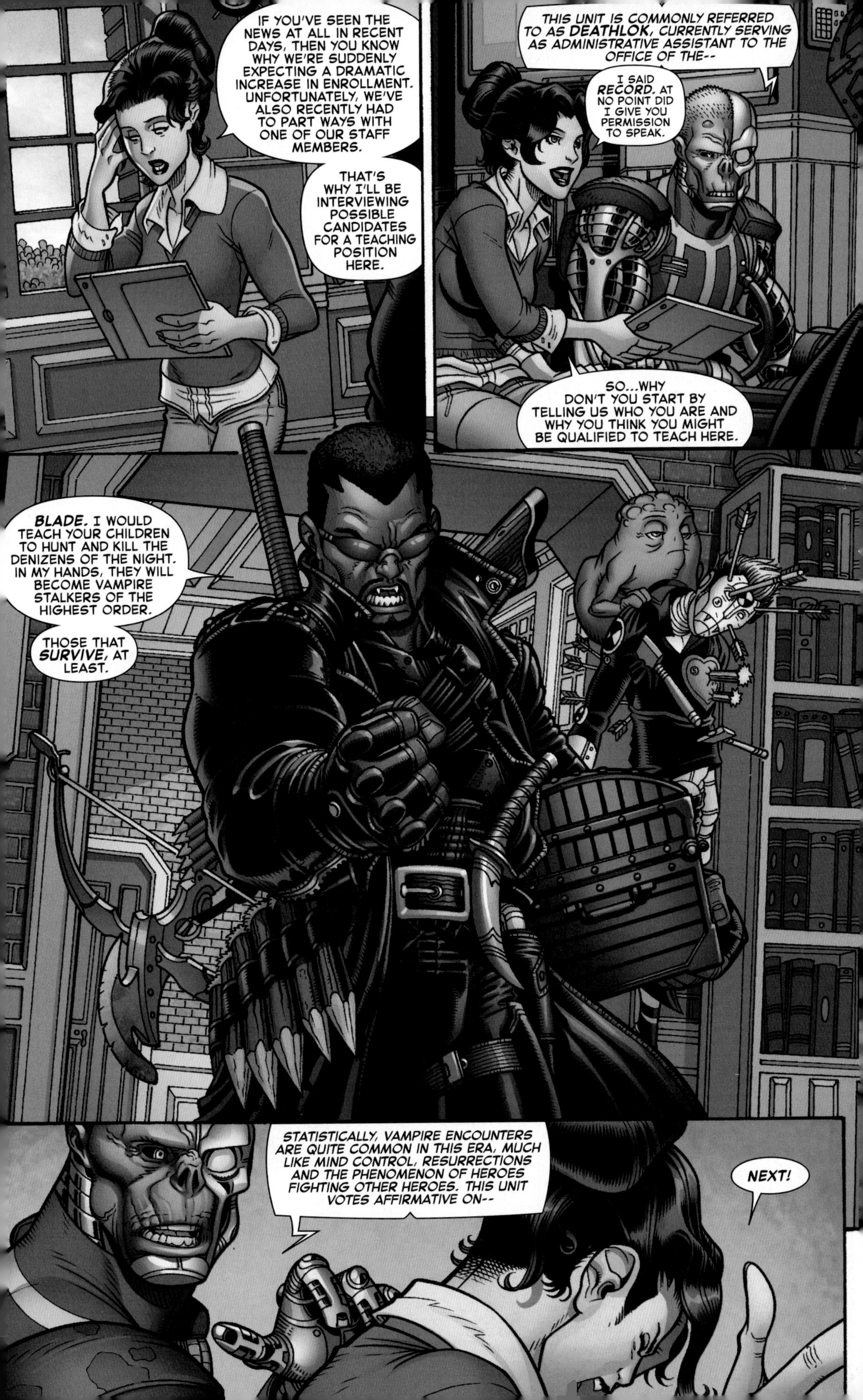
IF YOU'VE SEEN THE NEWS AT ALL IN RECENT DAYS, THEN YOU KNOW WHY WE'RE SUDDENLY EXPECTING A DRAMATIC INCREASE IN ENROLLMENT. UNFORTUNATELY, WE'VE ALSO RECENTLY HAD TO PART WAYS WITH ONE OF OUR STAFF MEMBERS.
THAT'S WHY I'LL BE INTERVIEWING POSSIBLE CANDIDATES FOR A TEACHING POSITION HERE.
THIS UNIT IS COMMONLY REFERRED TO AS DEATHLOK, CURRENTLY SERVING AS ADMINISTRATIVE ASSISTANT TO THE OFFICE OF THE--
I SAID RECORD. AT NO POINT DID I GIVE YOU PERMISSION TO SPEAK.
SO...WHY DON'T YOU START BY TELLING US WHO YOU ARE AND WHY YOU THINK YOU MIGHT BE QUALIFIED TO TEACH HERE.
BLADE. I WOULD TEACH YOUR CHILDREN TO HUNT AND KILL THE DENIZENS OF THE NIGHT. IN MY HANDS, THEY WILL BECOME VAMPIRE STALKERS OF THE HIGHEST ORDER.
THOSE THAT SURVIVE, AT LEAST.
STATISTICALLY, VAMPIRE ENCOUNTERS ARE QUITE COMMON IN THIS ERA, MUCH LIKE MIND CONTROL, RESURRECTIONS AND THE PHENOMENON OF HEROES FIGHTING OTHER HEROES. THIS UNIT VOTES AFFIRMATIVE ON--
NEXT!

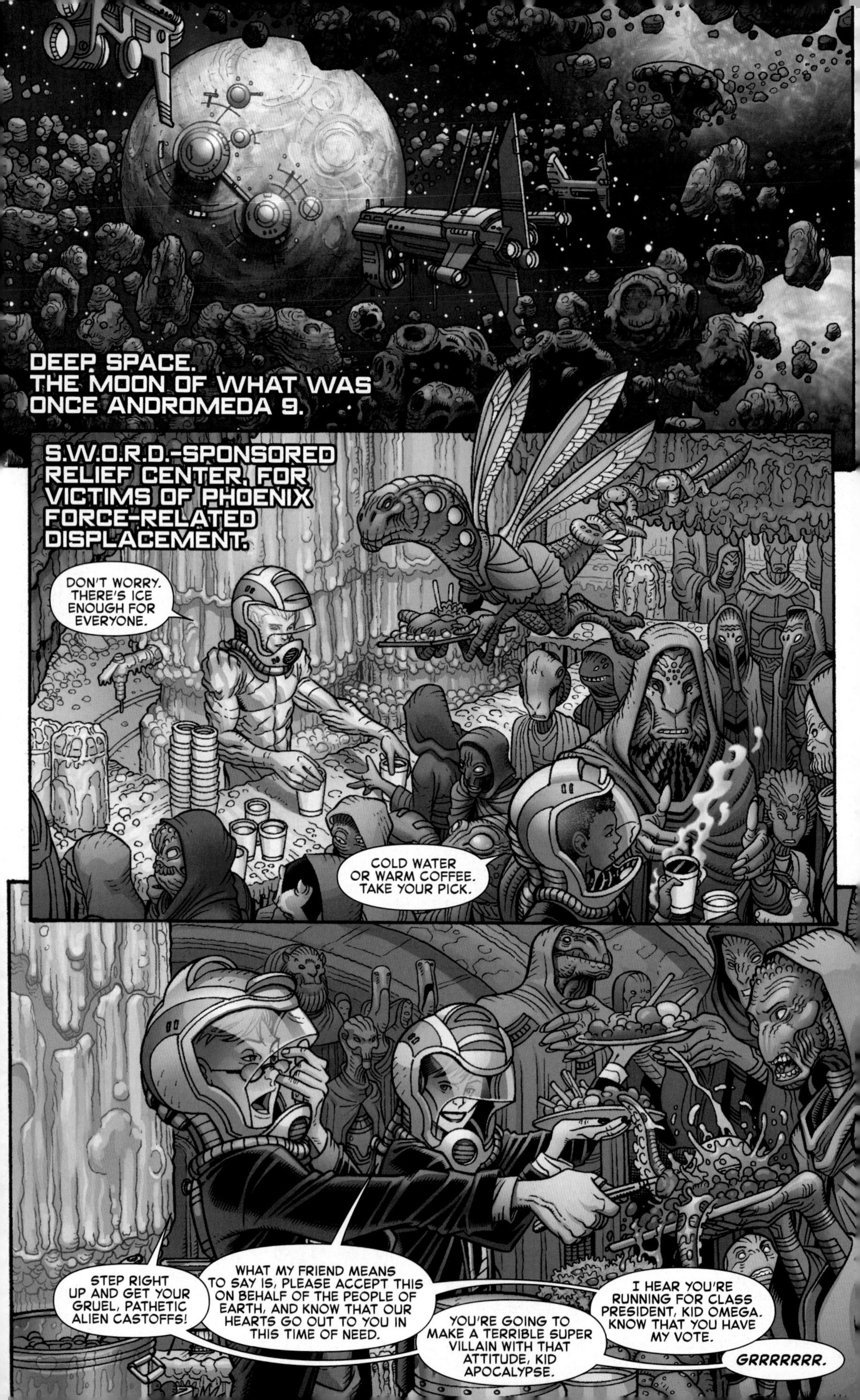
DEEP SPACE.
THE MOON OF WHAT WAS ONCE ANDROMEDA 9.
S.W.O.R.D.-SPONSORED RELIEF CENTER, FOR VICTIMS OF PHOENIX FORCE-RELATED DISPLACEMENT.
DON'T WORRY. THERE'S ICE ENOUGH FOR EVERYONE.
COLD WATER OR WARM COFFEE. TAKE YOUR PICK.
STEP RIGHT UP AND GET YOUR GRUEL, PATHETIC ALIEN CASTOFFS!
WHAT MY FRIEND MEANS TO SAY IS, PLEASE ACCEPT THIS ON BEHALF OF THE PEOPLE OF EARTH, AND KNOW THAT OUR HEARTS GO OUT TO YOU IN THIS TIME OF NEED.
YOU'RE GOING TO MAKE A TERRIBLE SUPER VILLAIN WITH THAT ATTITUDE, KID APOCALYPSE.
I HEAR YOU'RE RUNNING FOR CLASS PRESIDENT, KID OMEGA. KNOW THAT YOU HAVE MY VOTE.
GRRRRRRR.

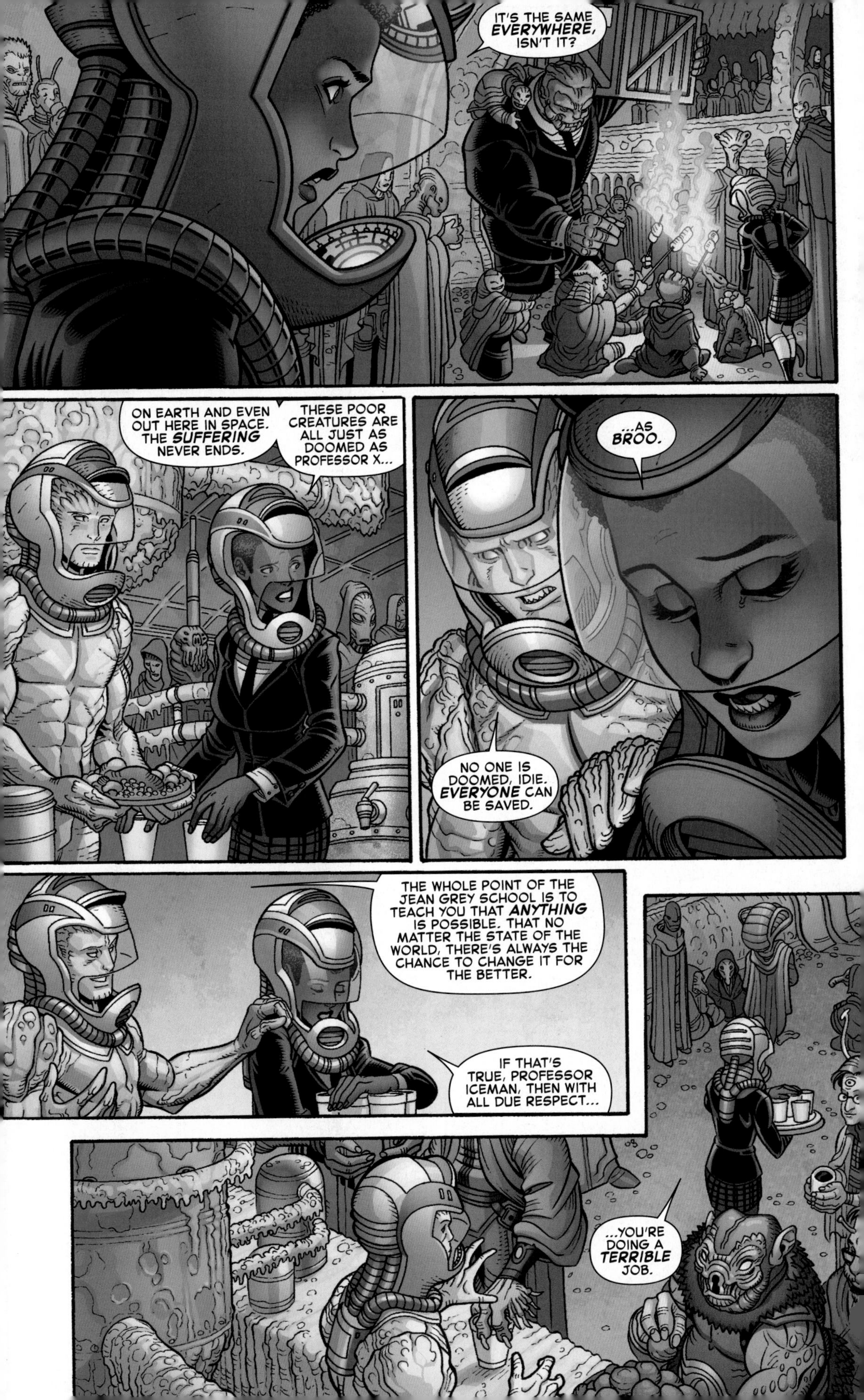
IT'S THE SAME EVERYWHERE, ISN'T IT?
ON EARTH AND EVEN OUT HERE IN SPACE. THE SUFFERING NEVER ENDS.
THESE POOR CREATURES ARE ALL JUST AS DOOMED AS PROFESSOR X...
...AS BROO.
NO ONE IS DOOMED, IDIE. EVERYONE CAN BE SAVED.
THE WHOLE POINT OF THE JEAN GREY SCHOOL IS TO TEACH YOU THAT ANYTHING IS POSSIBLE. THAT NO MATTER THE STATE OF THE WORLD, THERE'S ALWAYS THE CHANCE TO CHANGE IT FOR THE BETTER.
IF THAT'S TRUE, PROFESSOR ICEMAN, THEN WITH ALL DUE RESPECT...
...YOU'RE DOING A TERRIBLE JOB.

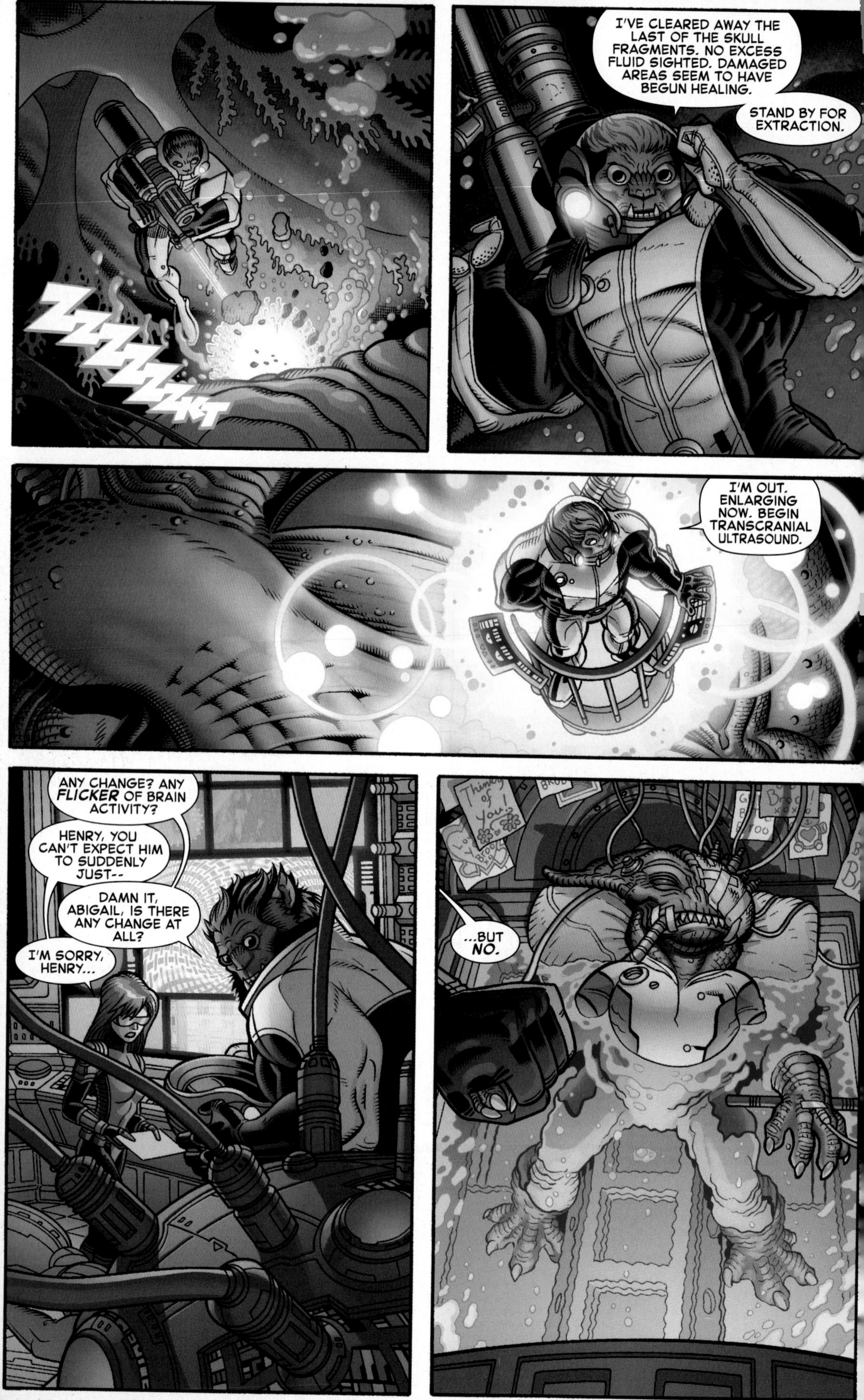
ZZZZZZKT
I'VE CLEARED AWAY THE LAST OF THE SKULL FRAGMENTS. NO EXCESS FLUID SIGHTED. DAMAGED AREAS SEEM TO HAVE BEGUN HEALING.
STAND BY FOR EXTRACTION.
I'M OUT. ENLARGING NOW. BEGIN TRANSCRANIAL ULTRASOUND.
ANY CHANGE? ANY *FLICKER* OF BRAIN ACTIVITY?
HENRY, YOU CAN'T EXPECT HIM TO SUDDENLY JUST--
DAMN IT, ABIGAIL, IS THERE ANY CHANGE AT ALL?
I'M SORRY, HENRY...
...BUT **NO.**
Thinking of You!

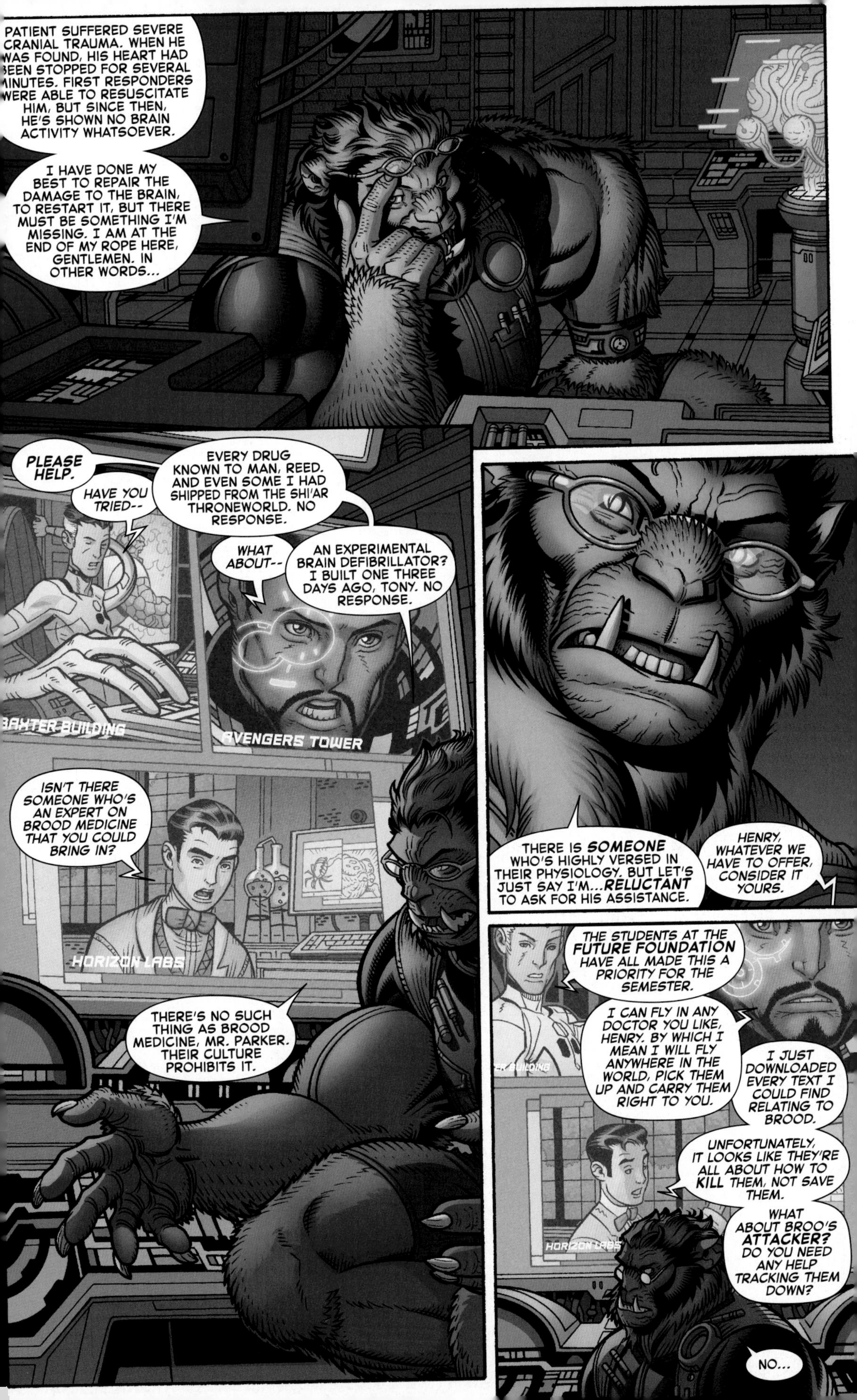
PATIENT SUFFERED SEVERE CRANIAL TRAUMA. WHEN HE WAS FOUND, HIS HEART HAD BEEN STOPPED FOR SEVERAL MINUTES. FIRST RESPONDERS WERE ABLE TO RESUSCITATE HIM, BUT SINCE THEN, HE'S SHOWN NO BRAIN ACTIVITY WHATSOEVER.
I HAVE DONE MY BEST TO REPAIR THE DAMAGE TO THE BRAIN, TO RESTART IT, BUT THERE MUST BE SOMETHING I'M MISSING. I AM AT THE END OF MY ROPE HERE, GENTLEMEN. IN OTHER WORDS...
PLEASE HELP.
HAVE YOU TRIED--
EVERY DRUG KNOWN TO MAN, REED. AND EVEN SOME I HAD SHIPPED FROM THE SHI'AR THRONEWORLD. NO RESPONSE.
WHAT ABOUT--
AN EXPERIMENTAL BRAIN DEFIBRILLATOR? I BUILT ONE THREE DAYS AGO, TONY. NO RESPONSE.
BAXTER BUILDING
AVENGERS TOWER
ISN'T THERE SOMEONE WHO'S AN EXPERT ON BROOD MEDICINE THAT YOU COULD BRING IN?
HORIZON LABS
THERE'S NO SUCH THING AS BROOD MEDICINE, MR. PARKER. THEIR CULTURE PROHIBITS IT.
THERE IS SOMEONE WHO'S HIGHLY VERSED IN THEIR PHYSIOLOGY. BUT LET'S JUST SAY I'M...RELUCTANT TO ASK FOR HIS ASSISTANCE.
HENRY, WHATEVER WE HAVE TO OFFER, CONSIDER IT YOURS.
THE STUDENTS AT THE FUTURE FOUNDATION HAVE ALL MADE THIS A PRIORITY FOR THE SEMESTER.
I CAN FLY IN ANY DOCTOR YOU LIKE, HENRY. BY WHICH I MEAN I WILL FLY ANYWHERE IN THE WORLD, PICK THEM UP AND CARRY THEM RIGHT TO YOU.
I JUST DOWNLOADED EVERY TEXT I COULD FIND RELATING TO BROOD.
UNFORTUNATELY, IT LOOKS LIKE THEY'RE ALL ABOUT HOW TO KILL THEM, NOT SAVE THEM.
HORIZON LABS
WHAT ABOUT BROO'S ATTACKER? DO YOU NEED ANY HELP TRACKING THEM DOWN?
NO...

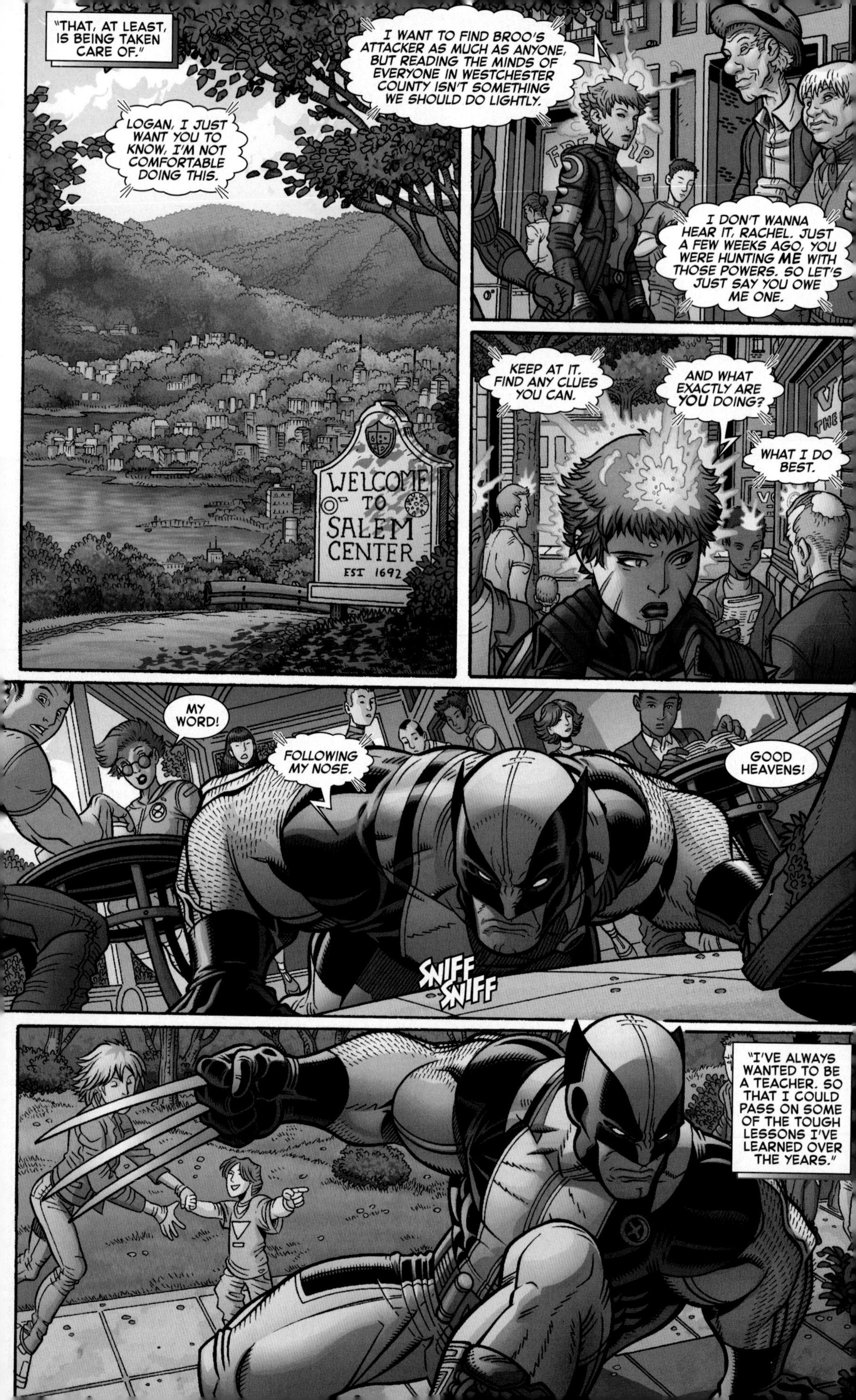
"THAT, AT LEAST, IS BEING TAKEN CARE OF."
LOGAN, I JUST WANT YOU TO KNOW. I'M NOT COMFORTABLE DOING THIS.
WELCOME TO SALEM CENTER EST 1692
I WANT TO FIND BROO'S ATTACKER AS MUCH AS ANYONE, BUT READING THE MINDS OF EVERYONE IN WESTCHESTER COUNTY ISN'T SOMETHING WE SHOULD DO LIGHTLY.
I DON'T WANNA HEAR IT, RACHEL. JUST A FEW WEEKS AGO, YOU WERE HUNTING ME WITH THOSE POWERS. SO LET'S JUST SAY YOU OWE ME ONE.
KEEP AT IT. FIND ANY CLUES YOU CAN.
AND WHAT EXACTLY ARE YOU DOING?
WHAT I DO BEST.
MY WORD!
FOLLOWING MY NOSE.
GOOD HEAVENS!
SNIFF SNIFF
"I'VE ALWAYS WANTED TO BE A TEACHER. SO THAT I COULD PASS ON SOME OF THE TOUGH LESSONS I'VE LEARNED OVER THE YEARS."

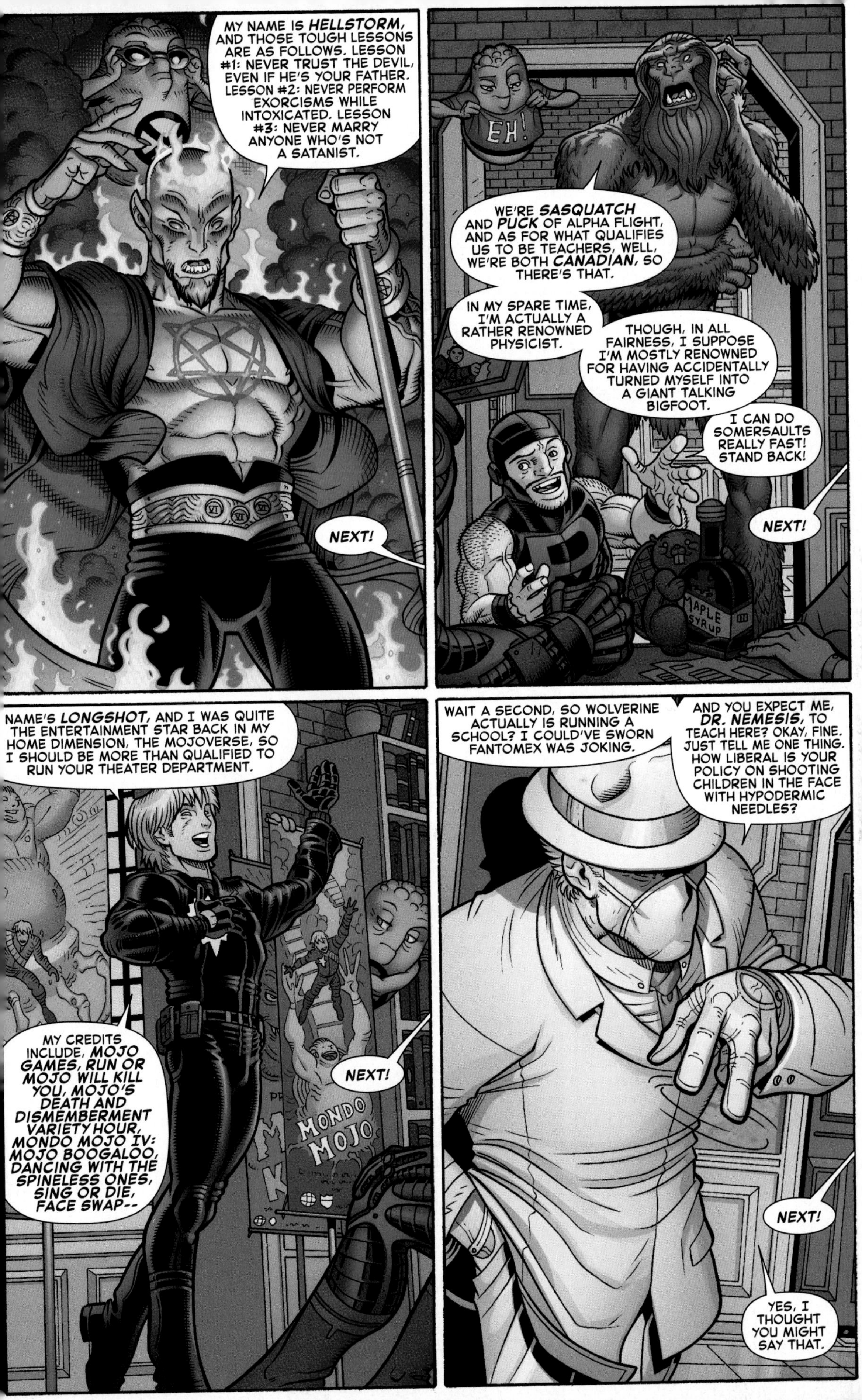

MY NAME IS **HELLSTORM**, AND THOSE TOUGH LESSONS ARE AS FOLLOWS. LESSON #1: NEVER TRUST THE DEVIL, EVEN IF HE'S YOUR FATHER. LESSON #2: NEVER PERFORM EXORCISMS WHILE INTOXICATED. LESSON #3: NEVER MARRY ANYONE WHO'S NOT A SATANIST.
NEXT!
EH!
WE'RE **SASQUATCH** AND **PUCK** OF ALPHA FLIGHT, AND AS FOR WHAT QUALIFIES US TO BE TEACHERS, WELL, WE'RE BOTH **CANADIAN**, SO THERE'S THAT.
IN MY SPARE TIME, I'M ACTUALLY A RATHER RENOWNED PHYSICIST.
THOUGH, IN ALL FAIRNESS, I SUPPOSE I'M MOSTLY RENOWNED FOR HAVING ACCIDENTALLY TURNED MYSELF INTO A GIANT TALKING BIGFOOT.
I CAN DO SOMERSAULTS REALLY FAST! STAND BACK!
MAPLE SYRUP
NEXT!
NAME'S **LONGSHOT**, AND I WAS QUITE THE ENTERTAINMENT STAR BACK IN MY HOME DIMENSION, THE MOJOVERSE, SO I SHOULD BE MORE THAN QUALIFIED TO RUN YOUR THEATER DEPARTMENT.
MY CREDITS INCLUDE, ***MOJO GAMES, RUN OR MOJO WILL KILL YOU, MOJO'S DEATH AND DISMEMBERMENT VARIETY HOUR, MONDO MOJO IV: MOJO BOOGALOO, DANCING WITH THE SPINELESS ONES, SING OR DIE, FACE SWAP--***
MONDO MOJO
NEXT!
WAIT A SECOND, SO WOLVERINE ACTUALLY IS RUNNING A SCHOOL? I COULD'VE SWORN FANTOMEX WAS JOKING.
AND YOU EXPECT ME, **DR. NEMESIS**, TO TEACH HERE? OKAY, FINE. JUST TELL ME ONE THING. HOW LIBERAL IS YOUR POLICY ON SHOOTING CHILDREN IN THE FACE WITH HYPODERMIC NEEDLES?
NEXT!
YES, I THOUGHT YOU MIGHT SAY THAT.

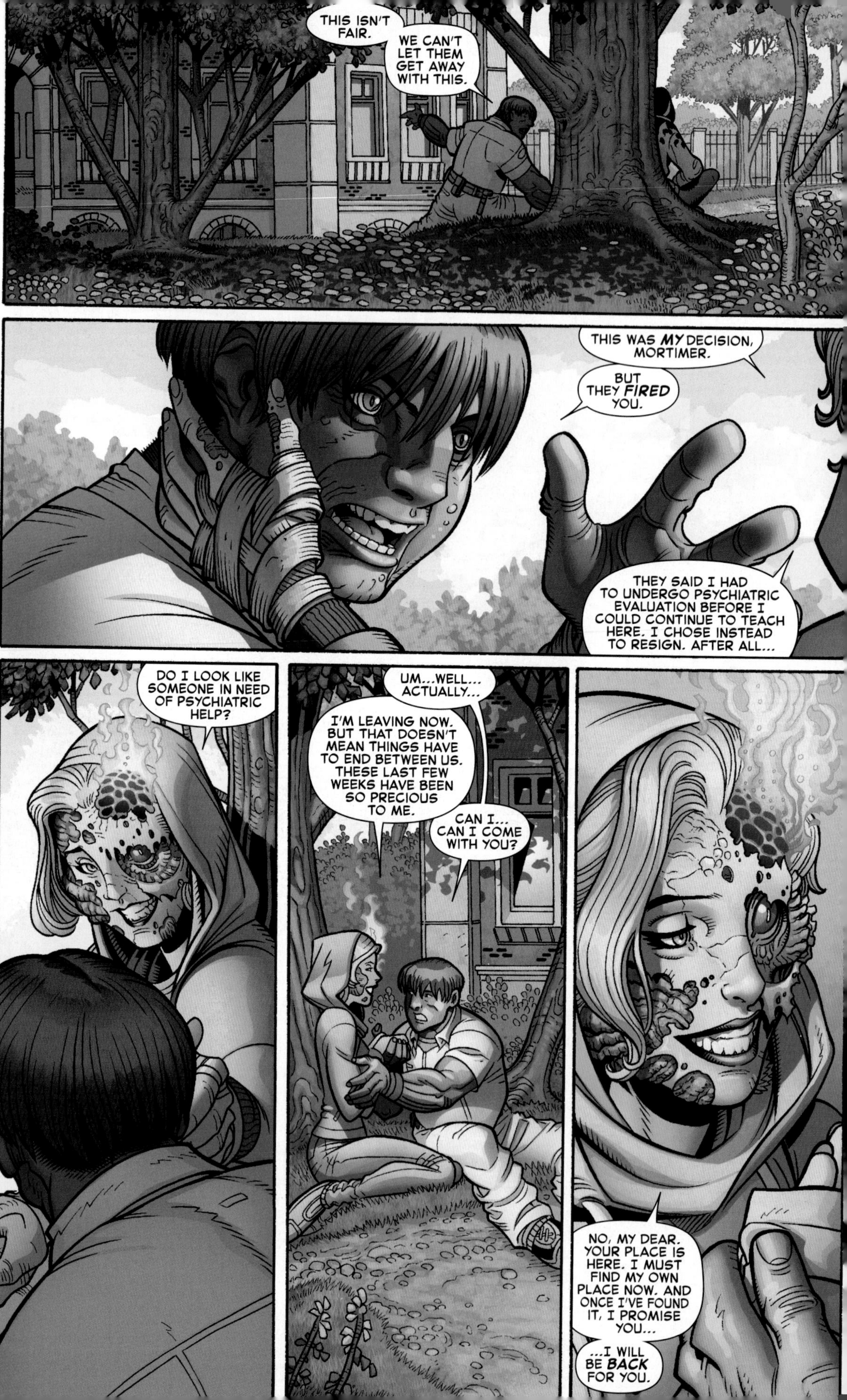
THIS ISN'T FAIR.
WE CAN'T LET THEM GET AWAY WITH THIS.
THIS WAS MY DECISION, MORTIMER.
BUT THEY FIRED YOU.
THEY SAID I HAD TO UNDERGO PSYCHIATRIC EVALUATION BEFORE I COULD CONTINUE TO TEACH HERE. I CHOSE INSTEAD TO RESIGN. AFTER ALL...
DO I LOOK LIKE SOMEONE IN NEED OF PSYCHIATRIC HELP?
UM...WELL... ACTUALLY...
I'M LEAVING NOW. BUT THAT DOESN'T MEAN THINGS HAVE TO END BETWEEN US. THESE LAST FEW WEEKS HAVE BEEN SO PRECIOUS TO ME.
CAN I... CAN I COME WITH YOU?
NO, MY DEAR. YOUR PLACE IS HERE. I MUST FIND MY OWN PLACE NOW. AND ONCE I'VE FOUND IT, I PROMISE YOU...
...I WILL BE BACK FOR YOU.

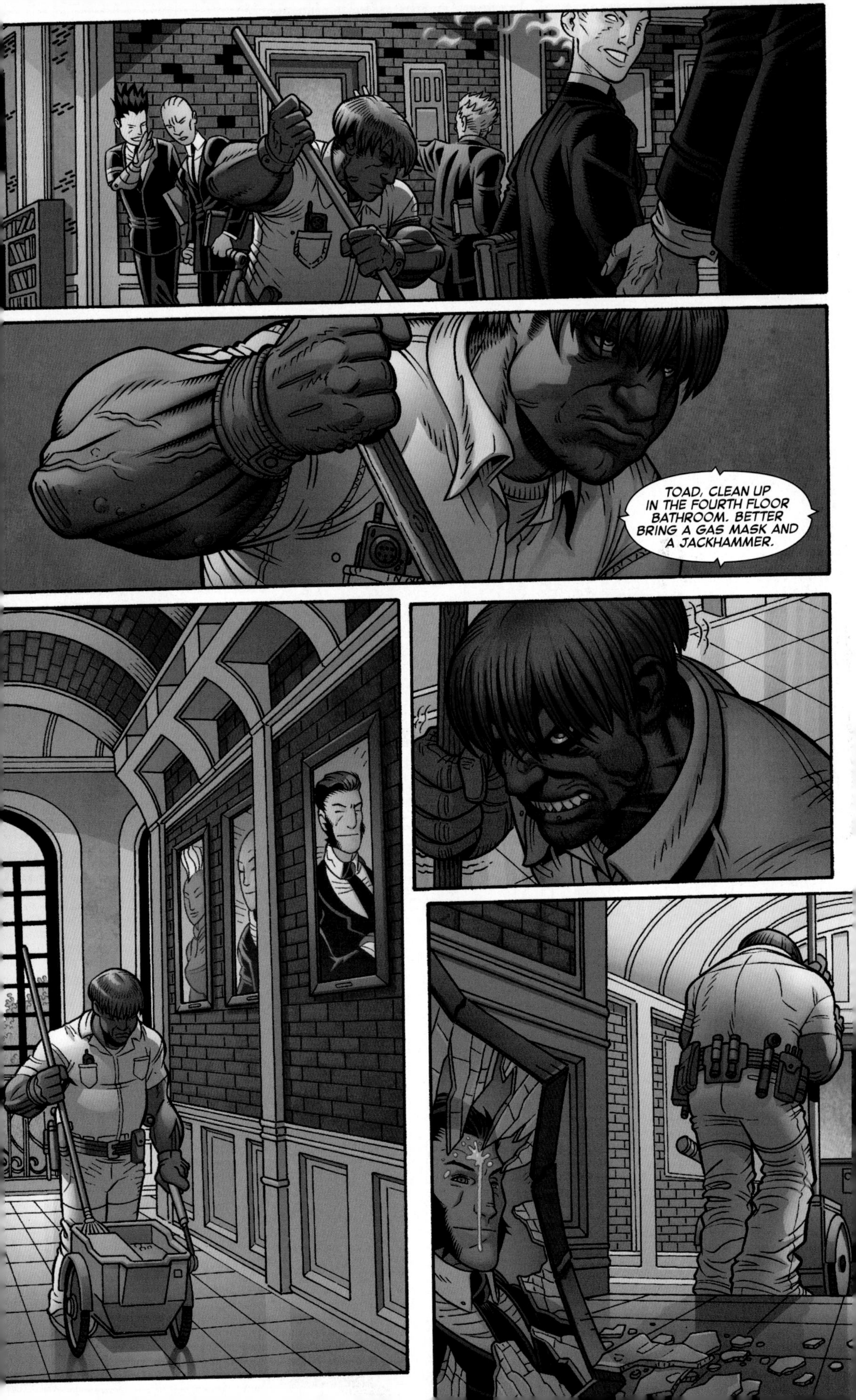
TOAD, CLEAN UP IN THE FOURTH FLOOR BATHROOM. BETTER BRING A GAS MASK AND A JACKHAMMER.

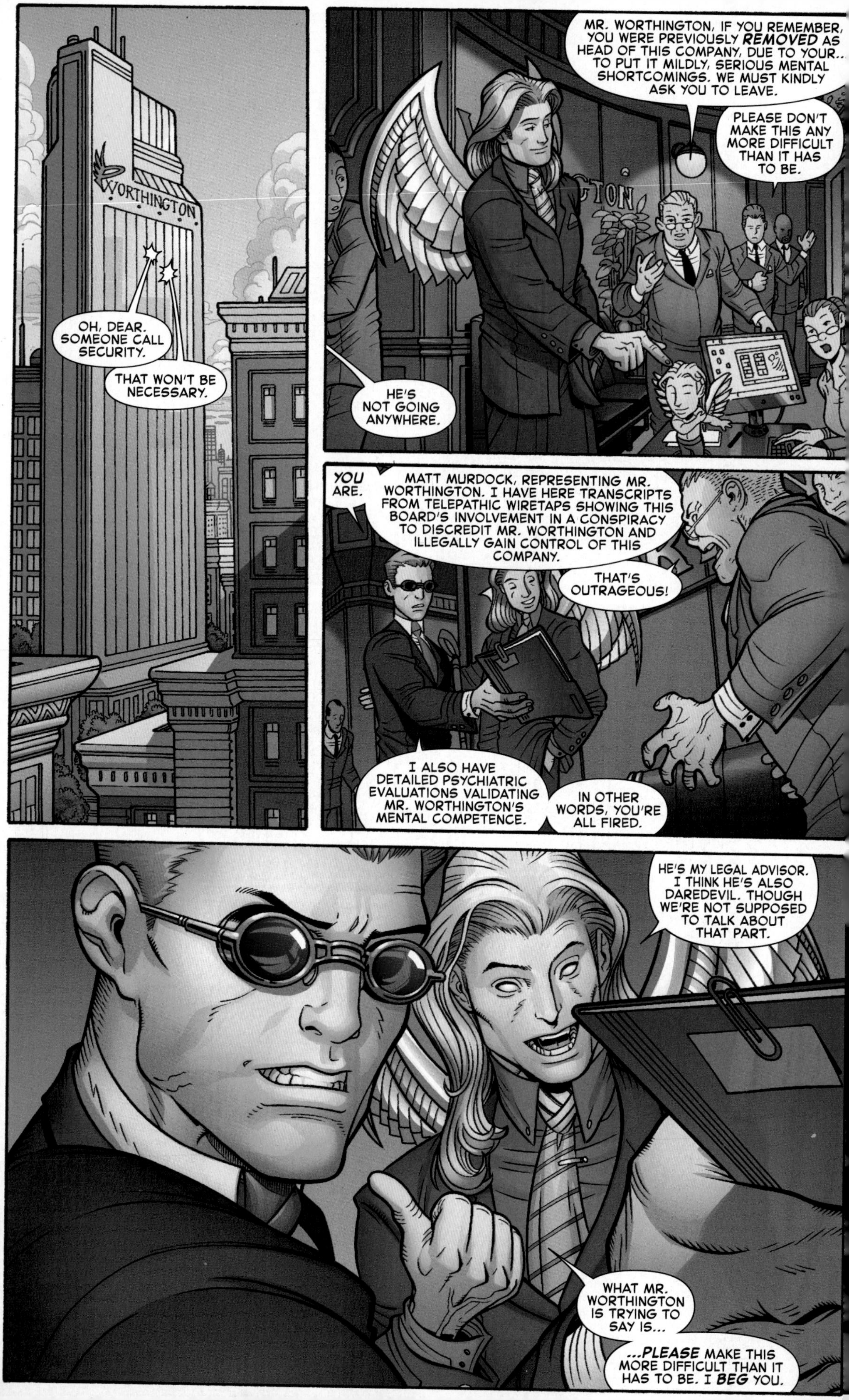
OH, DEAR. SOMEONE CALL SECURITY.
THAT WON'T BE NECESSARY.
MR. WORTHINGTON, IF YOU REMEMBER, YOU WERE PREVIOUSLY REMOVED AS HEAD OF THIS COMPANY, DUE TO YOUR.. TO PUT IT MILDLY, SERIOUS MENTAL SHORTCOMINGS. WE MUST KINDLY ASK YOU TO LEAVE.
PLEASE DON'T MAKE THIS ANY MORE DIFFICULT THAN IT HAS TO BE.
HE'S NOT GOING ANYWHERE.
YOU ARE.
MATT MURDOCK, REPRESENTING MR. WORTHINGTON. I HAVE HERE TRANSCRIPTS FROM TELEPATHIC WIRETAPS SHOWING THIS BOARD'S INVOLVEMENT IN A CONSPIRACY TO DISCREDIT MR. WORTHINGTON AND ILLEGALLY GAIN CONTROL OF THIS COMPANY.
THAT'S OUTRAGEOUS!
I ALSO HAVE DETAILED PSYCHIATRIC EVALUATIONS VALIDATING MR. WORTHINGTON'S MENTAL COMPETENCE.
IN OTHER WORDS, YOU'RE ALL FIRED.
HE'S MY LEGAL ADVISOR. I THINK HE'S ALSO DAREDEVIL. THOUGH WE'RE NOT SUPPOSED TO TALK ABOUT THAT PART.
WHAT MR. WORTHINGTON IS TRYING TO SAY IS...
...PLEASE MAKE THIS MORE DIFFICULT THAN IT HAS TO BE. I BEG YOU.

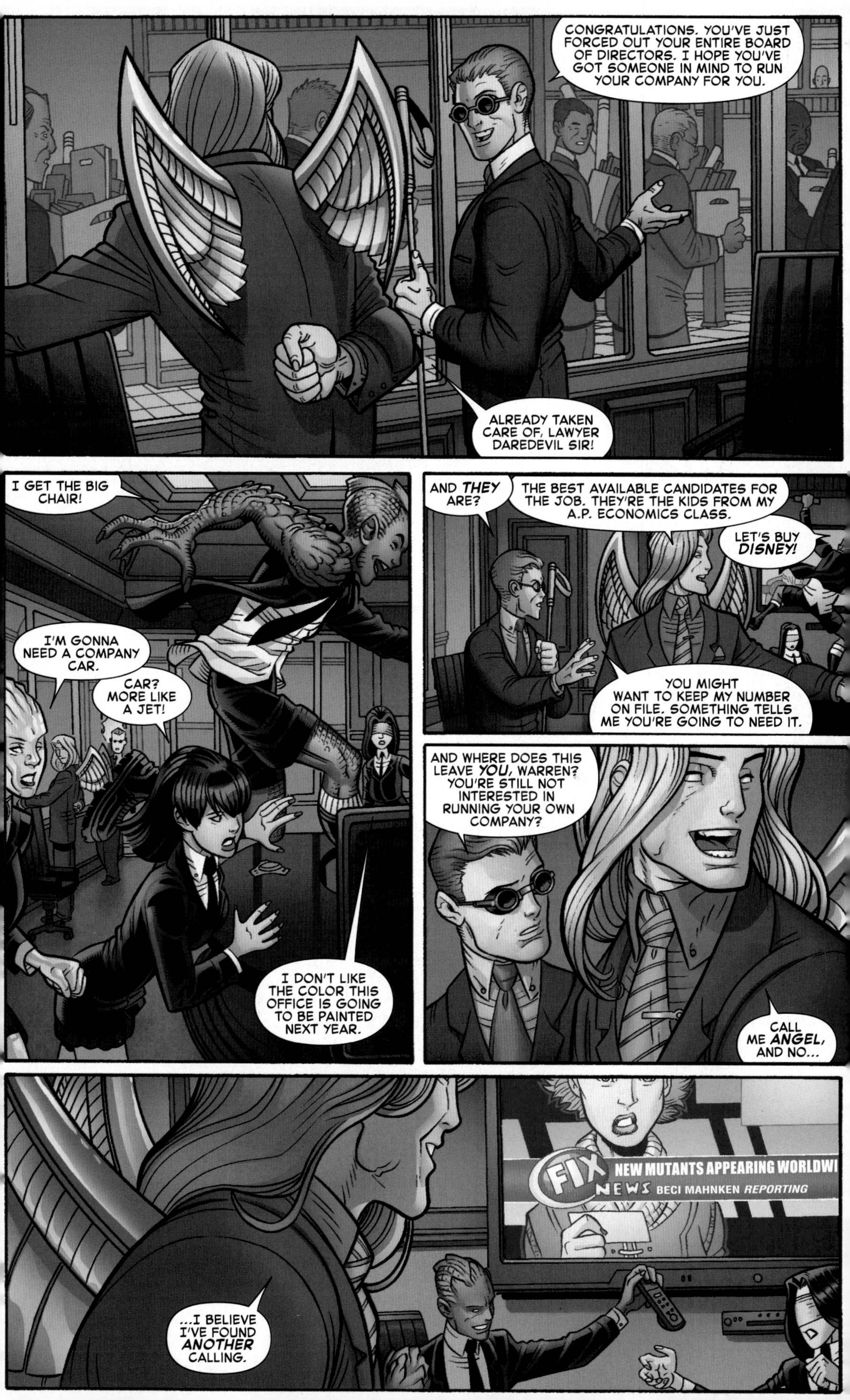
CONGRATULATIONS. YOU'VE JUST FORCED OUT YOUR ENTIRE BOARD OF DIRECTORS. I HOPE YOU'VE GOT SOMEONE IN MIND TO RUN YOUR COMPANY FOR YOU.
ALREADY TAKEN CARE OF, LAWYER DAREDEVIL SIR!
I GET THE BIG CHAIR!
I'M GONNA NEED A COMPANY CAR.
CAR? MORE LIKE A JET!
I DON'T LIKE THE COLOR THIS OFFICE IS GOING TO BE PAINTED NEXT YEAR.
AND THEY ARE?
THE BEST AVAILABLE CANDIDATES FOR THE JOB. THEY'RE THE KIDS FROM MY A.P. ECONOMICS CLASS.
LET'S BUY DISNEY!
YOU MIGHT WANT TO KEEP MY NUMBER ON FILE. SOMETHING TELLS ME YOU'RE GOING TO NEED IT.
AND WHERE DOES THIS LEAVE YOU, WARREN? YOU'RE STILL NOT INTERESTED IN RUNNING YOUR OWN COMPANY?
CALL ME ANGEL, AND NO...
FIX NEWS
NEW MUTANTS APPEARING WORLDWI
BECI MAHNKEN REPORTING
...I BELIEVE I'VE FOUND ANOTHER CALLING.

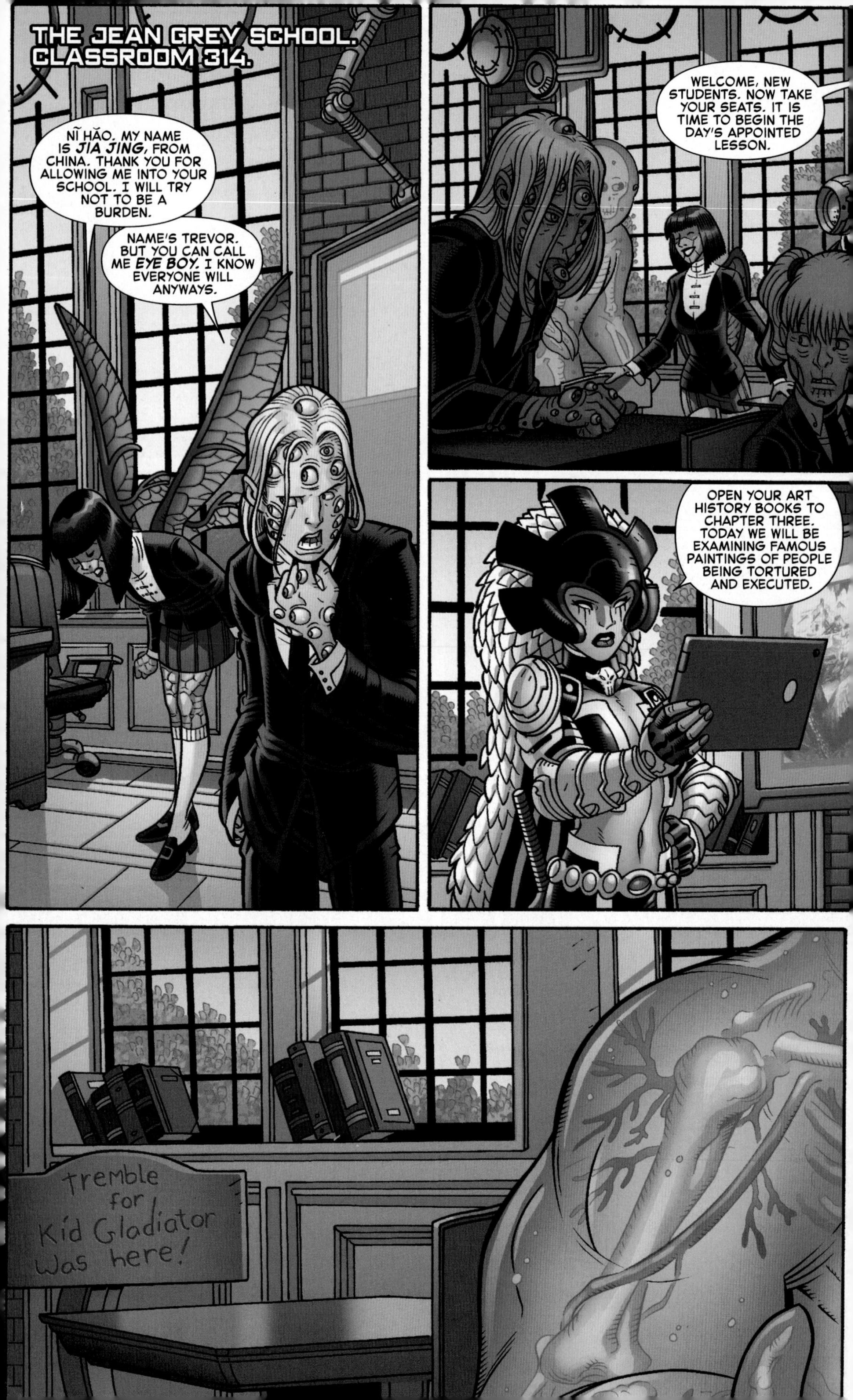
THE JEAN GREY SCHOOL. CLASSROOM 314.
NĬ HǍO. MY NAME IS JIA JING, FROM CHINA. THANK YOU FOR ALLOWING ME INTO YOUR SCHOOL. I WILL TRY NOT TO BE A BURDEN.
NAME'S TREVOR. BUT YOU CAN CALL ME EYE BOY. I KNOW EVERYONE WILL ANYWAYS.
WELCOME, NEW STUDENTS. NOW TAKE YOUR SEATS. IT IS TIME TO BEGIN THE DAY'S APPOINTED LESSON.
OPEN YOUR ART HISTORY BOOKS TO CHAPTER THREE. TODAY WE WILL BE EXAMINING FAMOUS PAINTINGS OF PEOPLE BEING TORTURED AND EXECUTED.
tremble for Kid Gladiator Was here!

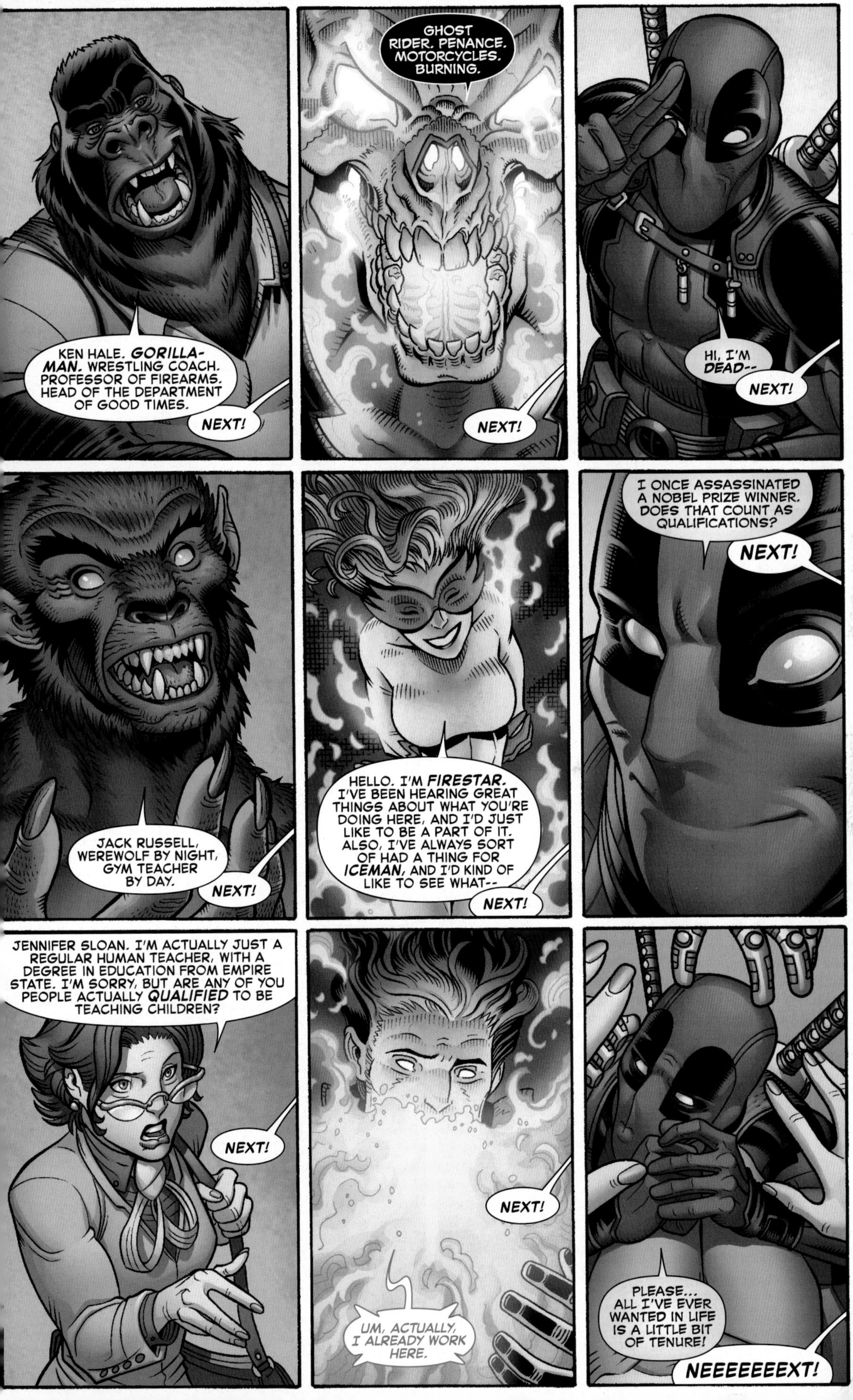

KEN HALE. GORILLA-MAN. WRESTLING COACH. PROFESSOR OF FIREARMS. HEAD OF THE DEPARTMENT OF GOOD TIMES.
NEXT!
GHOST RIDER. PENANCE. MOTORCYCLES. BURNING.
NEXT!
HI, I'M DEAD--
NEXT!
JACK RUSSELL, WEREWOLF BY NIGHT, GYM TEACHER BY DAY.
NEXT!
HELLO. I'M FIRESTAR. I'VE BEEN HEARING GREAT THINGS ABOUT WHAT YOU'RE DOING HERE, AND I'D JUST LIKE TO BE A PART OF IT. ALSO, I'VE ALWAYS SORT OF HAD A THING FOR ICEMAN, AND I'D KIND OF LIKE TO SEE WHAT--
NEXT!
I ONCE ASSASSINATED A NOBEL PRIZE WINNER. DOES THAT COUNT AS QUALIFICATIONS?
NEXT!
JENNIFER SLOAN. I'M ACTUALLY JUST A REGULAR HUMAN TEACHER, WITH A DEGREE IN EDUCATION FROM EMPIRE STATE. I'M SORRY, BUT ARE ANY OF YOU PEOPLE ACTUALLY QUALIFIED TO BE TEACHING CHILDREN?
NEXT!
NEXT!
UM, ACTUALLY, I ALREADY WORK HERE.
PLEASE... ALL I'VE EVER WANTED IN LIFE IS A LITTLE BIT OF TENURE!
NEEEEEEEXT!

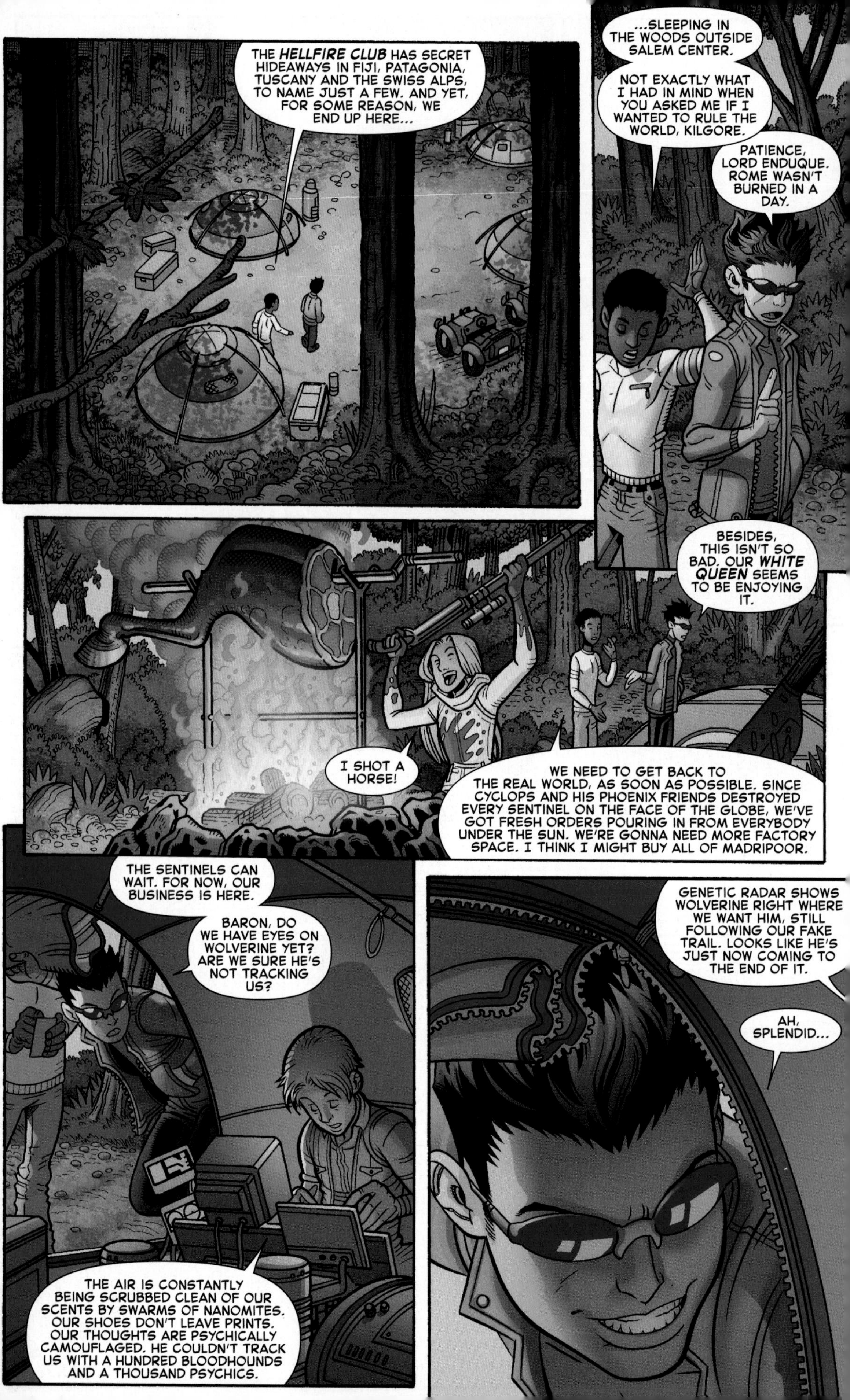

THE *HELLFIRE CLUB* HAS SECRET HIDEAWAYS IN FIJI, PATAGONIA, TUSCANY AND THE SWISS ALPS, TO NAME JUST A FEW. AND YET, FOR SOME REASON, WE END UP HERE...
...SLEEPING IN THE WOODS OUTSIDE SALEM CENTER.
NOT EXACTLY WHAT I HAD IN MIND WHEN YOU ASKED ME IF I WANTED TO RULE THE WORLD, KILGORE.
PATIENCE, LORD ENDUQUE. ROME WASN'T BURNED IN A DAY.
BESIDES, THIS ISN'T SO BAD. OUR *WHITE QUEEN* SEEMS TO BE ENJOYING IT.
I SHOT A HORSE!
WE NEED TO GET BACK TO THE REAL WORLD, AS SOON AS POSSIBLE. SINCE CYCLOPS AND HIS PHOENIX FRIENDS DESTROYED EVERY SENTINEL ON THE FACE OF THE GLOBE, WE'VE GOT FRESH ORDERS POURING IN FROM EVERYBODY UNDER THE SUN. WE'RE GONNA NEED MORE FACTORY SPACE. I THINK I MIGHT BUY ALL OF MADRIPOOR.
THE SENTINELS CAN WAIT. FOR NOW, OUR BUSINESS IS HERE.
BARON, DO WE HAVE EYES ON WOLVERINE YET? ARE WE SURE HE'S NOT TRACKING US?
THE AIR IS CONSTANTLY BEING SCRUBBED CLEAN OF OUR SCENTS BY SWARMS OF NANOMITES. OUR SHOES DON'T LEAVE PRINTS. OUR THOUGHTS ARE PSYCHICALLY CAMOUFLAGED. HE COULDN'T TRACK US WITH A HUNDRED BLOODHOUNDS AND A THOUSAND PSYCHICS.
GENETIC RADAR SHOWS WOLVERINE RIGHT WHERE WE WANT HIM, STILL FOLLOWING OUR FAKE TRAIL. LOOKS LIKE HE'S JUST NOW COMING TO THE END OF IT.
AH, SPLENDID...

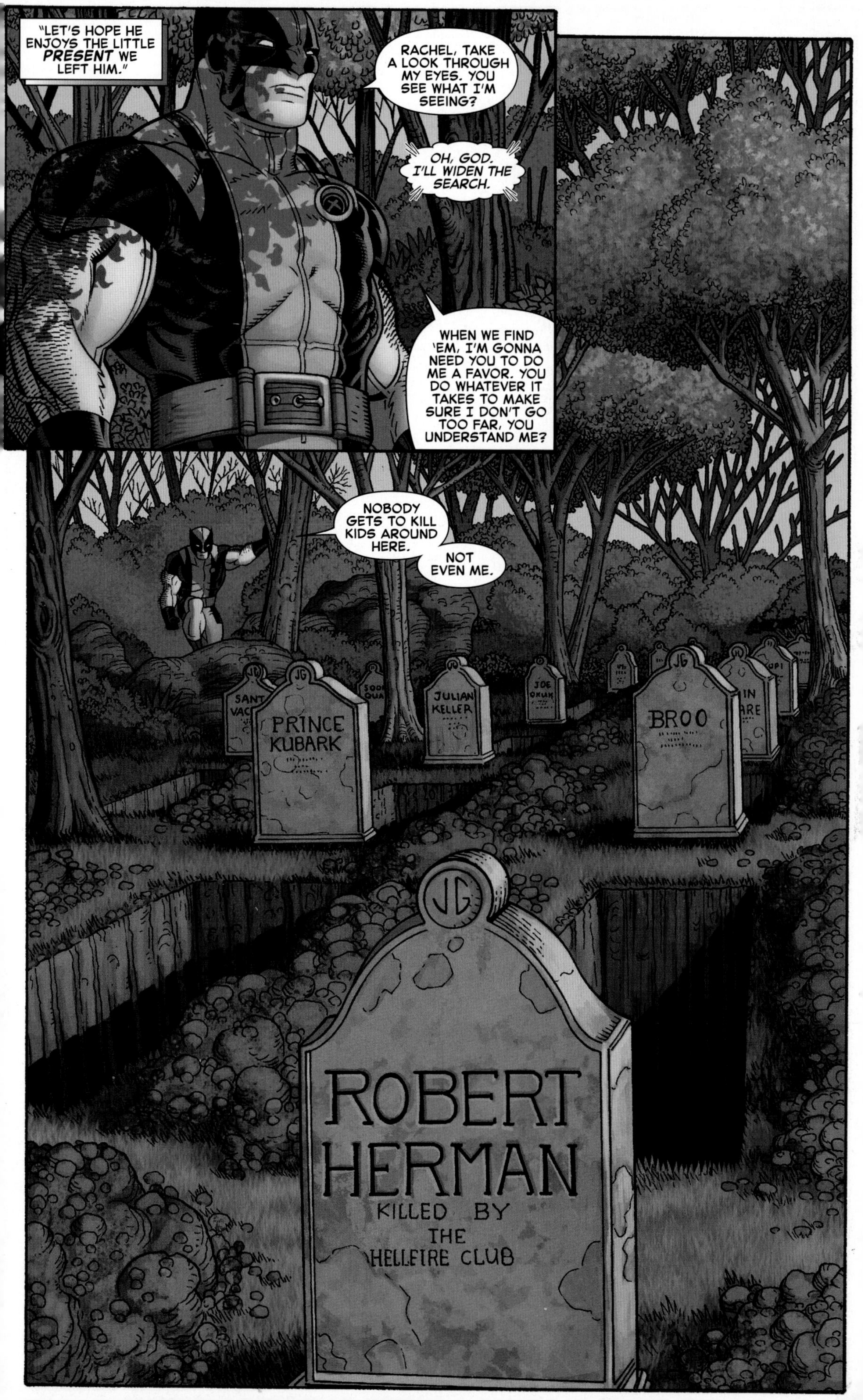
"LET'S HOPE HE ENJOYS THE LITTLE *PRESENT* WE LEFT HIM."
RACHEL, TAKE A LOOK THROUGH MY EYES. YOU SEE WHAT I'M SEEING?
OH, GOD. I'LL WIDEN THE SEARCH.
WHEN WE FIND 'EM, I'M GONNA NEED YOU TO DO ME A FAVOR. YOU DO WHATEVER IT TAKES TO MAKE SURE I DON'T GO TOO FAR, YOU UNDERSTAND ME?
NOBODY GETS TO KILL KIDS AROUND HERE.
NOT EVEN ME.
PRINCE KUBARK
JULIAN KELLER
BROO
ROBERT HERMAN
KILLED BY THE HELLFIRE CLUB

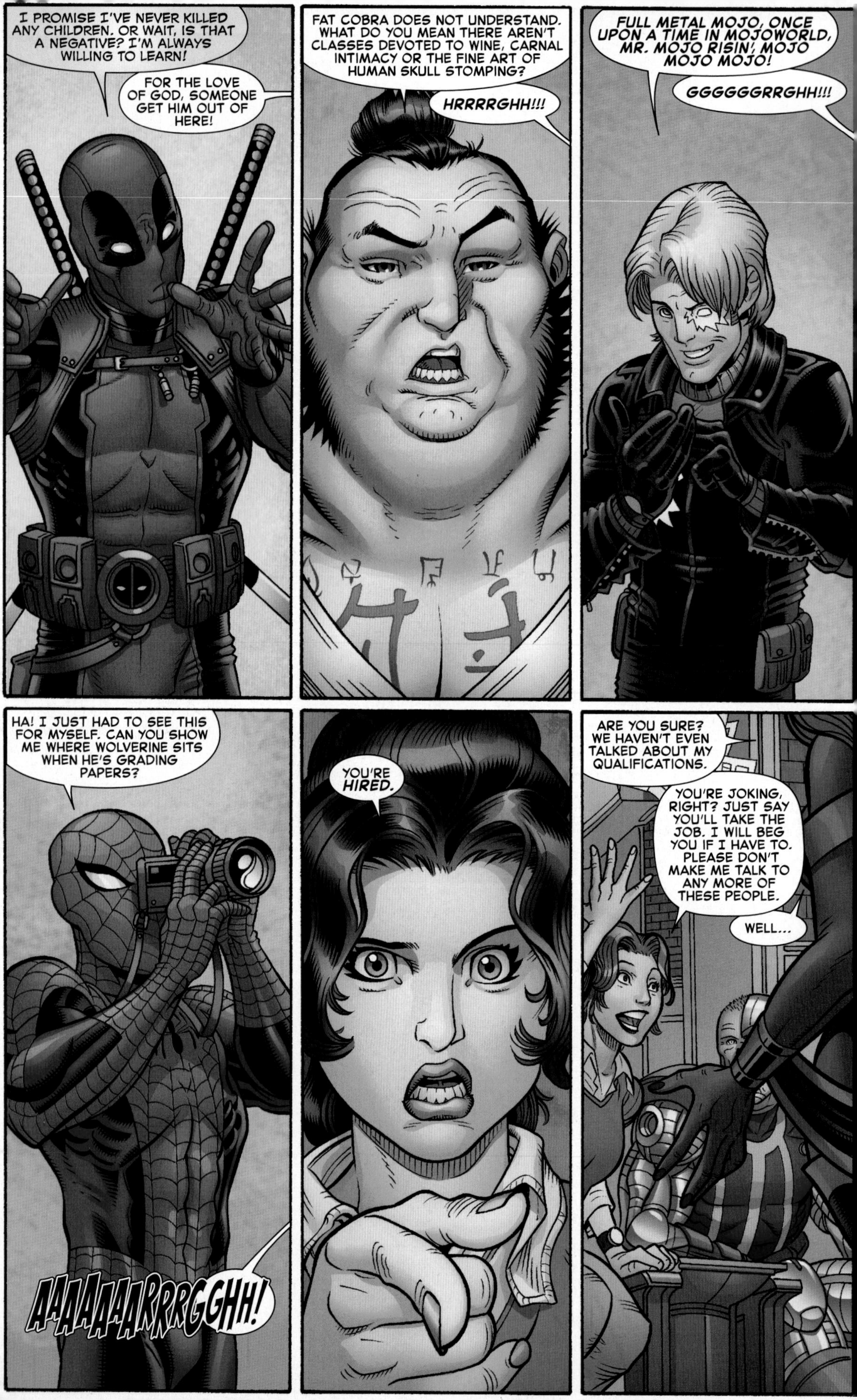
I PROMISE I'VE NEVER KILLED ANY CHILDREN. OR WAIT, IS THAT A NEGATIVE? I'M ALWAYS WILLING TO LEARN!
FOR THE LOVE OF GOD, SOMEONE GET HIM OUT OF HERE!
FAT COBRA DOES NOT UNDERSTAND. WHAT DO YOU MEAN THERE AREN'T CLASSES DEVOTED TO WINE, CARNAL INTIMACY OR THE FINE ART OF HUMAN SKULL STOMPING?
HRRRRGHH!!!
FULL METAL MOJO, ONCE UPON A TIME IN MOJOWORLD, MR. MOJO RISIN', MOJO MOJO MOJO!
GGGGGGRRGHH!!!
HA! I JUST HAD TO SEE THIS FOR MYSELF. CAN YOU SHOW ME WHERE WOLVERINE SITS WHEN HE'S GRADING PAPERS?
AAAAAAARRRGGHH!
YOU'RE HIRED.
ARE YOU SURE? WE HAVEN'T EVEN TALKED ABOUT MY QUALIFICATIONS.
YOU'RE JOKING, RIGHT? JUST SAY YOU'LL TAKE THE JOB. I WILL BEG YOU IF I HAVE TO. PLEASE DON'T MAKE ME TALK TO ANY MORE OF THESE PEOPLE.
WELL...

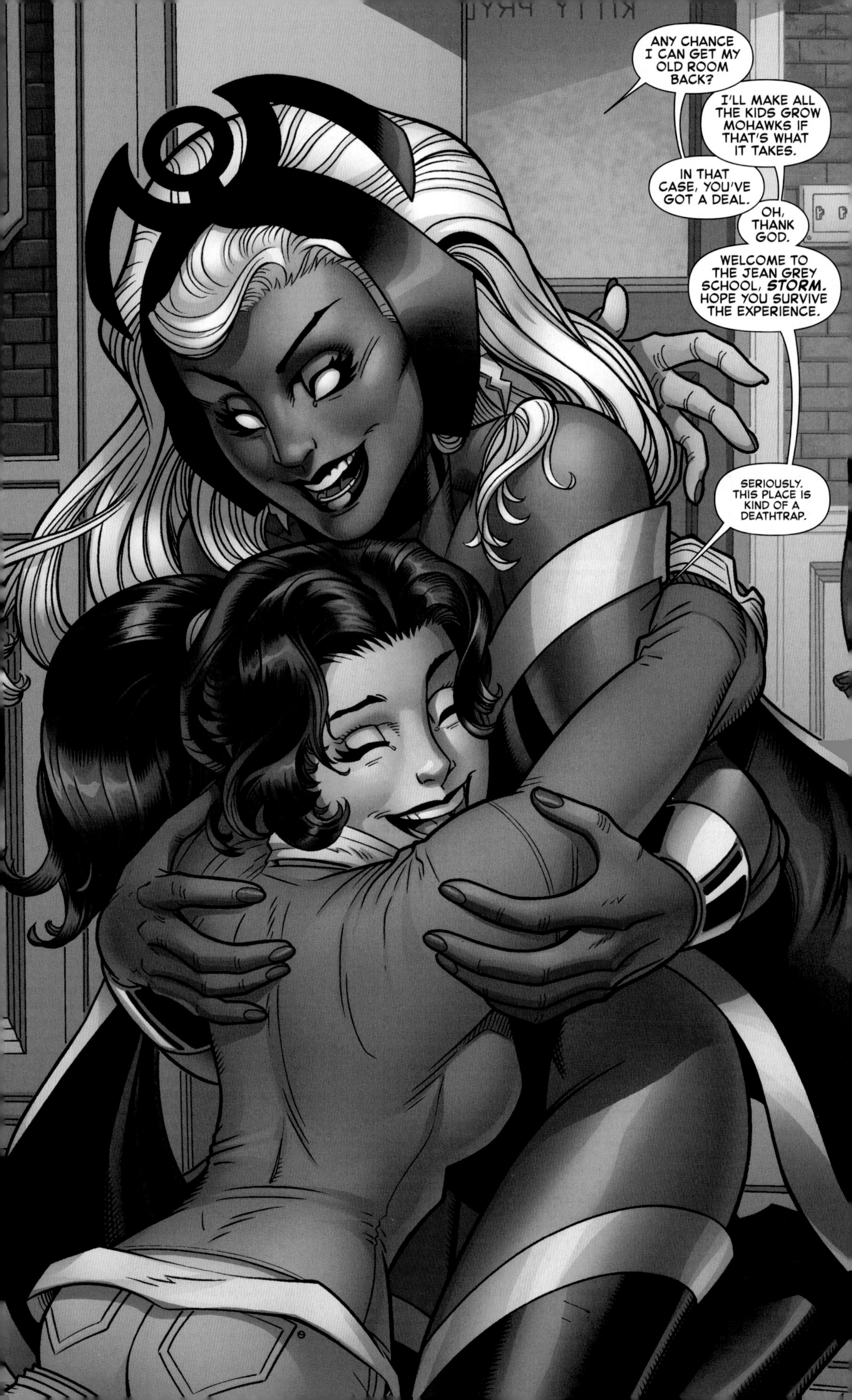
ANY CHANCE I CAN GET MY OLD ROOM BACK?
I'LL MAKE ALL THE KIDS GROW MOHAWKS IF THAT'S WHAT IT TAKES.
IN THAT CASE, YOU'VE GOT A DEAL.
OH, THANK GOD.
WELCOME TO THE JEAN GREY SCHOOL, STORM. HOPE YOU SURVIVE THE EXPERIENCE.
SERIOUSLY. THIS PLACE IS KIND OF A DEATHTRAP.

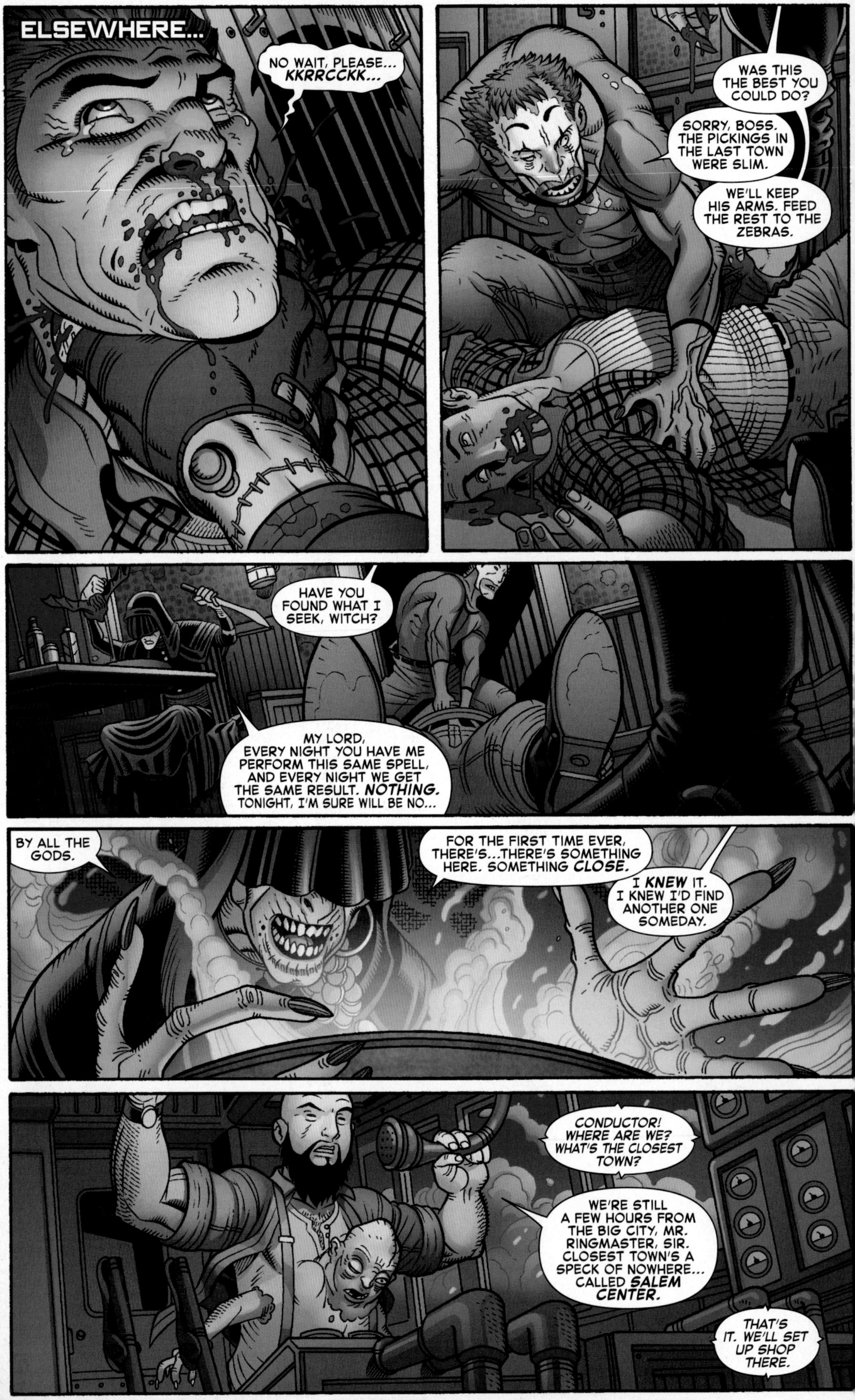
ELSEWHERE...
NO WAIT, PLEASE... KKRRCCKK...
WAS THIS THE BEST YOU COULD DO?
SORRY, BOSS. THE PICKINGS IN THE LAST TOWN WERE SLIM.
WE'LL KEEP HIS ARMS. FEED THE REST TO THE ZEBRAS.
HAVE YOU FOUND WHAT I SEEK, WITCH?
MY LORD, EVERY NIGHT YOU HAVE ME PERFORM THIS SAME SPELL, AND EVERY NIGHT WE GET THE SAME RESULT. NOTHING. TONIGHT, I'M SURE WILL BE NO...
BY ALL THE GODS.
FOR THE FIRST TIME EVER, THERE'S...THERE'S SOMETHING HERE. SOMETHING CLOSE.
I KNEW IT. I KNEW I'D FIND ANOTHER ONE SOMEDAY.
CONDUCTOR! WHERE ARE WE? WHAT'S THE CLOSEST TOWN?
WE'RE STILL A FEW HOURS FROM THE BIG CITY, MR. RINGMASTER, SIR. CLOSEST TOWN'S A SPECK OF NOWHERE... CALLED SALEM CENTER.
THAT'S IT. WE'LL SET UP SHOP THERE.

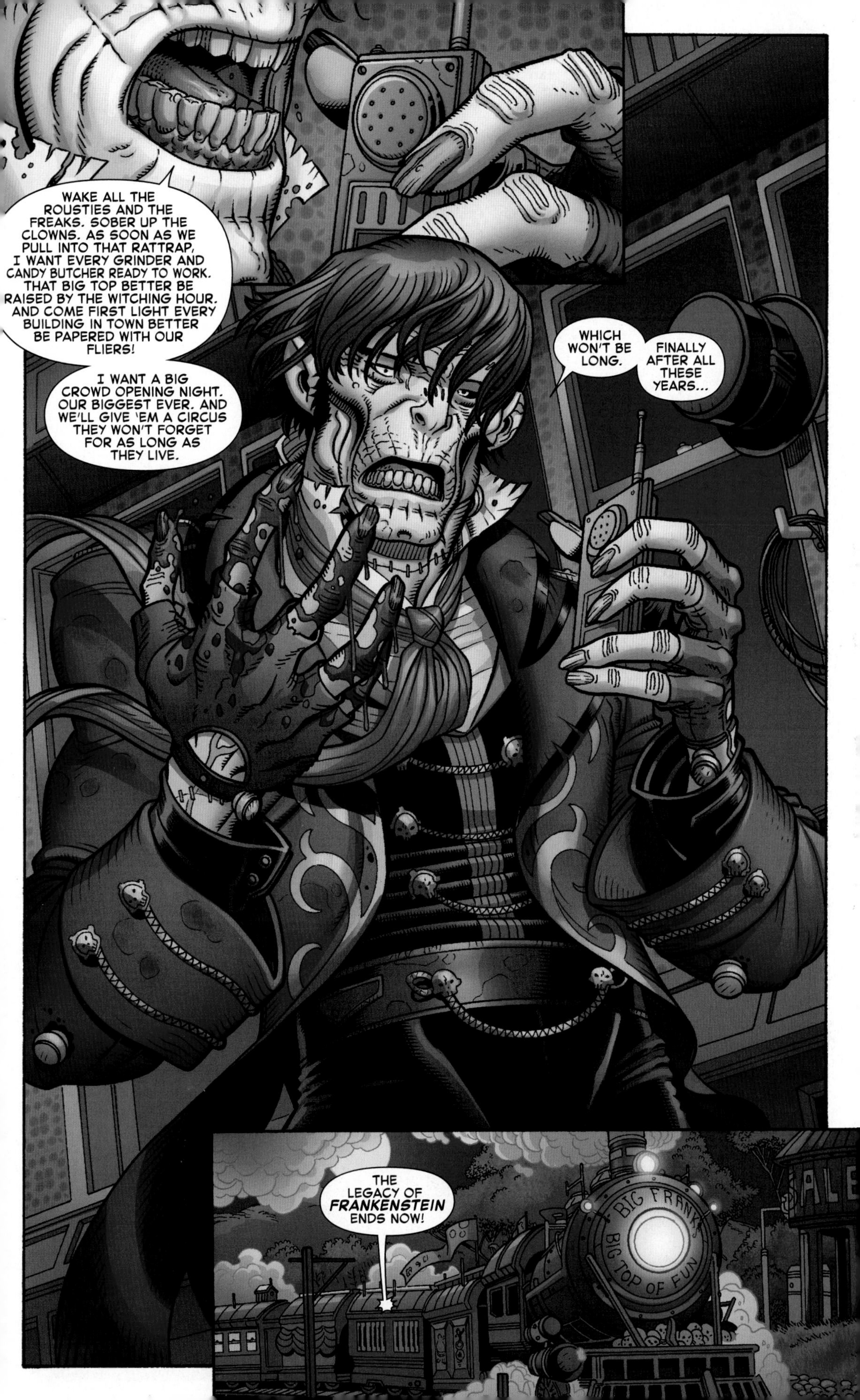

WAKE ALL THE ROUSTIES AND THE FREAKS. SOBER UP THE CLOWNS. AS SOON AS WE PULL INTO THAT RATTRAP, I WANT EVERY GRINDER AND CANDY BUTCHER READY TO WORK. THAT BIG TOP BETTER BE RAISED BY THE WITCHING HOUR. AND COME FIRST LIGHT EVERY BUILDING IN TOWN BETTER BE PAPERED WITH OUR FLIERS!
I WANT A BIG CROWD OPENING NIGHT. OUR BIGGEST EVER. AND WE'LL GIVE 'EM A CIRCUS THEY WON'T FORGET FOR AS LONG AS THEY LIVE.
WHICH WON'T BE LONG.
FINALLY AFTER ALL THESE YEARS...
THE LEGACY OF FRANKENSTEIN ENDS NOW!
BIG FRANK'S BIG TOP OF FUN

20 "THE SEARCH FOR SOMETHING NEW"

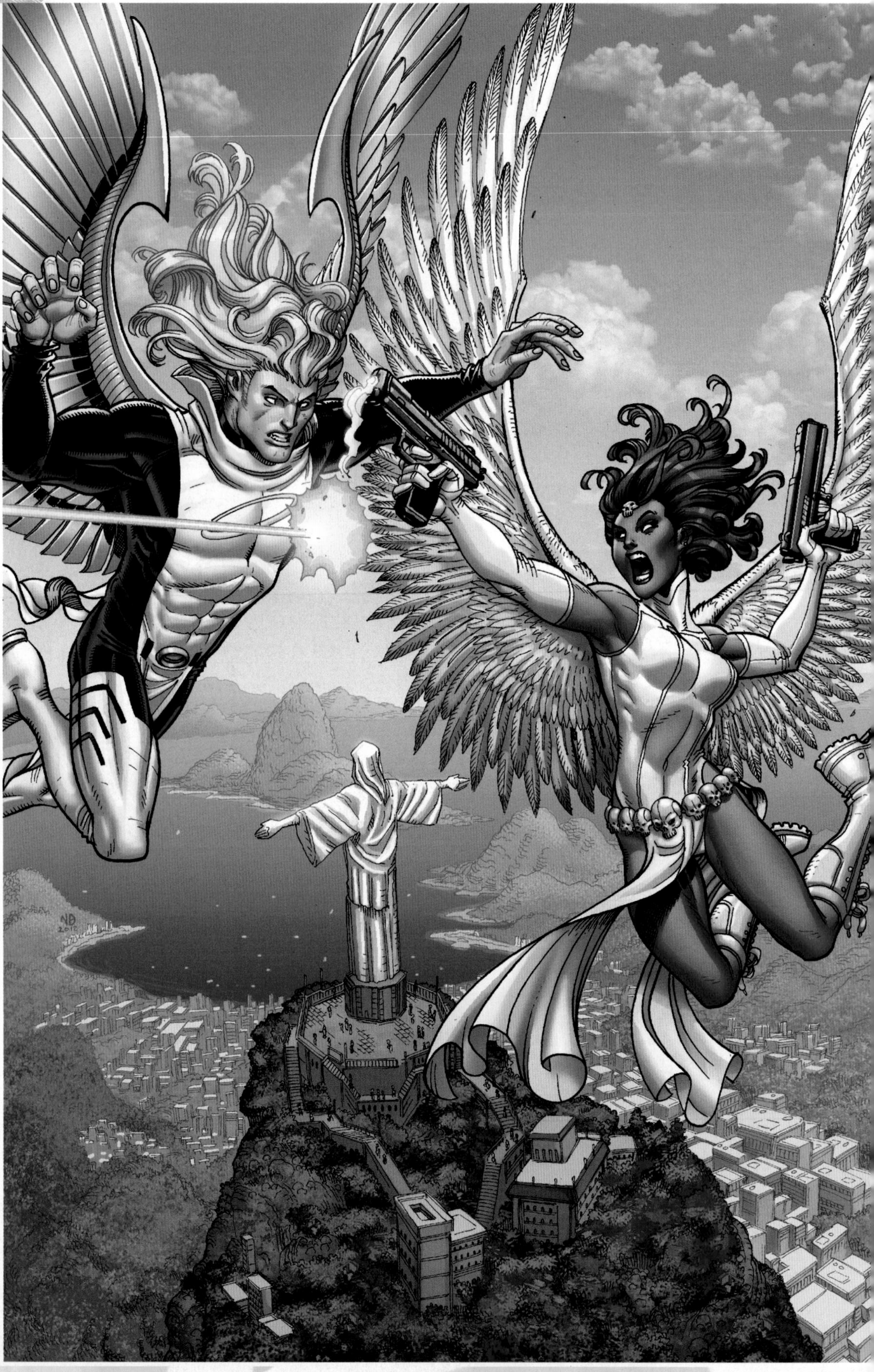

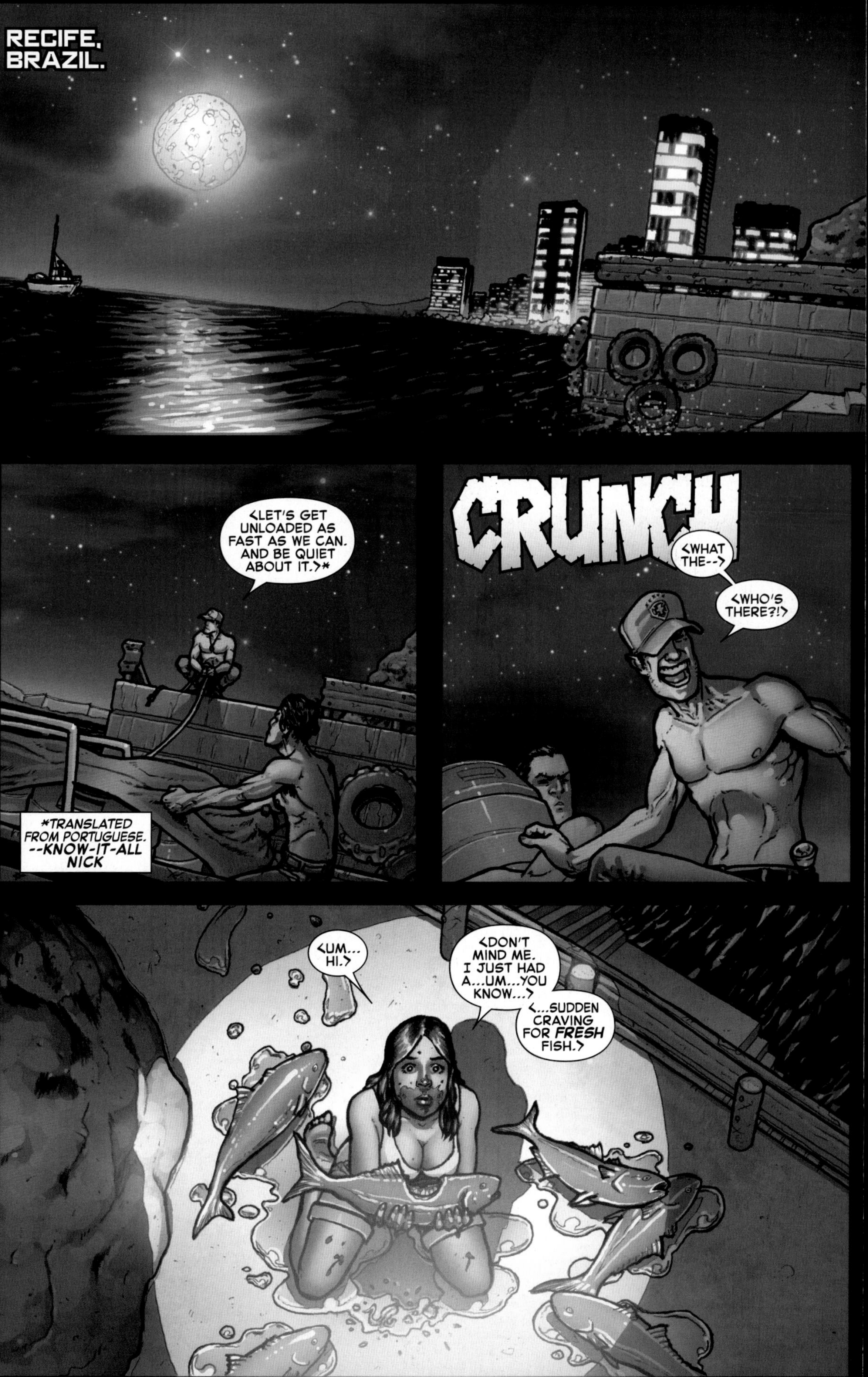
RECIFE, BRAZIL.
<LET'S GET UNLOADED AS FAST AS WE CAN. AND BE QUIET ABOUT IT.>*
*TRANSLATED FROM PORTUGUESE. --KNOW-IT-ALL NICK
CRUNCH
<WHAT THE-->
<WHO'S THERE?!>
<UM... HI.>
<DON'T MIND ME. I JUST HAD A...UM...YOU KNOW...>
<...SUDDEN CRAVING FOR FRESH FISH.>

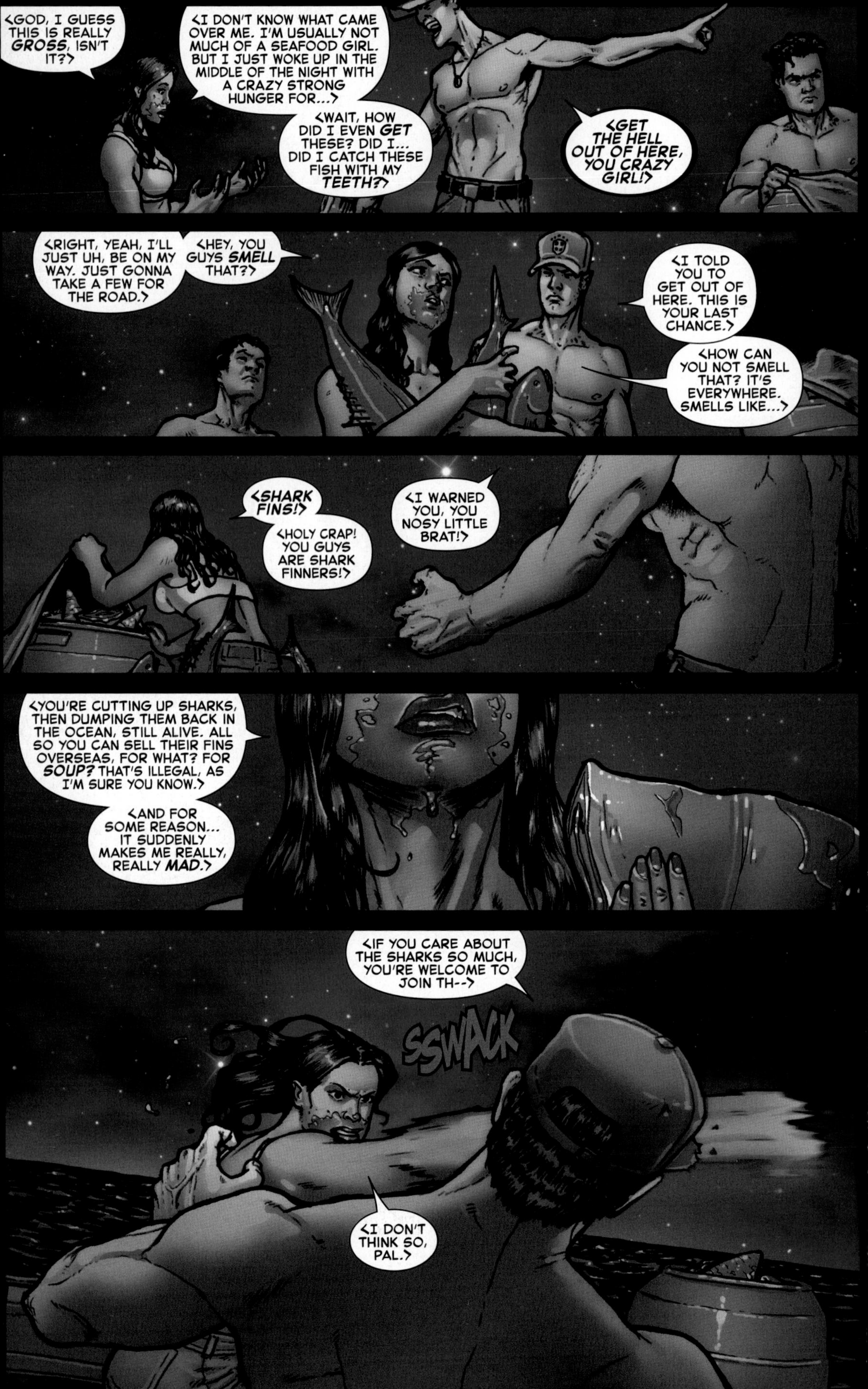
<GOD, I GUESS THIS IS REALLY ***GROSS***, ISN'T IT?>
<I DON'T KNOW WHAT CAME OVER ME. I'M USUALLY NOT MUCH OF A SEAFOOD GIRL. BUT I JUST WOKE UP IN THE MIDDLE OF THE NIGHT WITH A CRAZY STRONG HUNGER FOR...>
<WAIT, HOW DID I EVEN ***GET*** THESE? DID I... DID I CATCH THESE FISH WITH MY ***TEETH?***>
<***GET THE HELL OUT OF HERE, YOU CRAZY GIRL!***>
<RIGHT, YEAH, I'LL JUST UH, BE ON MY WAY. JUST GONNA TAKE A FEW FOR THE ROAD.>
<HEY, YOU GUYS ***SMELL*** THAT?>
<I TOLD YOU TO GET OUT OF HERE. THIS IS YOUR LAST CHANCE.>
<HOW CAN YOU NOT SMELL THAT? IT'S EVERYWHERE. SMELLS LIKE...>
<***SHARK FINS!***>
<HOLY CRAP! YOU GUYS ARE SHARK FINNERS!>
<I WARNED YOU, YOU NOSY LITTLE BRAT!>
<YOU'RE CUTTING UP SHARKS, THEN DUMPING THEM BACK IN THE OCEAN, STILL ALIVE. ALL SO YOU CAN SELL THEIR FINS OVERSEAS, FOR WHAT? FOR ***SOUP?*** THAT'S ILLEGAL, AS I'M SURE YOU KNOW.>
<AND FOR SOME REASON... IT SUDDENLY MAKES ME REALLY, REALLY ***MAD***.>
<IF YOU CARE ABOUT THE SHARKS SO MUCH, YOU'RE WELCOME TO JOIN TH-->
SSWACK
<I DON'T THINK SO, PAL.>

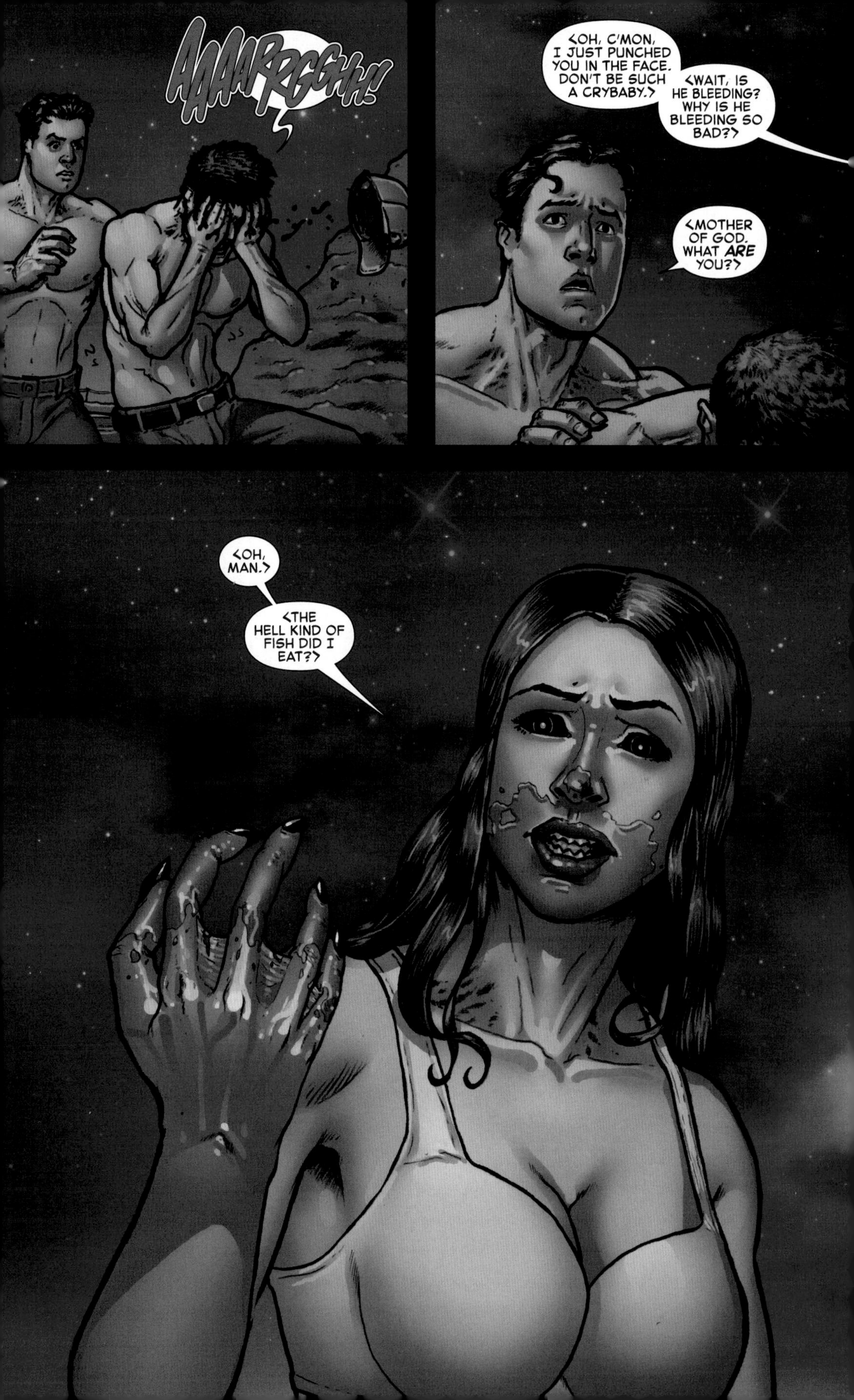
AAAARRGGHH!
<OH, C'MON, I JUST PUNCHED YOU IN THE FACE. DON'T BE SUCH A CRYBABY.>
<WAIT, IS HE BLEEDING? WHY IS HE BLEEDING SO BAD?>
<MOTHER OF GOD. WHAT *ARE* YOU?>
<OH, MAN.>
<THE HELL KIND OF FISH DID I EAT?>

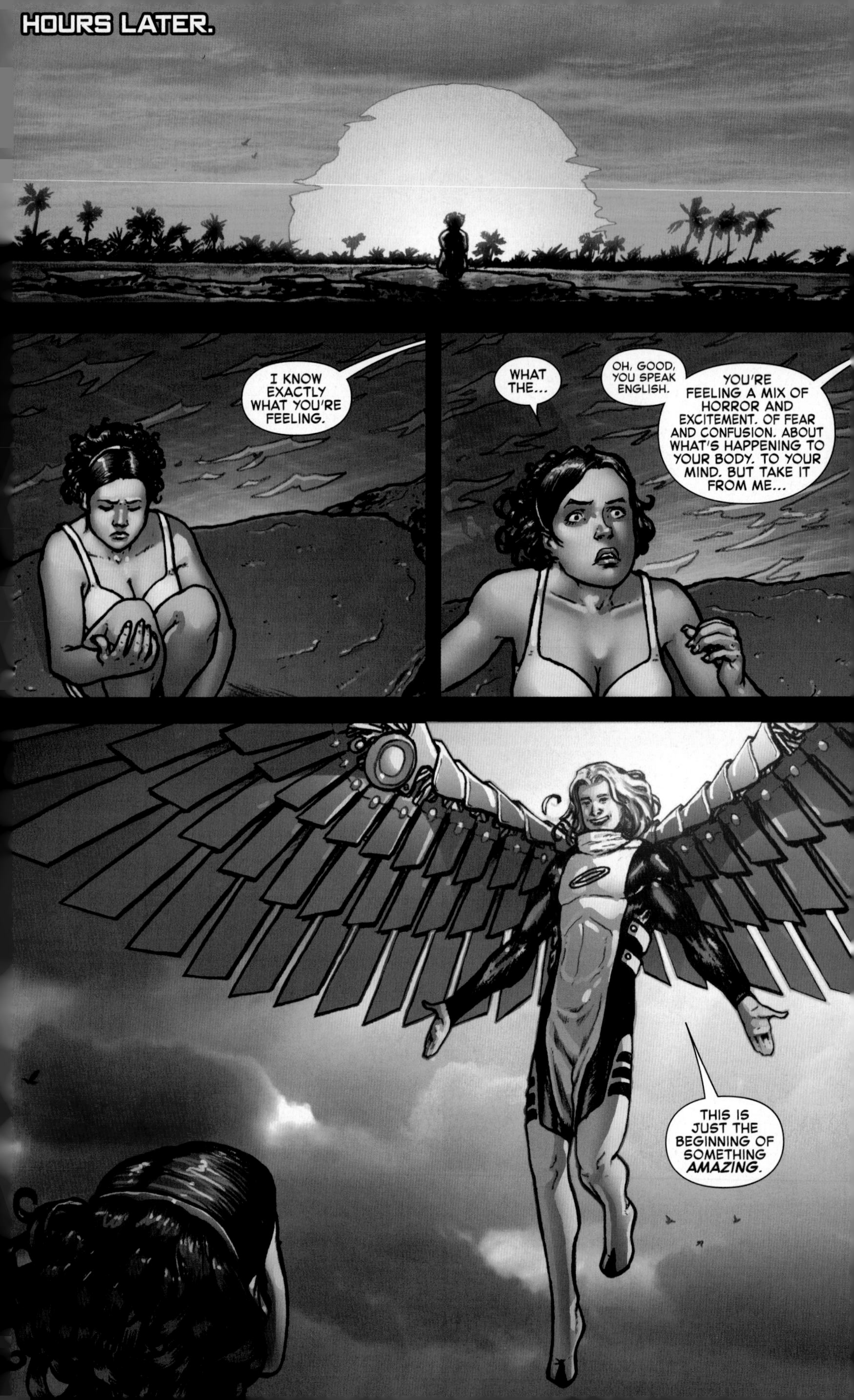
HOURS LATER.
I KNOW EXACTLY WHAT YOU'RE FEELING.
WHAT THE...
OH, GOOD, YOU SPEAK ENGLISH.
YOU'RE FEELING A MIX OF HORROR AND EXCITEMENT. OF FEAR AND CONFUSION. ABOUT WHAT'S HAPPENING TO YOUR BODY. TO YOUR MIND. BUT TAKE IT FROM ME...
THIS IS JUST THE BEGINNING OF SOMETHING *AMAZING*.

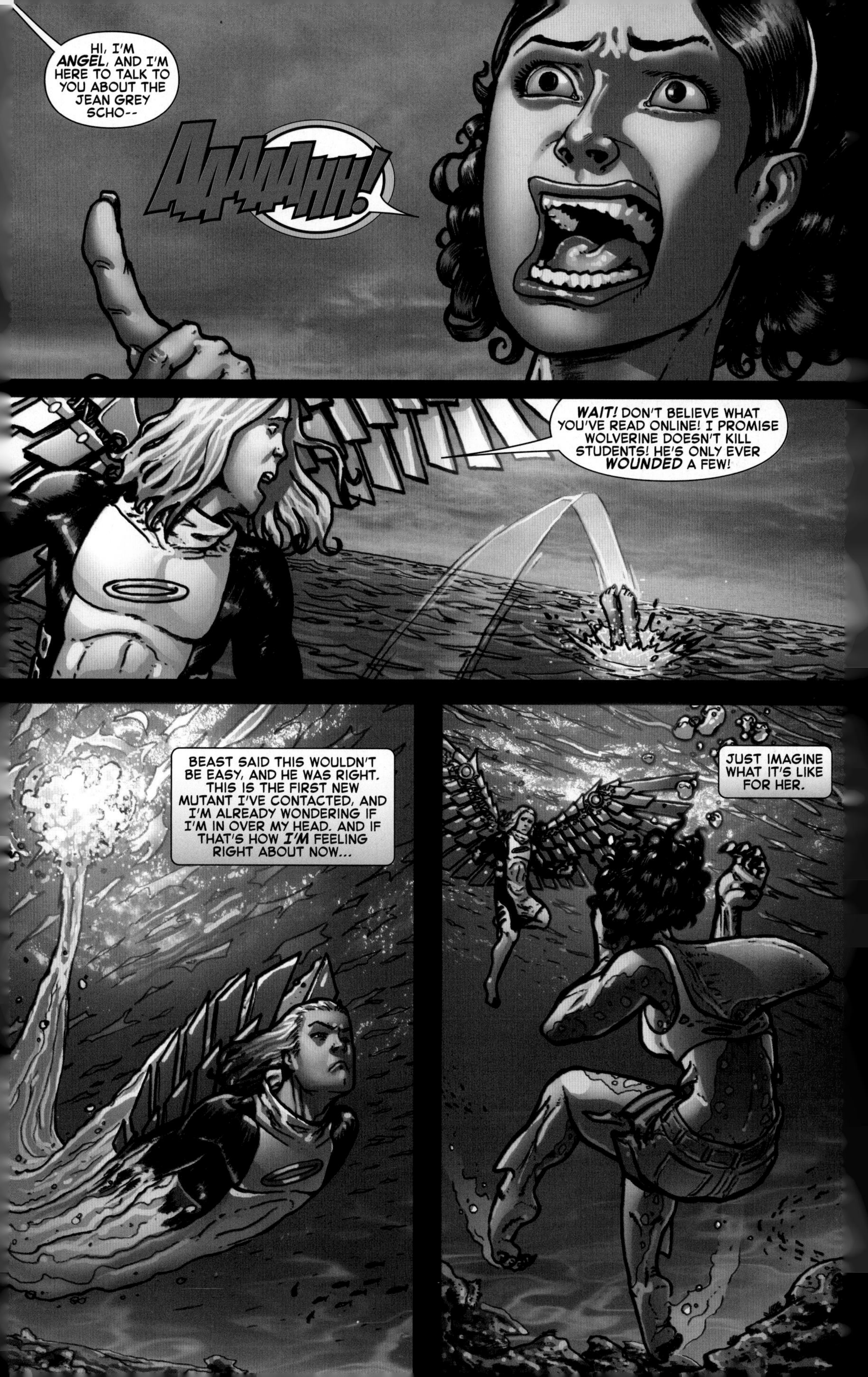
HI, I'M ANGEL, AND I'M HERE TO TALK TO YOU ABOUT THE JEAN GREY SCHO--
AAAAAHH!
WAIT! DON'T BELIEVE WHAT YOU'VE READ ONLINE! I PROMISE WOLVERINE DOESN'T KILL STUDENTS! HE'S ONLY EVER WOUNDED A FEW!
BEAST SAID THIS WOULDN'T BE EASY, AND HE WAS RIGHT. THIS IS THE FIRST NEW MUTANT I'VE CONTACTED, AND I'M ALREADY WONDERING IF I'M IN OVER MY HEAD. AND IF THAT'S HOW I'M FEELING RIGHT ABOUT NOW...
JUST IMAGINE WHAT IT'S LIKE FOR HER.

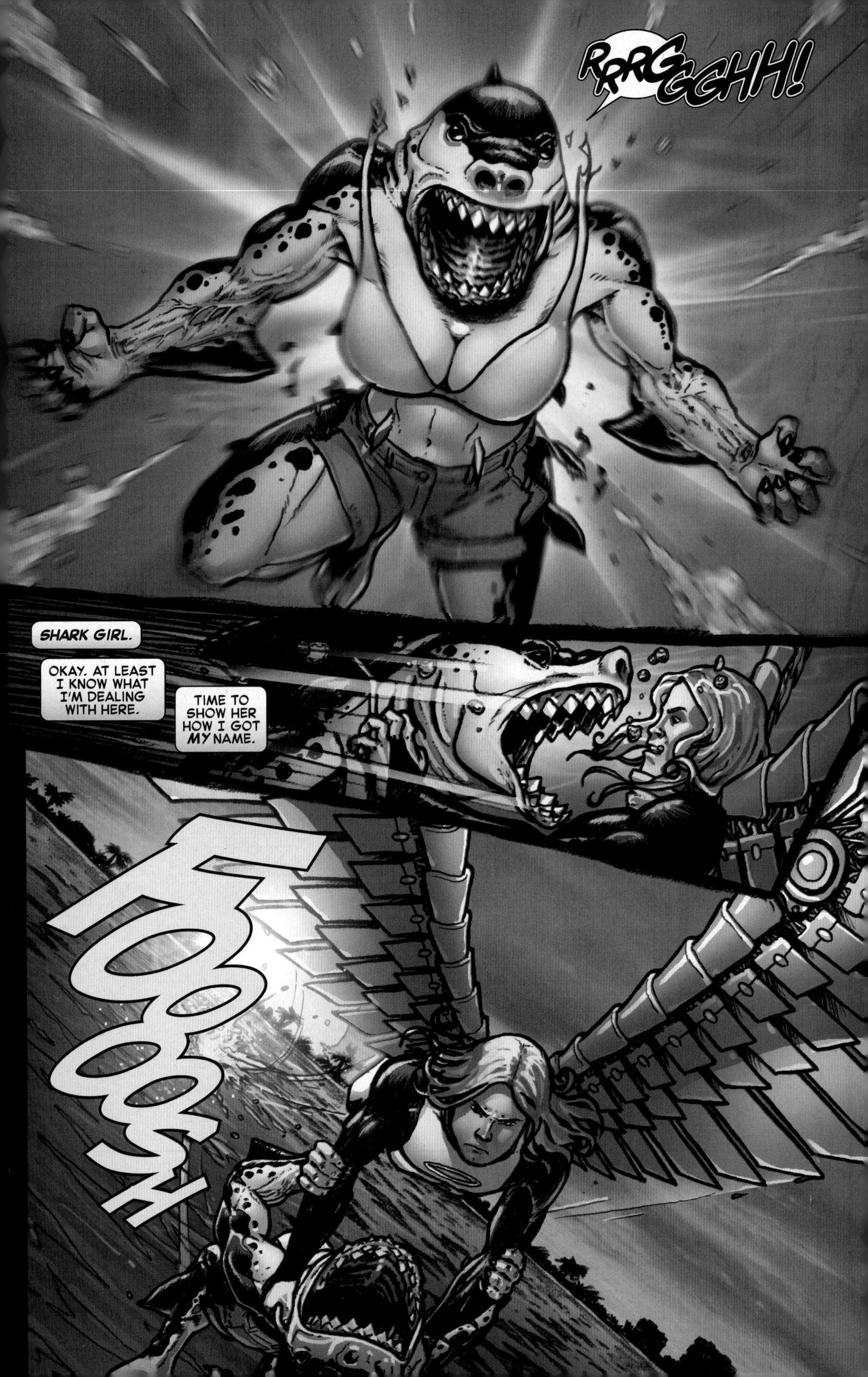
RRRGGGHH!
SHARK GIRL.
OKAY. AT LEAST I KNOW WHAT I'M DEALING WITH HERE.
TIME TO SHOW HER HOW I GOT MY NAME.
FOOOOSH

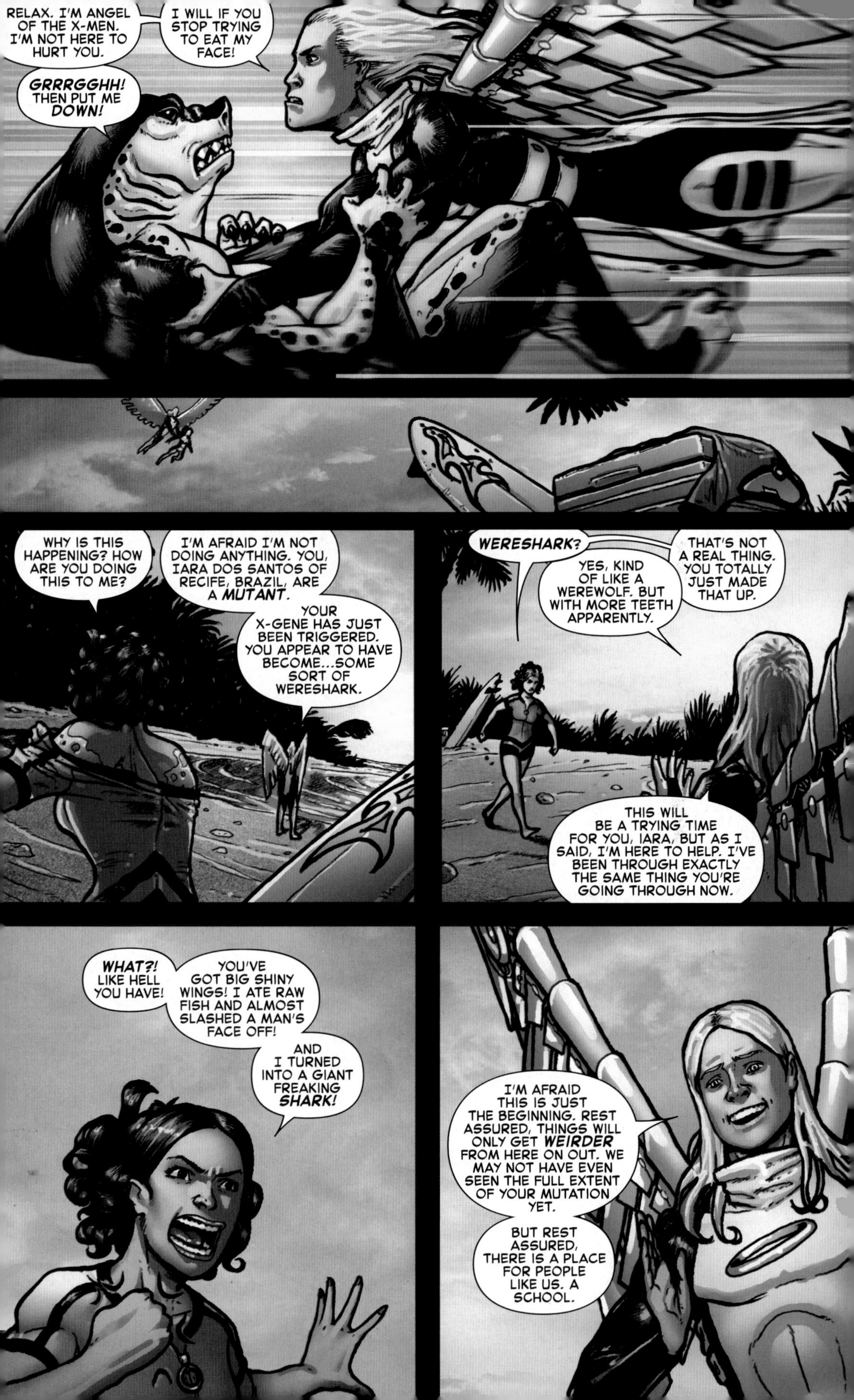

RELAX. I'M ANGEL OF THE X-MEN. I'M NOT HERE TO HURT YOU.
I WILL IF YOU STOP TRYING TO EAT MY FACE!
GRRRGGHH! THEN PUT ME DOWN!
WHY IS THIS HAPPENING? HOW ARE YOU DOING THIS TO ME?
I'M AFRAID I'M NOT DOING ANYTHING. YOU, IARA DOS SANTOS OF RECIFE, BRAZIL, ARE A MUTANT.
YOUR X-GENE HAS JUST BEEN TRIGGERED. YOU APPEAR TO HAVE BECOME...SOME SORT OF WERESHARK.
WERESHARK?
YES, KIND OF LIKE A WEREWOLF. BUT WITH MORE TEETH APPARENTLY.
THAT'S NOT A REAL THING. YOU TOTALLY JUST MADE THAT UP.
THIS WILL BE A TRYING TIME FOR YOU, IARA, BUT AS I SAID, I'M HERE TO HELP. I'VE BEEN THROUGH EXACTLY THE SAME THING YOU'RE GOING THROUGH NOW.
WHAT?! LIKE HELL YOU HAVE!
YOU'VE GOT BIG SHINY WINGS! I ATE RAW FISH AND ALMOST SLASHED A MAN'S FACE OFF!
AND I TURNED INTO A GIANT FREAKING SHARK!
I'M AFRAID THIS IS JUST THE BEGINNING. REST ASSURED, THINGS WILL ONLY GET WEIRDER FROM HERE ON OUT. WE MAY NOT HAVE EVEN SEEN THE FULL EXTENT OF YOUR MUTATION YET.
BUT REST ASSURED, THERE IS A PLACE FOR PEOPLE LIKE US. A SCHOOL.

"THE MOST ASTOUNDING SCHOOL YOU CAN IMAGINE."

HOURS EARLIER.

WARREN, I'M NOT SO SURE THIS IS A GOOD IDEA.

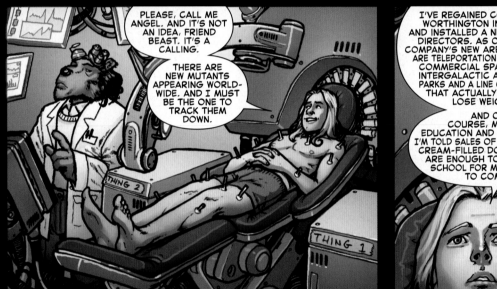

PLEASE, CALL ME ANGEL. AND IT'S NOT AN IDEA, FRIEND BEAST. IT'S A CALLING.

THERE ARE NEW MUTANTS APPEARING WORLD-WIDE. AND I MUST BE THE ONE TO TRACK THEM DOWN.

I'VE REGAINED CONTROL OF WORTHINGTON INDUSTRIES AND INSTALLED A NEW BOARD OF DIRECTORS. AS OF NOW, THE COMPANY'S NEW AREAS OF FOCUS ARE TELEPORTATION TECHNOLOGY, COMMERCIAL SPACE FLIGHT, INTERGALACTIC AMUSEMENT PARKS AND A LINE OF PASTRIES THAT ACTUALLY HELP YOU LOSE WEIGHT.

AND OF COURSE, MUTANT EDUCATION AND INTEGRATION. I'M TOLD SALES OF THE FAT-FREE CREAM-FILLED DONUTS ALONE ARE ENOUGH TO FUND THIS SCHOOL FOR MANY YEARS TO COME.

NO ONE DOUBTS YOUR HEART, ANGEL, BUT YOU ONLY JUST GRADUATED FROM THIS SCHOOL YOURSELF.

WHICH MAKES ME THE PERFECT AMBASSADOR. I'M NOT ASKING FOR MUCH, DR. MCCOY. I'LL NEED MS. GREY TO TRACK THE NEW MUTANTS WITH CEREBRA AND DIRECT ME ACCORDINGLY. AND THEN WHATEVER LOCAL CONTACTS YOU CAN OFFER. I'LL HANDLE THE REST.

ANGEL, PLEASE.

DO YOU KNOW WHO WE HAVE TO THANK FOR THAT MULTI-MILLION DOLLAR PASTRY LINE I MENTIONED? *BROO*. IT WAS HIS SCIENCE FAIR PROJECT, FINISHED RIGHT BEFORE HE WAS...

I *LOVE* THIS SCHOOL, *DR. MCCOY*, AND I'M WILLING TO DO WHATEVER IT TAKES TO SEE THAT ITS STUDENTS HAVE THE CHANCE TO THRIVE.

HOW IS BROO? ANY CHANGE IN HIS CONDITION? IF YOU PERMIT ME, I WOULD LIKE TO LAY HANDS ON HIM AND ATTEMPT TO--

BROO IS BEING CARED FOR. ANGEL, LISTEN TO ME...

YOU NEED TO BE WORRIED ABOUT *YOUR* CONDITION.

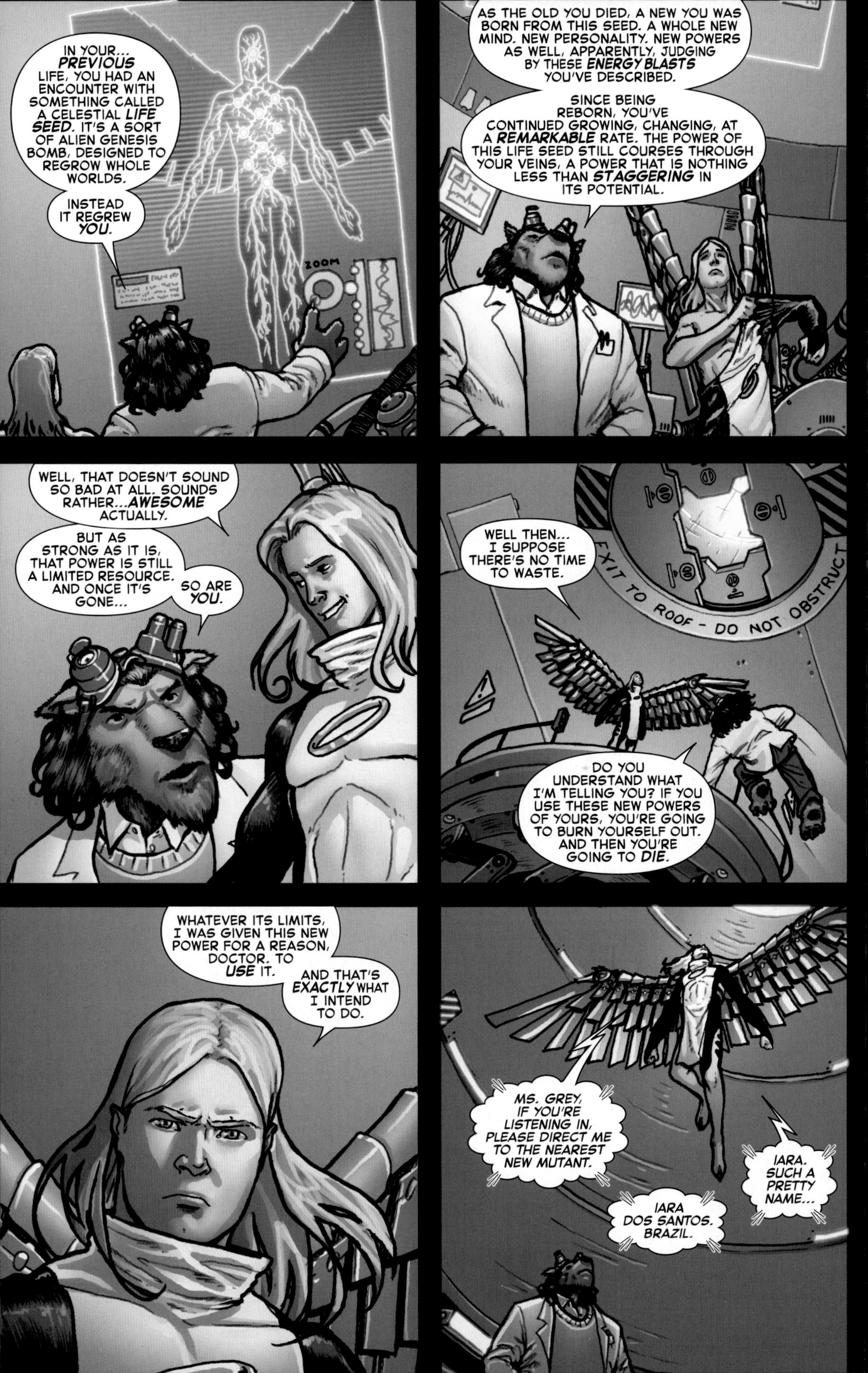
IN YOUR... PREVIOUS LIFE, YOU HAD AN ENCOUNTER WITH SOMETHING CALLED A CELESTIAL LIFE SEED. IT'S A SORT OF ALIEN GENESIS BOMB, DESIGNED TO REGROW WHOLE WORLDS.
INSTEAD IT REGREW YOU.
ZOOM
AS THE OLD YOU DIED, A NEW YOU WAS BORN FROM THIS SEED. A WHOLE NEW MIND. NEW PERSONALITY. NEW POWERS AS WELL, APPARENTLY, JUDGING BY THESE ENERGY BLASTS YOU'VE DESCRIBED.
SINCE BEING REBORN, YOU'VE CONTINUED GROWING, CHANGING, AT A REMARKABLE RATE. THE POWER OF THIS LIFE SEED STILL COURSES THROUGH YOUR VEINS, A POWER THAT IS NOTHING LESS THAN STAGGERING IN ITS POTENTIAL.
WELL, THAT DOESN'T SOUND SO BAD AT ALL. SOUNDS RATHER...AWESOME ACTUALLY.
BUT AS STRONG AS IT IS, THAT POWER IS STILL A LIMITED RESOURCE. AND ONCE IT'S GONE...
SO ARE YOU.
WELL THEN... I SUPPOSE THERE'S NO TIME TO WASTE.
EXIT TO ROOF - DO NOT OBSTRUCT
DO YOU UNDERSTAND WHAT I'M TELLING YOU? IF YOU USE THESE NEW POWERS OF YOURS, YOU'RE GOING TO BURN YOURSELF OUT. AND THEN YOU'RE GOING TO DIE.
WHATEVER ITS LIMITS, I WAS GIVEN THIS NEW POWER FOR A REASON, DOCTOR. TO USE IT.
AND THAT'S EXACTLY WHAT I INTEND TO DO.
MS. GREY, IF YOU'RE LISTENING IN, PLEASE DIRECT ME TO THE NEAREST NEW MUTANT.
IARA DOS SANTOS. BRAZIL.
IARA. SUCH A PRETTY NAME...

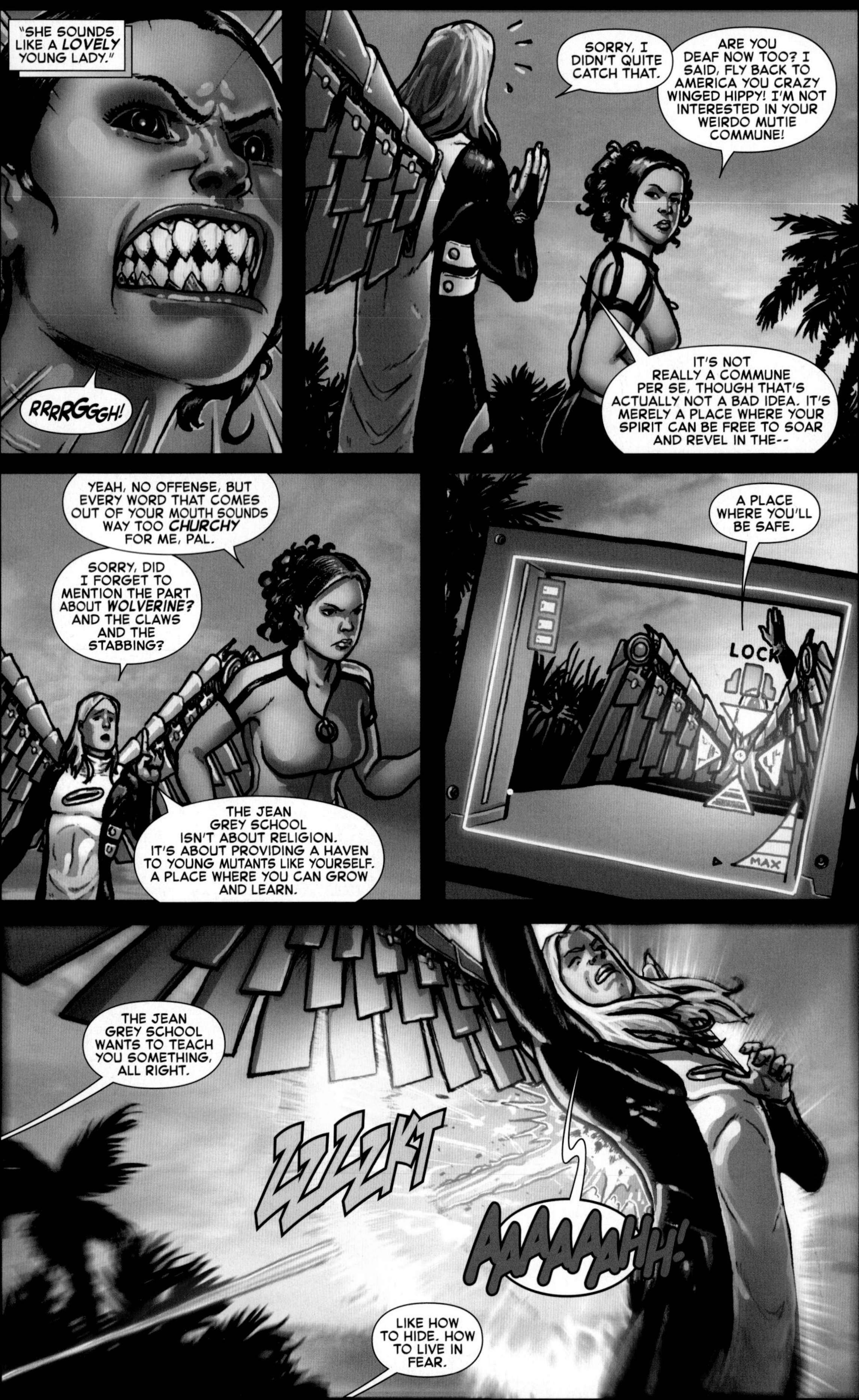
"SHE SOUNDS LIKE A LOVELY YOUNG LADY."
RRRRGGGH!
SORRY, I DIDN'T QUITE CATCH THAT.
ARE YOU DEAF NOW TOO? I SAID, FLY BACK TO AMERICA YOU CRAZY WINGED HIPPY! I'M NOT INTERESTED IN YOUR WEIRDO MUTIE COMMUNE!
IT'S NOT REALLY A COMMUNE PER SE, THOUGH THAT'S ACTUALLY NOT A BAD IDEA. IT'S MERELY A PLACE WHERE YOUR SPIRIT CAN BE FREE TO SOAR AND REVEL IN THE--
YEAH, NO OFFENSE, BUT EVERY WORD THAT COMES OUT OF YOUR MOUTH SOUNDS WAY TOO CHURCHY FOR ME, PAL.
SORRY, DID I FORGET TO MENTION THE PART ABOUT WOLVERINE? AND THE CLAWS AND THE STABBING?
THE JEAN GREY SCHOOL ISN'T ABOUT RELIGION. IT'S ABOUT PROVIDING A HAVEN TO YOUNG MUTANTS LIKE YOURSELF. A PLACE WHERE YOU CAN GROW AND LEARN.
A PLACE WHERE YOU'LL BE SAFE.
LOCK
MAX
THE JEAN GREY SCHOOL WANTS TO TEACH YOU SOMETHING, ALL RIGHT.
ZZZZKT
AAAAAAHH!
LIKE HOW TO HIDE. HOW TO LIVE IN FEAR.

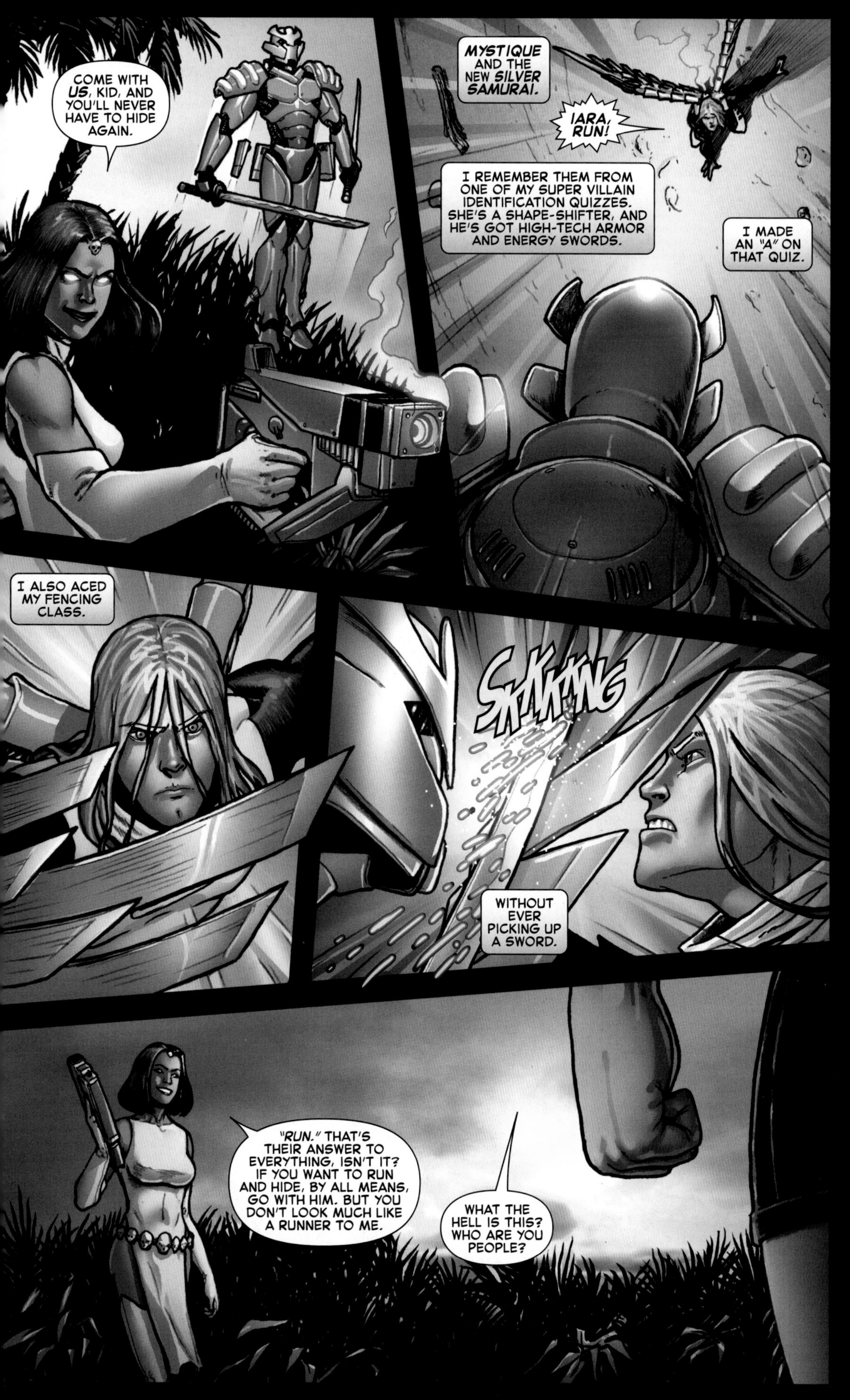
COME WITH *US*, KID, AND YOU'LL NEVER HAVE TO HIDE AGAIN.
MYSTIQUE AND THE NEW *SILVER SAMURAI*.
IARA, RUN!
I REMEMBER THEM FROM ONE OF MY SUPER VILLAIN IDENTIFICATION QUIZZES. SHE'S A SHAPE-SHIFTER, AND HE'S GOT HIGH-TECH ARMOR AND ENERGY SWORDS.
I MADE AN "A" ON THAT QUIZ.
I ALSO ACED MY FENCING CLASS.
SKKKKING
WITHOUT EVER PICKING UP A SWORD.
"*RUN.*" THAT'S THEIR ANSWER TO EVERYTHING, ISN'T IT? IF YOU WANT TO RUN AND HIDE, BY ALL MEANS, GO WITH HIM. BUT YOU DON'T LOOK MUCH LIKE A RUNNER TO ME.
WHAT THE HELL IS THIS? WHO ARE YOU PEOPLE?

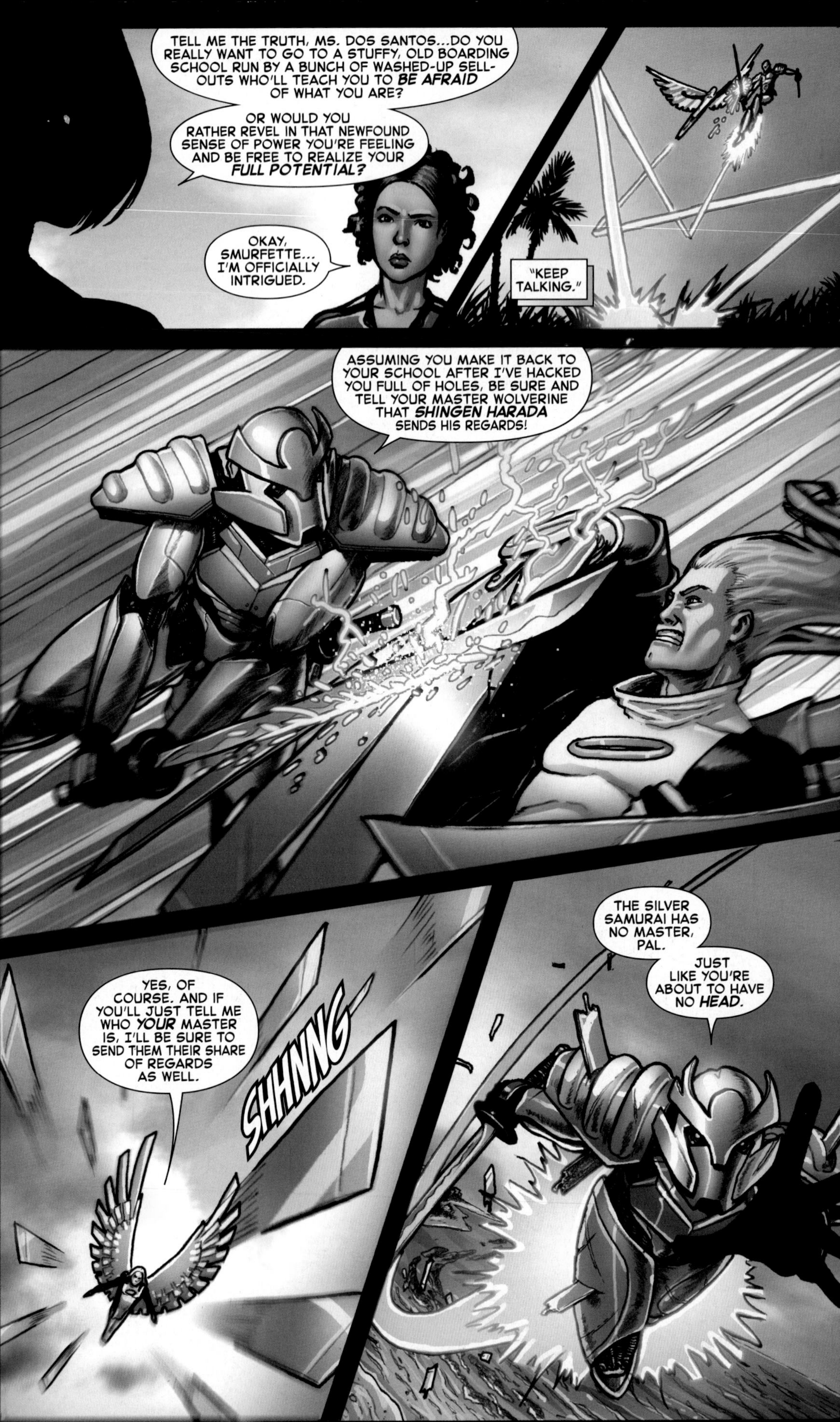
TELL ME THE TRUTH, MS. DOS SANTOS...DO YOU REALLY WANT TO GO TO A STUFFY, OLD BOARDING SCHOOL RUN BY A BUNCH OF WASHED-UP SELL-OUTS WHO'LL TEACH YOU TO BE AFRAID OF WHAT YOU ARE?
OR WOULD YOU RATHER REVEL IN THAT NEWFOUND SENSE OF POWER YOU'RE FEELING AND BE FREE TO REALIZE YOUR FULL POTENTIAL?
OKAY, SMURFETTE... I'M OFFICIALLY INTRIGUED.
"KEEP TALKING."
ASSUMING YOU MAKE IT BACK TO YOUR SCHOOL AFTER I'VE HACKED YOU FULL OF HOLES, BE SURE AND TELL YOUR MASTER WOLVERINE THAT SHINGEN HARADA SENDS HIS REGARDS!
YES, OF COURSE. AND IF YOU'LL JUST TELL ME WHO YOUR MASTER IS, I'LL BE SURE TO SEND THEM THEIR SHARE OF REGARDS AS WELL.
SHHNNG
THE SILVER SAMURAI HAS NO MASTER, PAL.
JUST LIKE YOU'RE ABOUT TO HAVE NO HEAD.

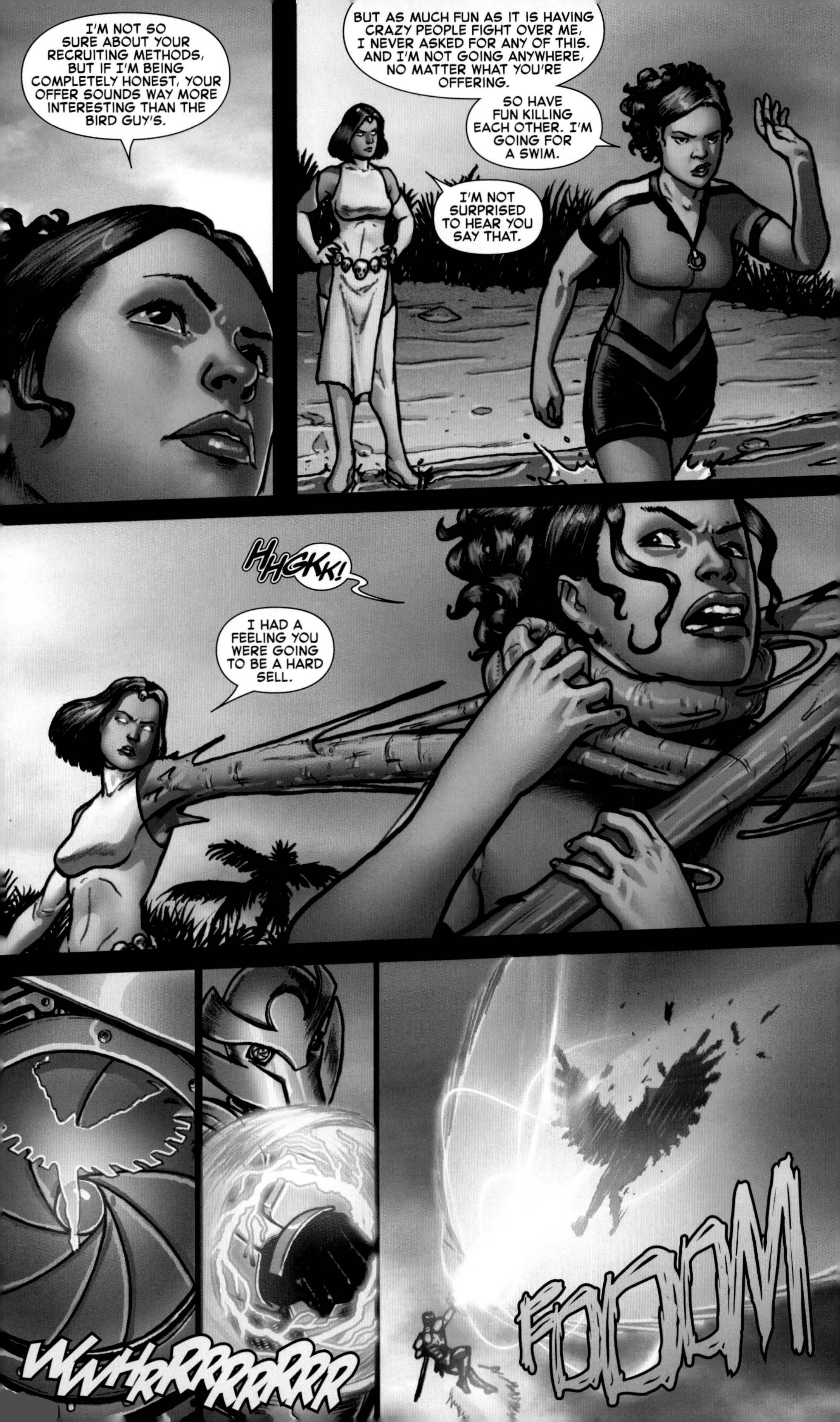
I'M NOT SO SURE ABOUT YOUR RECRUITING METHODS, BUT IF I'M BEING COMPLETELY HONEST, YOUR OFFER SOUNDS WAY MORE INTERESTING THAN THE BIRD GUY'S.
BUT AS MUCH FUN AS IT IS HAVING CRAZY PEOPLE FIGHT OVER ME, I NEVER ASKED FOR ANY OF THIS. AND I'M NOT GOING ANYWHERE, NO MATTER WHAT YOU'RE OFFERING.
SO HAVE FUN KILLING EACH OTHER. I'M GOING FOR A SWIM.
I'M NOT SURPRISED TO HEAR YOU SAY THAT.
HHGKK!
I HAD A FEELING YOU WERE GOING TO BE A HARD SELL.
WWHRRRRRRRRRR
FOOOM

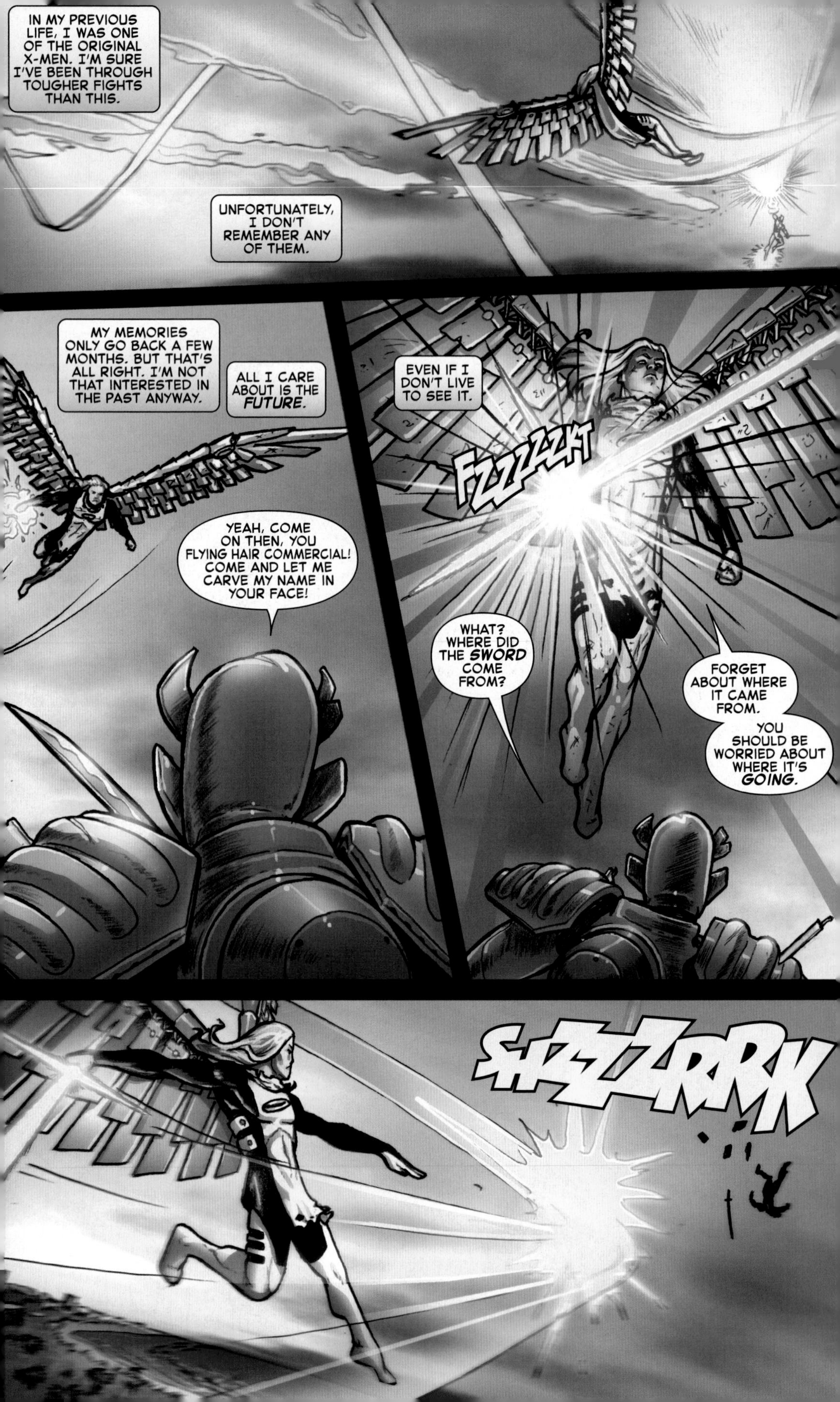
IN MY PREVIOUS LIFE, I WAS ONE OF THE ORIGINAL X-MEN. I'M SURE I'VE BEEN THROUGH TOUGHER FIGHTS THAN THIS.
UNFORTUNATELY, I DON'T REMEMBER ANY OF THEM.
MY MEMORIES ONLY GO BACK A FEW MONTHS. BUT THAT'S ALL RIGHT. I'M NOT THAT INTERESTED IN THE PAST ANYWAY.
ALL I CARE ABOUT IS THE *FUTURE.*
YEAH, COME ON THEN, YOU FLYING HAIR COMMERCIAL! COME AND LET ME CARVE MY NAME IN YOUR FACE!
EVEN IF I DON'T LIVE TO SEE IT.
FZZZZZKT
WHAT? WHERE DID THE *SWORD* COME FROM?
FORGET ABOUT WHERE IT CAME FROM.
YOU SHOULD BE WORRIED ABOUT WHERE IT'S *GOING.*
SHZZZRRK

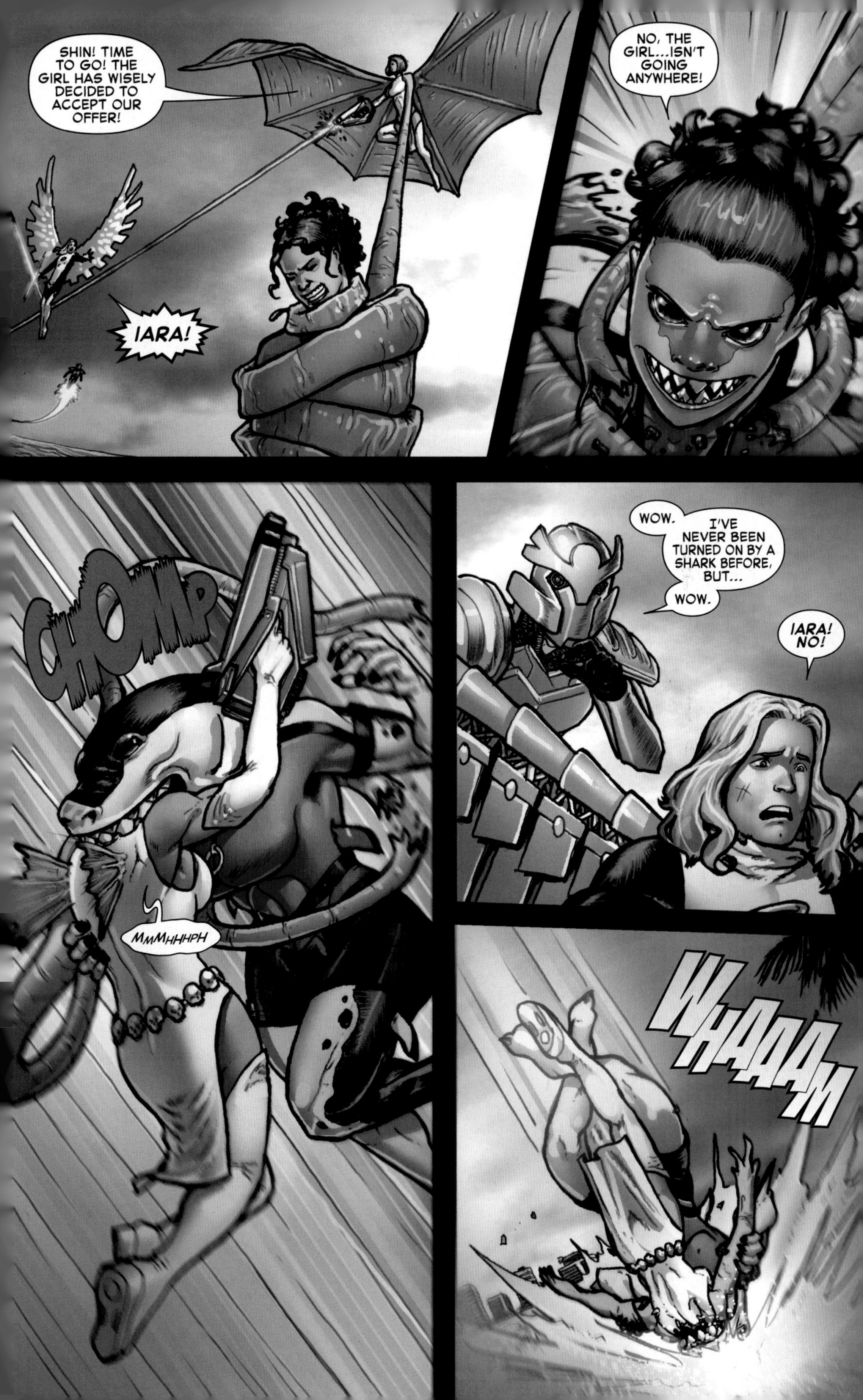
SHIN! TIME TO GO! THE GIRL HAS WISELY DECIDED TO ACCEPT OUR OFFER!
¡ARA!
NO, THE GIRL...ISN'T GOING ANYWHERE!
CHOMP
MMMHHHPH
WOW.
I'VE NEVER BEEN TURNED ON BY A SHARK BEFORE, BUT...
WOW.
¡ARA! NO!
WHAAAM

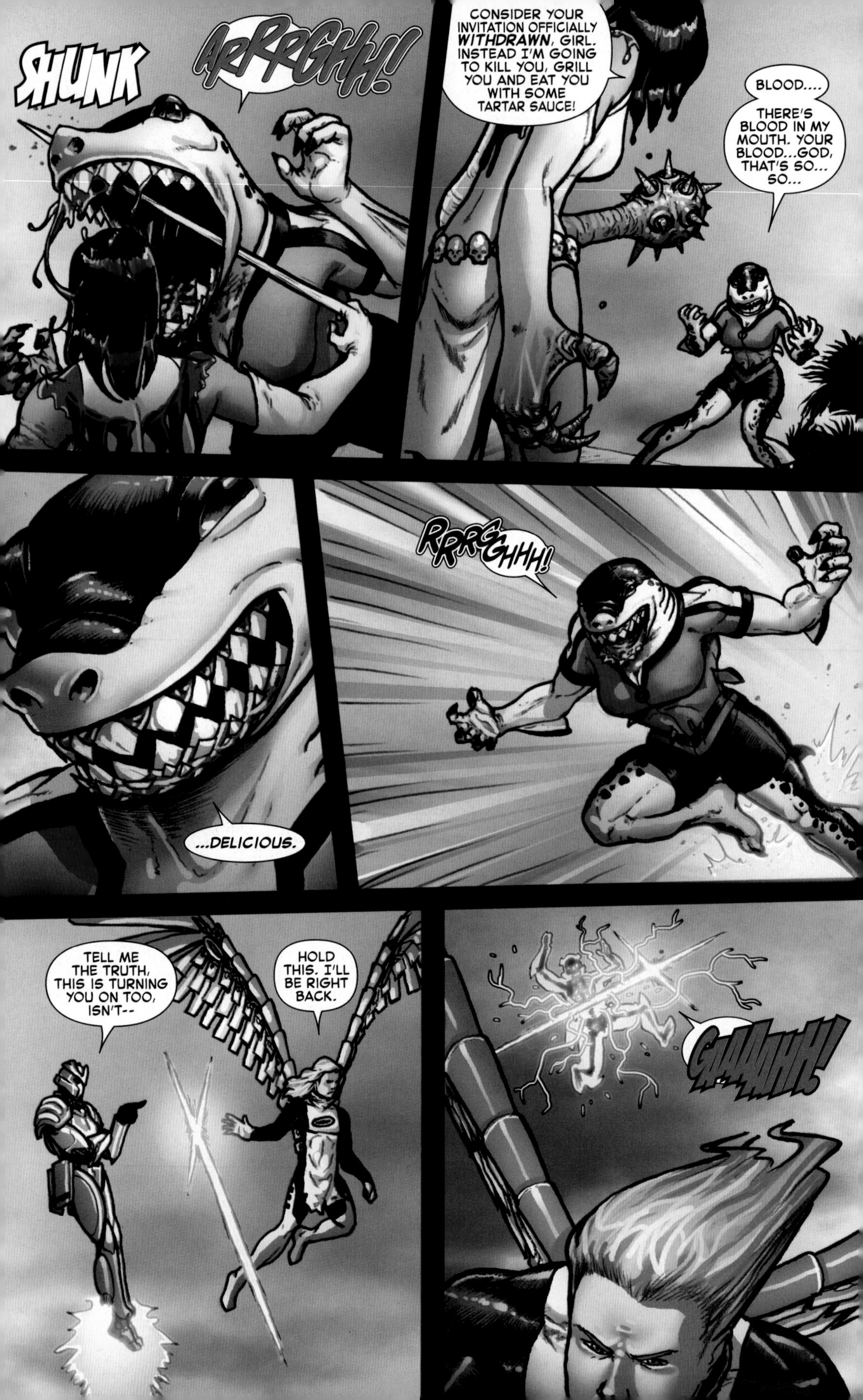
SHUNK
ARRRGHH!
CONSIDER YOUR INVITATION OFFICIALLY *WITHDRAWN*, GIRL. INSTEAD I'M GOING TO KILL YOU, GRILL YOU AND EAT YOU WITH SOME TARTAR SAUCE!
BLOOD....
THERE'S BLOOD IN MY MOUTH. YOUR BLOOD...GOD, THAT'S SO... SO...
...DELICIOUS.
RRRGHHH!
TELL ME THE TRUTH, THIS IS TURNING YOU ON TOO, ISN'T--
HOLD THIS. I'LL BE RIGHT BACK.
GAAAAHH!

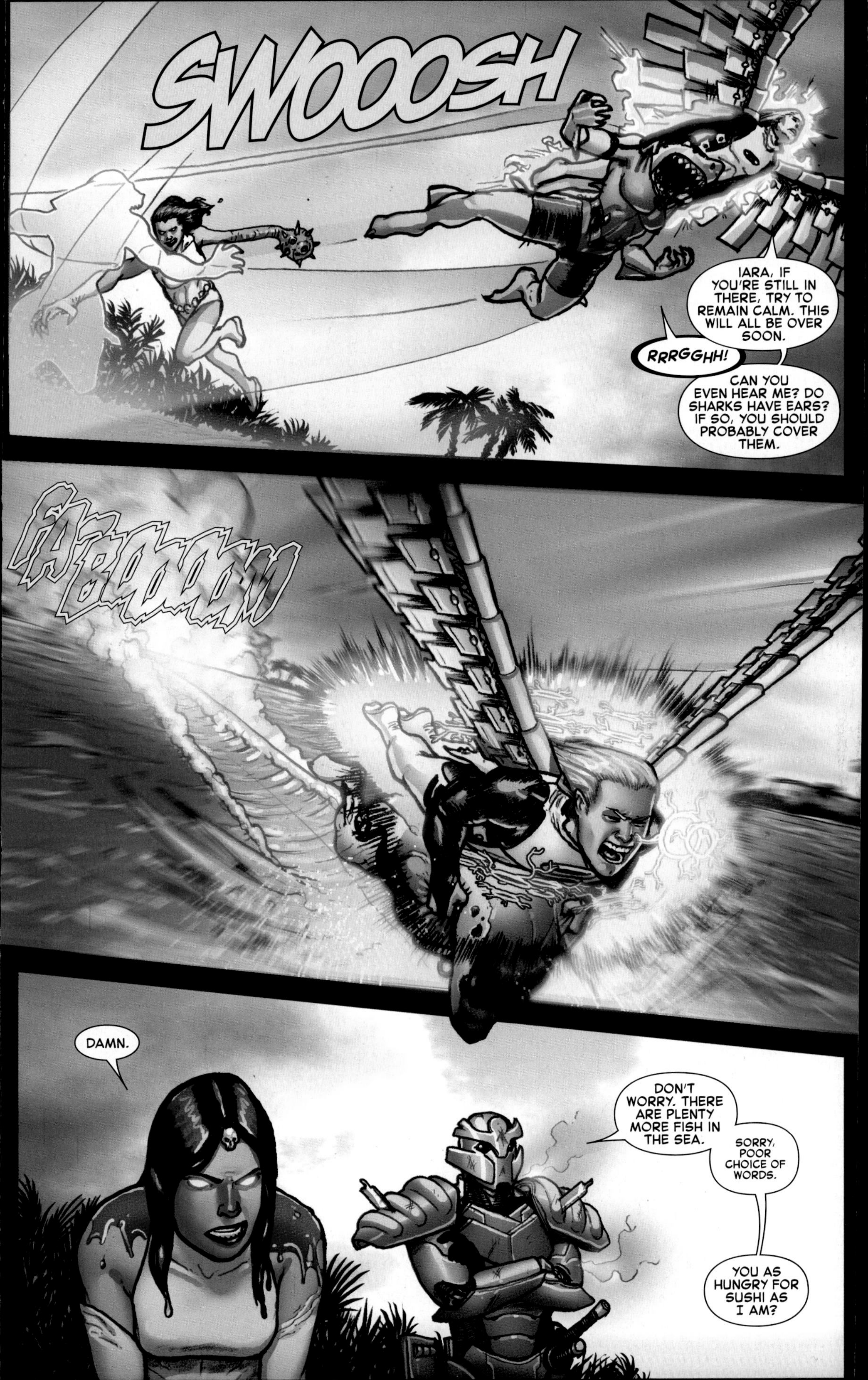

SWOOOSH
IARA, IF YOU'RE STILL IN THERE, TRY TO REMAIN CALM. THIS WILL ALL BE OVER SOON.
RRRGGHH!
CAN YOU EVEN HEAR ME? DO SHARKS HAVE EARS? IF SO, YOU SHOULD PROBABLY COVER THEM.
DAMN.
DON'T WORRY. THERE ARE PLENTY MORE FISH IN THE SEA.
SORRY, POOR CHOICE OF WORDS.
YOU AS HUNGRY FOR SUSHI AS I AM?

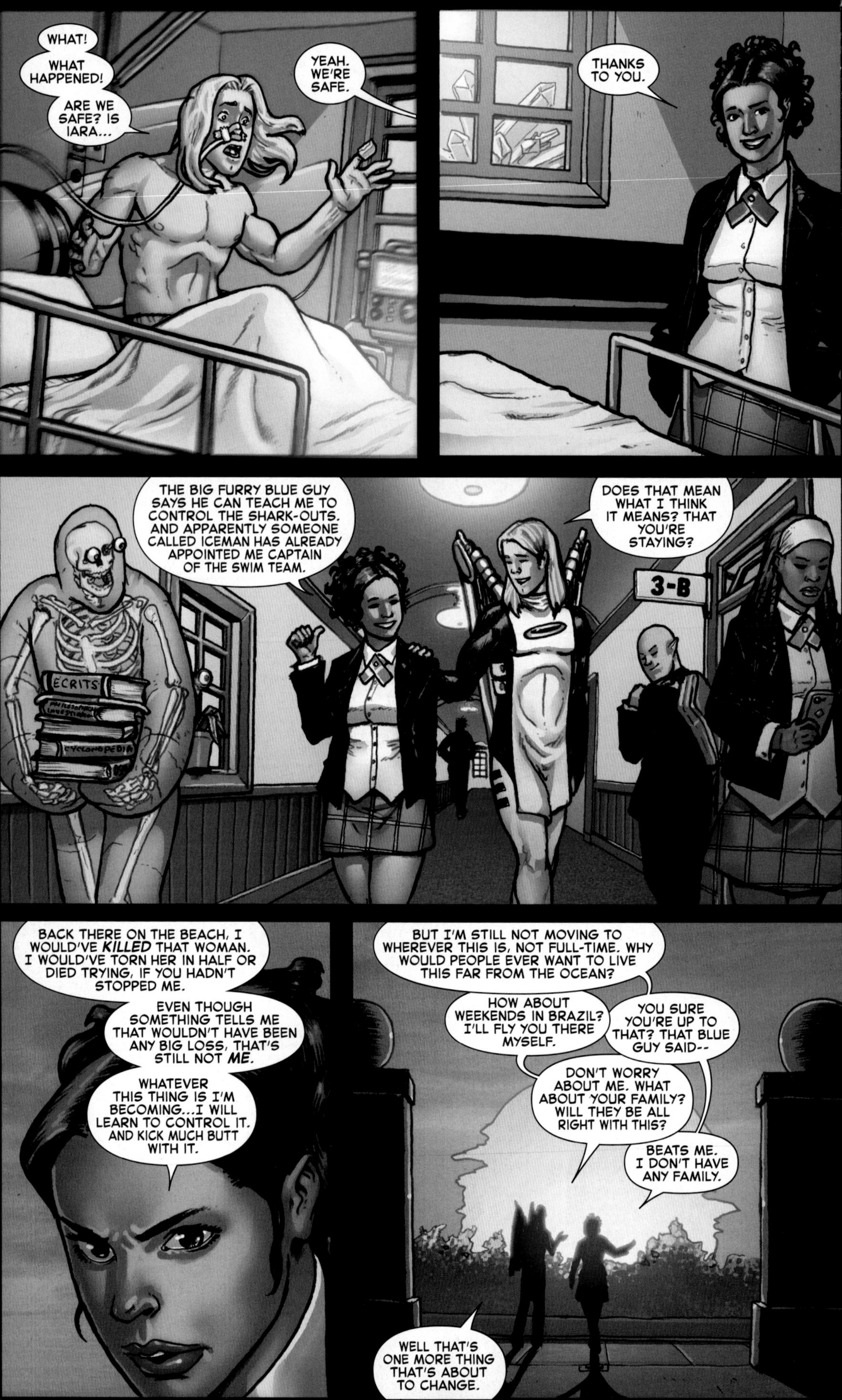
WHAT!
WHAT HAPPENED!
ARE WE SAFE? IS IARA...
YEAH. WE'RE SAFE.
THANKS TO YOU.
ECRITS
CYCLOPEDIA
THE BIG FURRY BLUE GUY SAYS HE CAN TEACH ME TO CONTROL THE SHARK-OUTS. AND APPARENTLY SOMEONE CALLED ICEMAN HAS ALREADY APPOINTED ME CAPTAIN OF THE SWIM TEAM.
DOES THAT MEAN WHAT I THINK IT MEANS? THAT YOU'RE STAYING?
3-B
BACK THERE ON THE BEACH, I WOULD'VE *KILLED* THAT WOMAN. I WOULD'VE TORN HER IN HALF OR DIED TRYING, IF YOU HADN'T STOPPED ME.
EVEN THOUGH SOMETHING TELLS ME THAT WOULDN'T HAVE BEEN ANY BIG LOSS, THAT'S STILL NOT *ME*.
WHATEVER THIS THING IS I'M BECOMING...I WILL LEARN TO CONTROL IT. AND KICK MUCH BUTT WITH IT.
BUT I'M STILL NOT MOVING TO WHEREVER THIS IS, NOT FULL-TIME. WHY WOULD PEOPLE EVER WANT TO LIVE THIS FAR FROM THE OCEAN?
HOW ABOUT WEEKENDS IN BRAZIL? I'LL FLY YOU THERE MYSELF.
YOU SURE YOU'RE UP TO THAT? THAT BLUE GUY SAID--
DON'T WORRY ABOUT ME. WHAT ABOUT YOUR FAMILY? WILL THEY BE ALL RIGHT WITH THIS?
BEATS ME. I DON'T HAVE ANY FAMILY.
WELL THAT'S ONE MORE THING THAT'S ABOUT TO CHANGE.

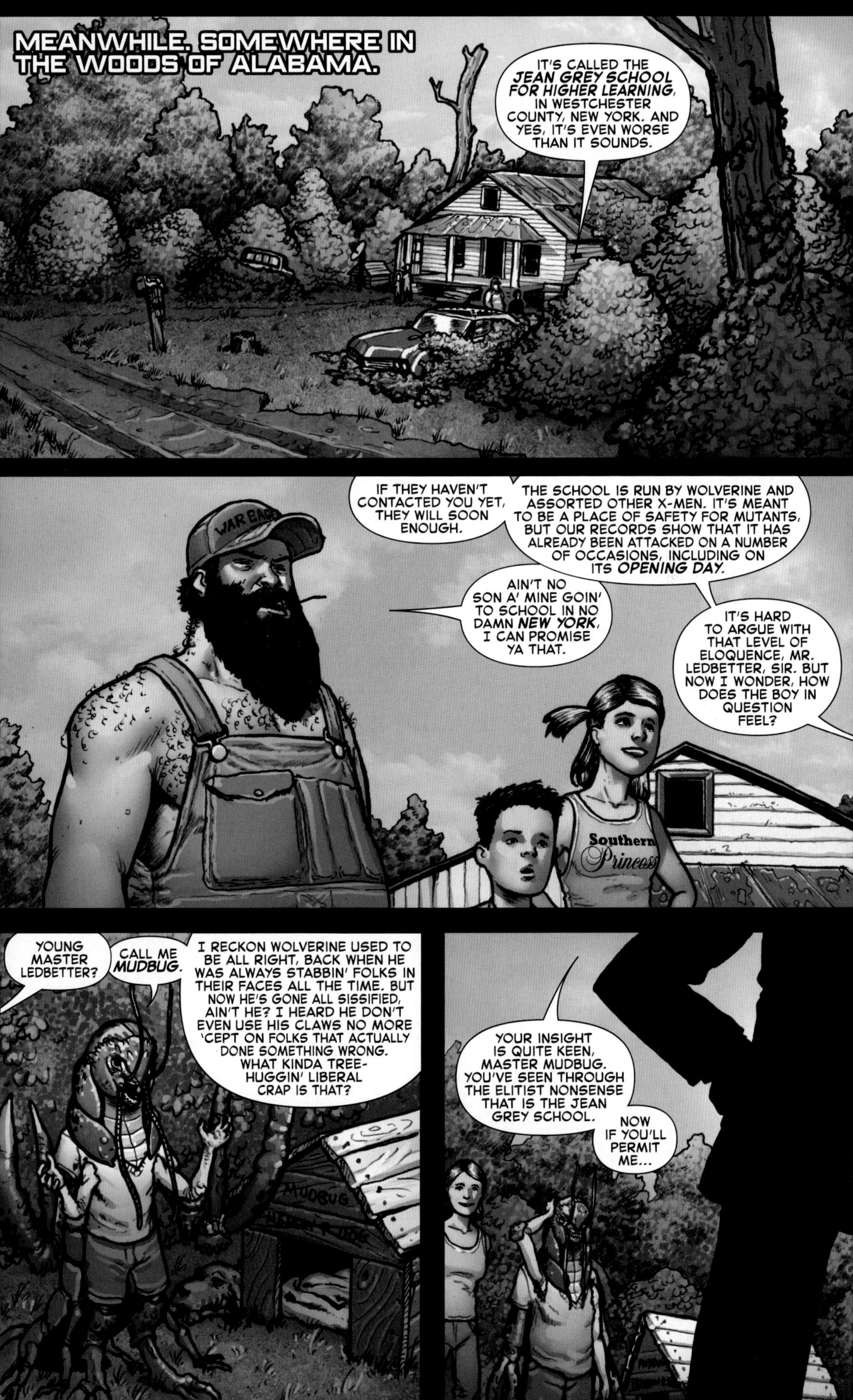
MEANWHILE. SOMEWHERE IN THE WOODS OF ALABAMA.
IT'S CALLED THE JEAN GREY SCHOOL FOR HIGHER LEARNING, IN WESTCHESTER COUNTY, NEW YORK. AND YES, IT'S EVEN WORSE THAN IT SOUNDS.
IF THEY HAVEN'T CONTACTED YOU YET, THEY WILL SOON ENOUGH.
THE SCHOOL IS RUN BY WOLVERINE AND ASSORTED OTHER X-MEN. IT'S MEANT TO BE A PLACE OF SAFETY FOR MUTANTS, BUT OUR RECORDS SHOW THAT IT HAS ALREADY BEEN ATTACKED ON A NUMBER OF OCCASIONS, INCLUDING ON ITS OPENING DAY.
AIN'T NO SON A' MINE GOIN' TO SCHOOL IN NO DAMN NEW YORK, I CAN PROMISE YA THAT.
IT'S HARD TO ARGUE WITH THAT LEVEL OF ELOQUENCE, MR. LEDBETTER, SIR. BUT NOW I WONDER, HOW DOES THE BOY IN QUESTION FEEL?
WAR EAGLE
Southern Princess
YOUNG MASTER LEDBETTER?
CALL ME MUDBUG.
I RECKON WOLVERINE USED TO BE ALL RIGHT, BACK WHEN HE WAS ALWAYS STABBIN' FOLKS IN THEIR FACES ALL THE TIME. BUT NOW HE'S GONE ALL SISSIFIED, AIN'T HE? I HEARD HE DON'T EVEN USE HIS CLAWS NO MORE 'CEPT ON FOLKS THAT ACTUALLY DONE SOMETHING WRONG. WHAT KINDA TREE-HUGGIN' LIBERAL CRAP IS THAT?
MUDBUG
YOUR INSIGHT IS QUITE KEEN, MASTER MUDBUG. YOU'VE SEEN THROUGH THE ELITIST NONSENSE THAT IS THE JEAN GREY SCHOOL.
NOW IF YOU'LL PERMIT ME...

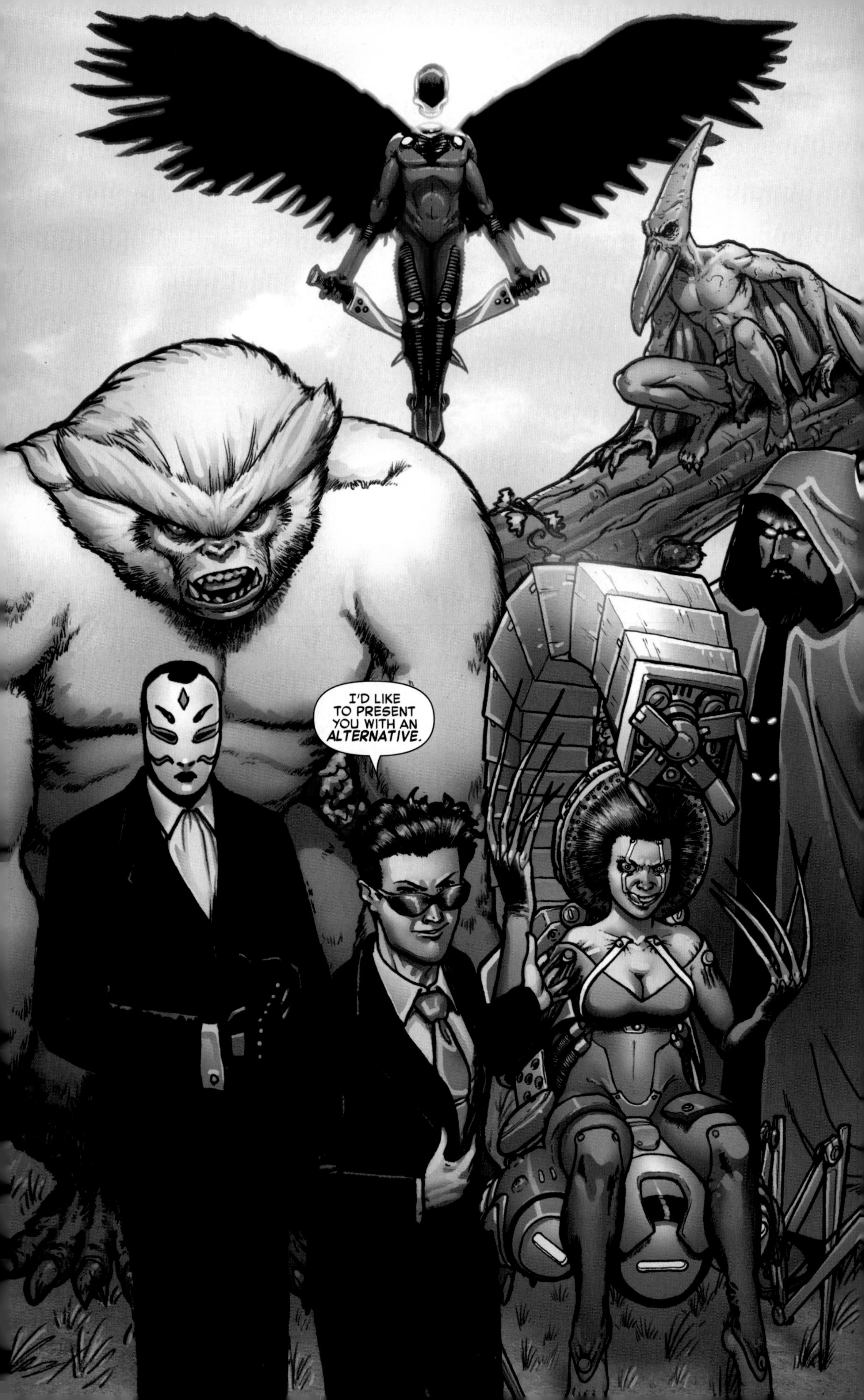
I'D LIKE TO PRESENT YOU WITH AN *ALTERNATIVE*.

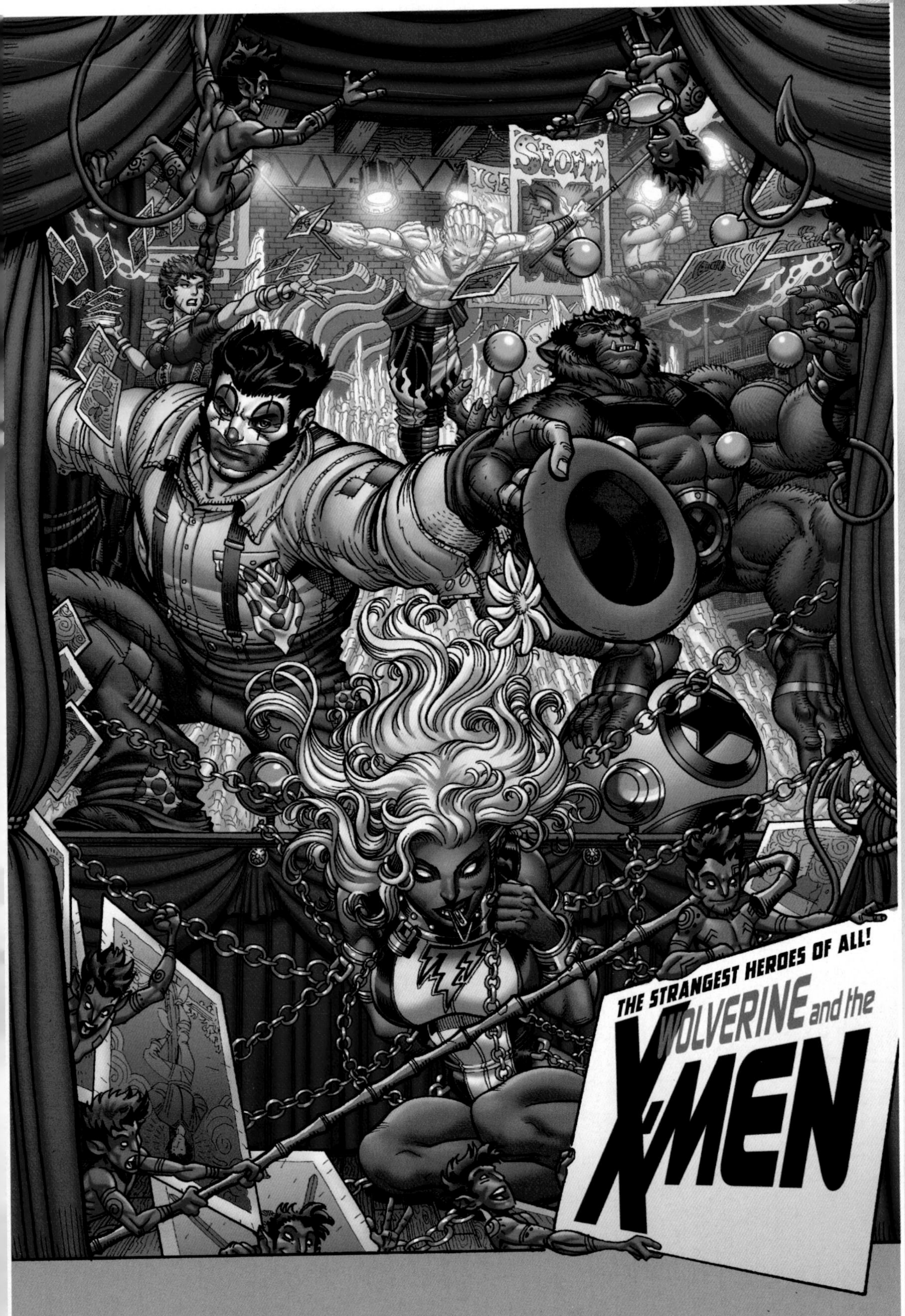
STORM
ICE
THE STRANGEST HEROES OF ALL!
WOLVERINE and the
X-MEN

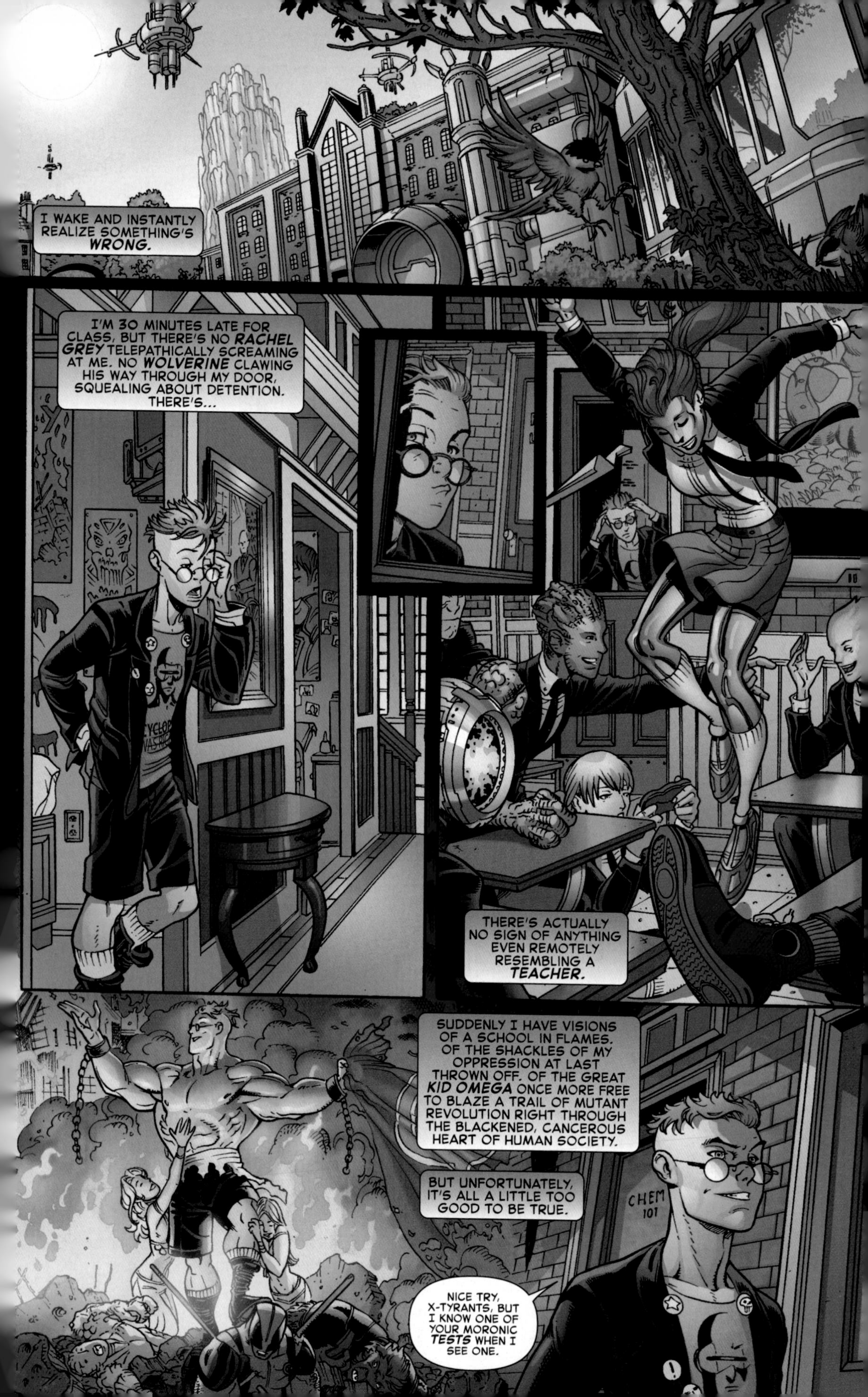
I WAKE AND INSTANTLY REALIZE SOMETHING'S WRONG.
I'M 30 MINUTES LATE FOR CLASS, BUT THERE'S NO RACHEL GREY TELEPATHICALLY SCREAMING AT ME. NO WOLVERINE CLAWING HIS WAY THROUGH MY DOOR, SQUEALING ABOUT DETENTION. THERE'S...
THERE'S ACTUALLY NO SIGN OF ANYTHING EVEN REMOTELY RESEMBLING A TEACHER.
SUDDENLY I HAVE VISIONS OF A SCHOOL IN FLAMES. OF THE SHACKLES OF MY OPPRESSION AT LAST THROWN OFF. OF THE GREAT KID OMEGA ONCE MORE FREE TO BLAZE A TRAIL OF MUTANT REVOLUTION RIGHT THROUGH THE BLACKENED, CANCEROUS HEART OF HUMAN SOCIETY.
BUT UNFORTUNATELY, IT'S ALL A LITTLE TOO GOOD TO BE TRUE.
CHEM 101
NICE TRY, X-TYRANTS, BUT I KNOW ONE OF YOUR MORONIC TESTS WHEN I SEE ONE.

KNEAD EDGUKASHUN

NO TEACHERS! RIOT AT THE GREY SCHOOL!

SHUT UP, YOU MORON.

MINDSCANNING THE GROUNDS. THEY MUST BE HERE SOMEWHERE.

I'VE BEEN QUIETLY READING TO MYSELF IN AN EMPTY PSYCHOLOGY CLASS FOR *TWO HOURS* NOW. DID DR. McCOY GET TRAPPED IN HIS OFFICE BY BAMFS AGAIN?

ANYBODY SEEN PROFESSOR DRAKE AROUND? ALL THE ICE DOORS IN THE EAST WING ARE MELTING SHUT. I HAD TO SMASH MY WAY OUT THROUGH THE GIRL'S LOCKER ROOM. IT WAS HORRIBLE.

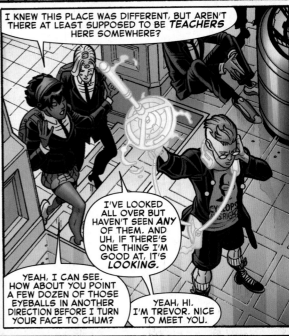

I KNEW THIS PLACE WAS DIFFERENT, BUT AREN'T THERE AT LEAST SUPPOSED TO BE *TEACHERS* HERE SOMEWHERE?

I'VE LOOKED ALL OVER BUT HAVEN'T SEEN *ANY* OF THEM. AND UH, IF THERE'S ONE THING I'M GOOD AT, IT'S *LOOKING.*

YEAH, I CAN SEE. HOW ABOUT YOU POINT A FEW DOZEN OF THOSE EYEBALLS IN ANOTHER DIRECTION BEFORE I TURN YOUR FACE TO CHUM?

YEAH, HI. I'M TREVOR. NICE TO MEET YOU.

THEY'RE GONE. THE ENTIRE STAFF. THEY'RE NOT ANYWHERE ON SCHOOL GROUNDS.

BUT... WHERE *ARE* THEY? WHAT DOES THIS MEAN?

AVENGERS VS. X-MEN 2? THE RETURN OF THE SKRULLS? CHILDREN OF THE CORN?

WHAT IT MEANS IS, THE FRONT DOORS ARE WIDE OPEN...

AND I, FOR ONE, AM WALKING THROUGH THEM.

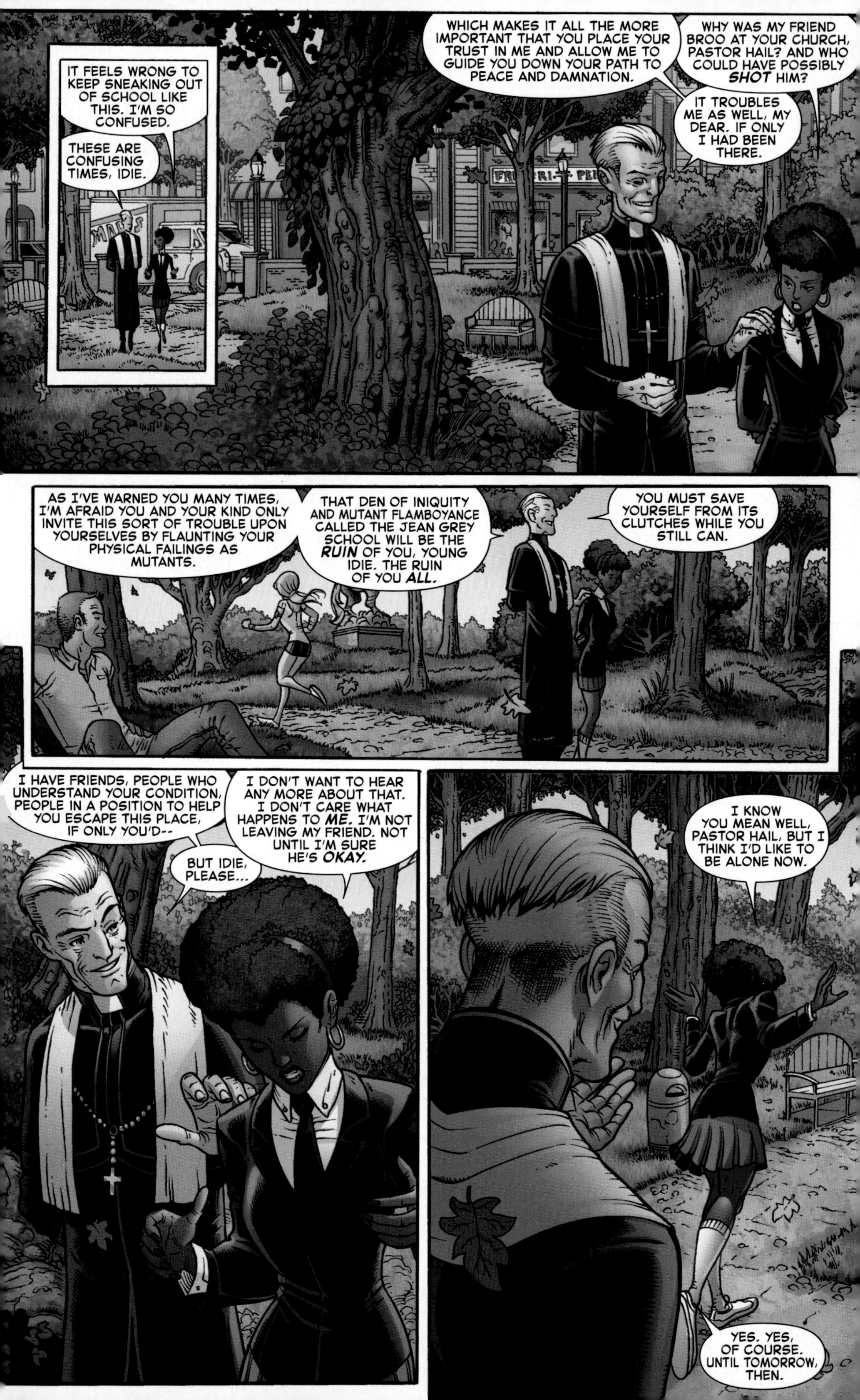
IT FEELS WRONG TO KEEP SNEAKING OUT OF SCHOOL LIKE THIS. I'M SO CONFUSED.
THESE ARE CONFUSING TIMES, IDIE.
WHICH MAKES IT ALL THE MORE IMPORTANT THAT YOU PLACE YOUR TRUST IN ME AND ALLOW ME TO GUIDE YOU DOWN YOUR PATH TO PEACE AND DAMNATION.
WHY WAS MY FRIEND BROO AT YOUR CHURCH, PASTOR HAIL? AND WHO COULD HAVE POSSIBLY SHOT HIM?
IT TROUBLES ME AS WELL, MY DEAR. IF ONLY I HAD BEEN THERE.
AS I'VE WARNED YOU MANY TIMES, I'M AFRAID YOU AND YOUR KIND ONLY INVITE THIS SORT OF TROUBLE UPON YOURSELVES BY FLAUNTING YOUR PHYSICAL FAILINGS AS MUTANTS.
THAT DEN OF INIQUITY AND MUTANT FLAMBOYANCE CALLED THE JEAN GREY SCHOOL WILL BE THE RUIN OF YOU, YOUNG IDIE. THE RUIN OF YOU ALL.
YOU MUST SAVE YOURSELF FROM ITS CLUTCHES WHILE YOU STILL CAN.
I HAVE FRIENDS, PEOPLE WHO UNDERSTAND YOUR CONDITION, PEOPLE IN A POSITION TO HELP YOU ESCAPE THIS PLACE, IF ONLY YOU'D--
I DON'T WANT TO HEAR ANY MORE ABOUT THAT. I DON'T CARE WHAT HAPPENS TO ME. I'M NOT LEAVING MY FRIEND. NOT UNTIL I'M SURE HE'S OKAY.
BUT IDIE, PLEASE...
I KNOW YOU MEAN WELL, PASTOR HAIL, BUT I THINK I'D LIKE TO BE ALONE NOW.
YES. YES, OF COURSE. UNTIL TOMORROW, THEN.

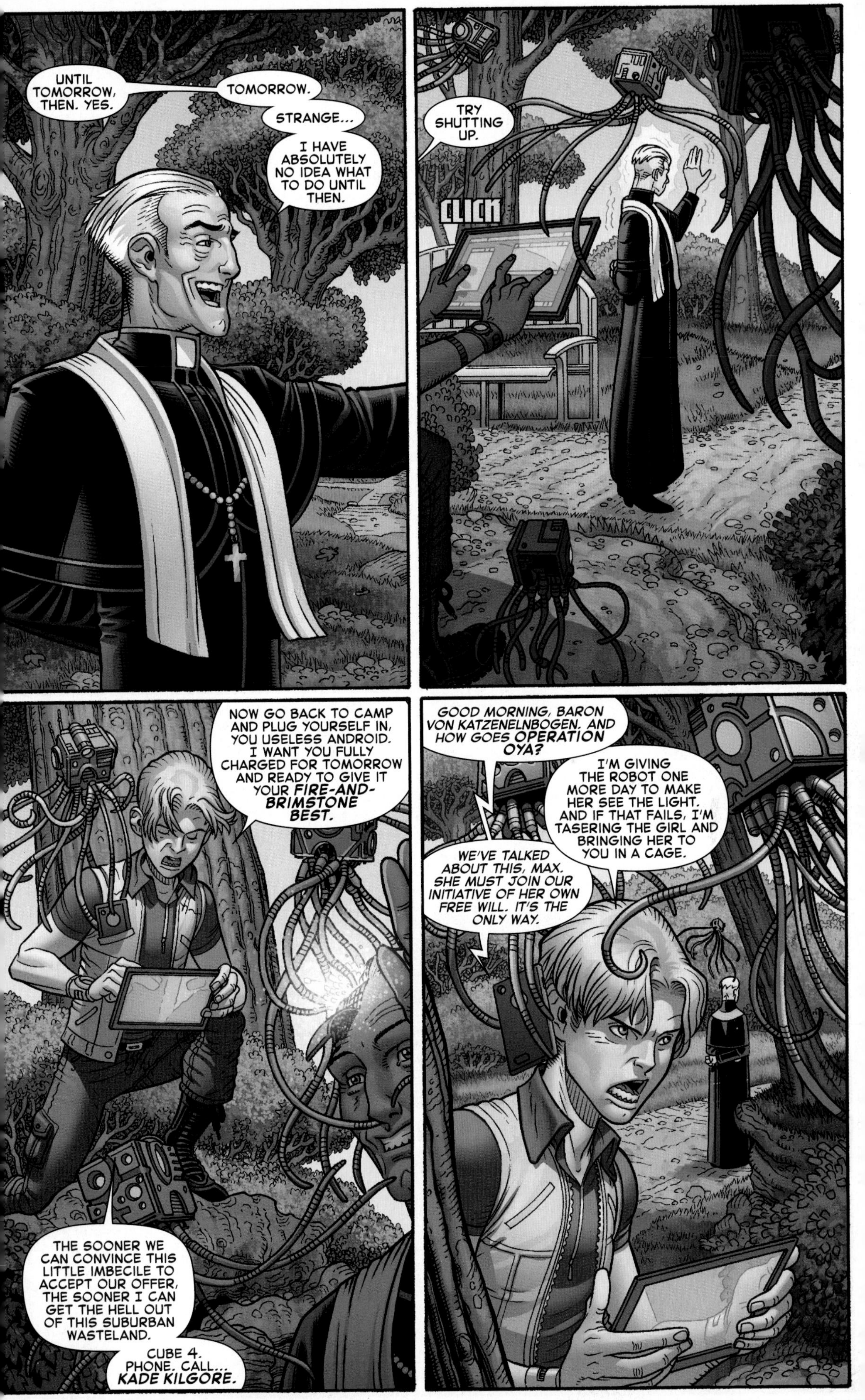
UNTIL TOMORROW, THEN. YES.
TOMORROW.
STRANGE...
I HAVE ABSOLUTELY NO IDEA WHAT TO DO UNTIL THEN.
TRY SHUTTING UP.
CLICK
NOW GO BACK TO CAMP AND PLUG YOURSELF IN, YOU USELESS ANDROID. I WANT YOU FULLY CHARGED FOR TOMORROW AND READY TO GIVE IT YOUR *FIRE-AND-BRIMSTONE BEST.*
THE SOONER WE CAN CONVINCE THIS LITTLE IMBECILE TO ACCEPT OUR OFFER, THE SOONER I CAN GET THE HELL OUT OF THIS SUBURBAN WASTELAND.
CUBE 4. PHONE. CALL... *KADE KILGORE.*
GOOD MORNING, BARON VON KATZENELNBOGEN. AND HOW GOES OPERATION OYA?
I'M GIVING THE ROBOT ONE MORE DAY TO MAKE HER SEE THE LIGHT. AND IF THAT FAILS, I'M TASERING THE GIRL AND BRINGING HER TO YOU IN A CAGE.
WE'VE TALKED ABOUT THIS, MAX. SHE MUST JOIN OUR INITIATIVE OF HER OWN FREE WILL. IT'S THE ONLY WAY.

ONE MORE DAY, KILGORE. IF I HAVE TO SPEND ANY LONGER THAN THAT IN THIS WRETCHED PLACE, THERE WILL BE A BODY COUNT, I CAN ASSURE YOU.

GO TO HELL.

GOOD MORNING.

EXCUSE ME?

NEVER MIND. HOW ARE OPERATIONS PROGRESSING ON YOUR END?

OH, SPLENDIDLY. WE'VE MADE CONTACT WITH MANY PROMISING CANDIDATES.

LOOK OUT, WORLD! HERE COMES MUDBUG!

AND... OTHERS AS WELL.

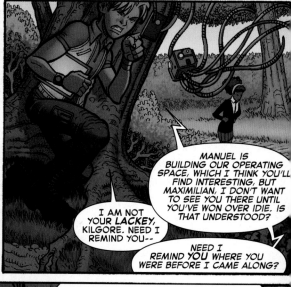

MANUEL IS BUILDING OUR OPERATING SPACE, WHICH I THINK YOU'LL FIND INTERESTING, BUT MAXIMILIAN, I DON'T WANT TO SEE YOU THERE UNTIL YOU'VE WON OVER IDIE. IS THAT UNDERSTOOD?

I AM NOT YOUR LACKEY, KILGORE. NEED I REMIND YOU--

NEED I REMIND YOU WHERE YOU WERE BEFORE I CAME ALONG?

DISGRACED. PENNILESS. A LIFE ALREADY IN RUIN BY THE AGE OF TWELVE. NO DOUBT SOON TO END IN A FILTHY ROADSIDE DITCH SOMEWHERE IN THE BACKWOODS OF ROMANIA.

TO BE REMEMBERED ONLY AS THE PATHETIC, FINAL WHIMPER IN A LONG, FOUL LEGACY OF FAILURE AND SHAME. THE LEGACY OF THE FAMILY FRANKEN--

YOU SAY THAT NAME, AND I PROMISE YOU, KILGORE, I WILL SLAUGHTER THIS ENTIRE TOWN, YOUR PRECIOUS MUTANTS INCLUDED.

AND THEN I WILL COME FOR YOU.

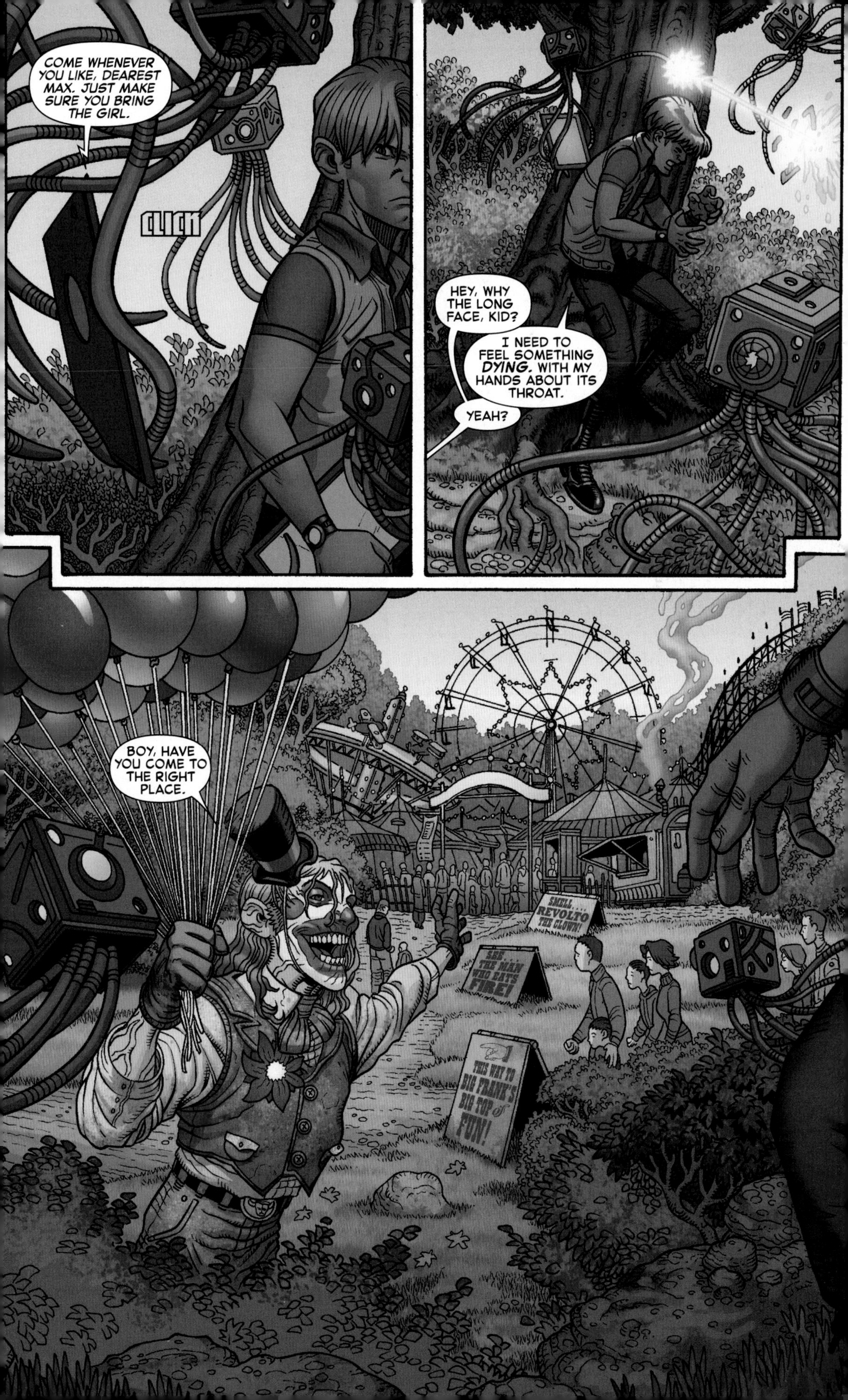
COME WHENEVER YOU LIKE, DEAREST MAX. JUST MAKE SURE YOU BRING THE GIRL.
CLICK
HEY, WHY THE LONG FACE, KID?
I NEED TO FEEL SOMETHING DYING. WITH MY HANDS ABOUT ITS THROAT.
YEAH?
BOY, HAVE YOU COME TO THE RIGHT PLACE.
SMELL... REVOLTO THE CLOWN!
SEE... THE MAN WHO EATS FIRE!
THIS WAY TO BIG FRANK'S BIG TOP of FUN!

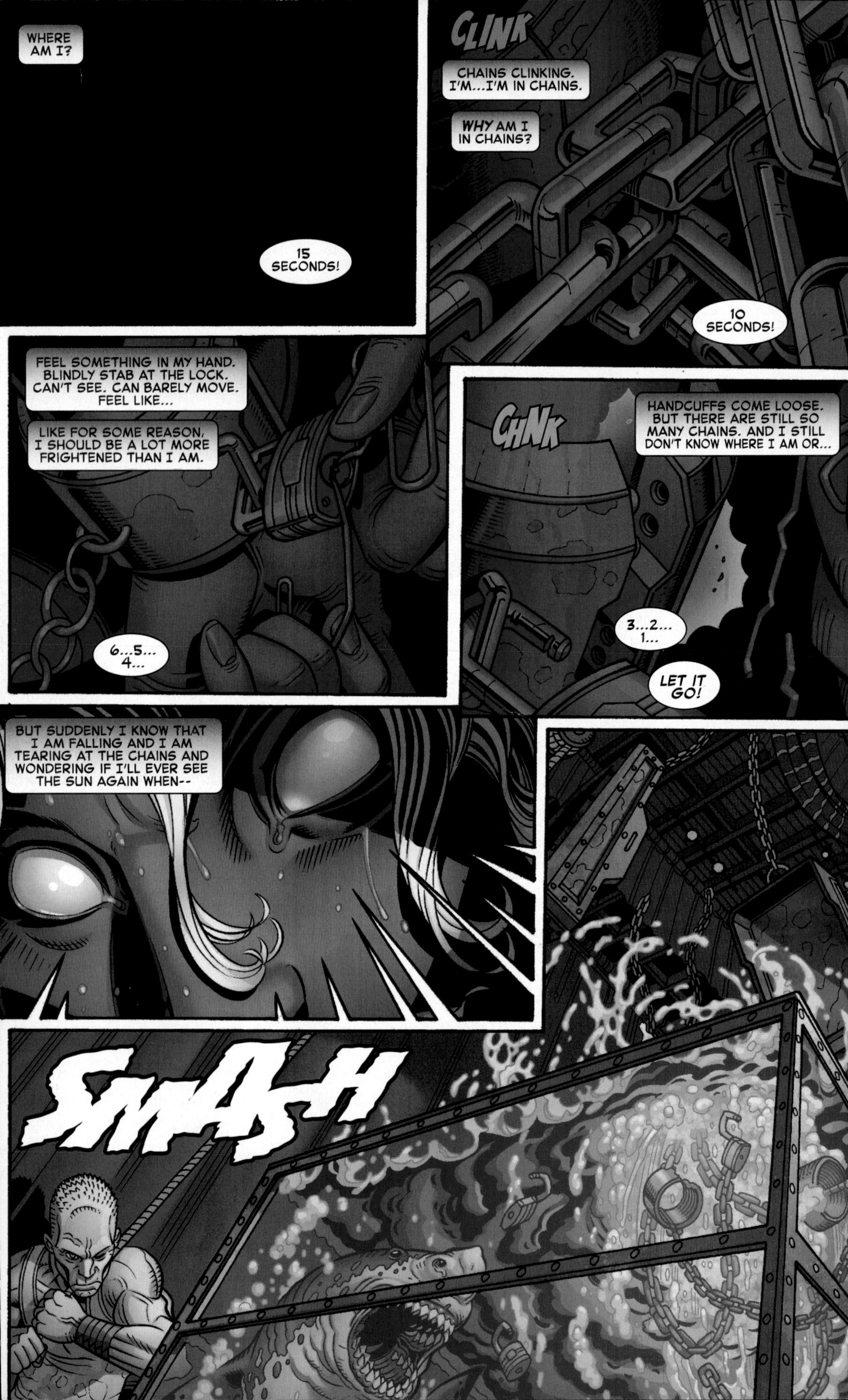
WHERE AM I?
15 SECONDS!
CLINK
CHAINS CLINKING. I'M...I'M IN CHAINS.
WHY AM I IN CHAINS?
10 SECONDS!
FEEL SOMETHING IN MY HAND. BLINDLY STAB AT THE LOCK. CAN'T SEE. CAN BARELY MOVE. FEEL LIKE...
LIKE FOR SOME REASON, I SHOULD BE A LOT MORE FRIGHTENED THAN I AM.
6...5... 4...
CHNK
HANDCUFFS COME LOOSE. BUT THERE ARE STILL SO MANY CHAINS. AND I STILL DON'T KNOW WHERE I AM OR...
3...2... 1...
LET IT GO!
BUT SUDDENLY I KNOW THAT I AM FALLING AND I AM TEARING AT THE CHAINS AND WONDERING IF I'LL EVER SEE THE SUN AGAIN WHEN--
SMASH

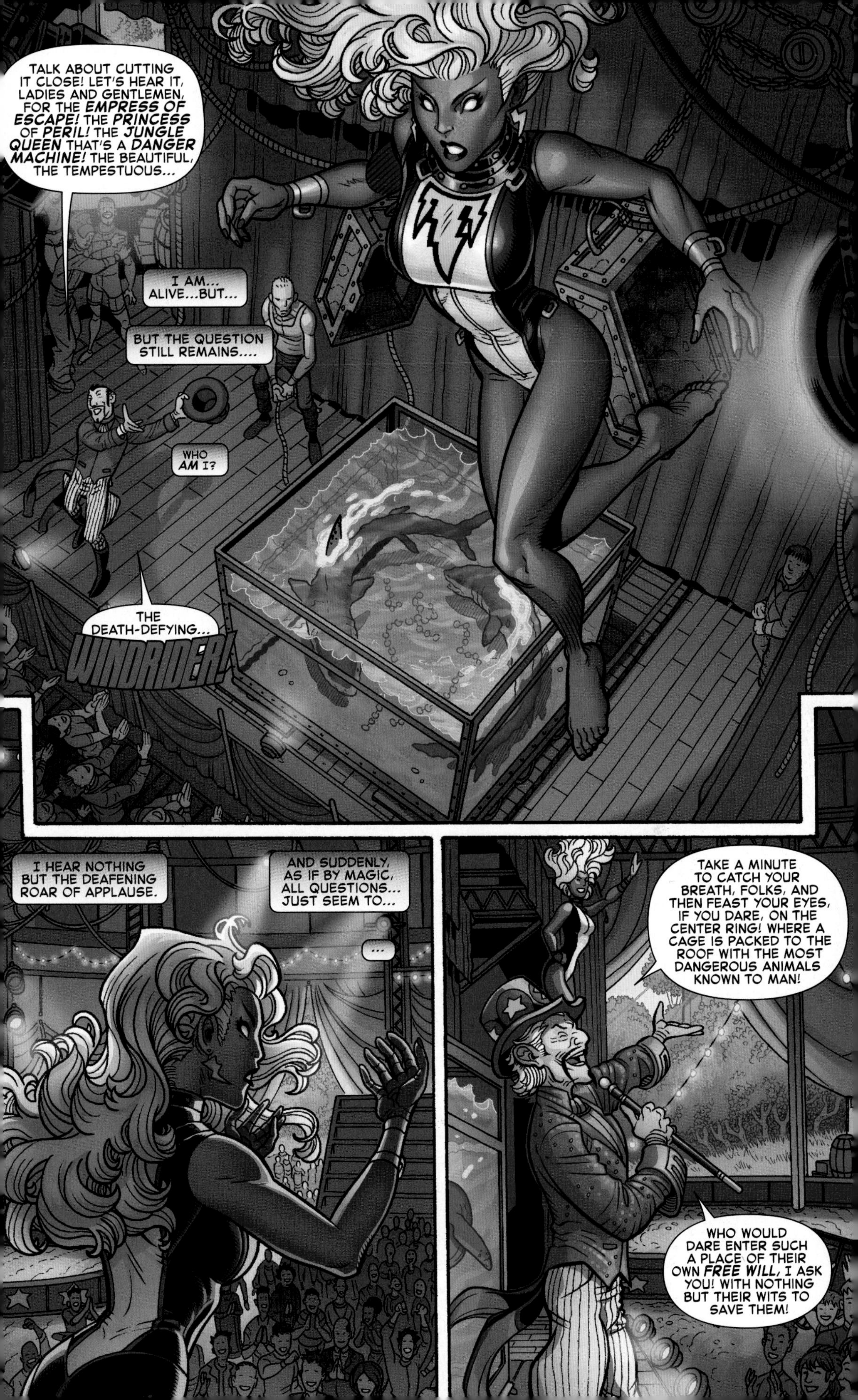
TALK ABOUT CUTTING IT CLOSE! LET'S HEAR IT, LADIES AND GENTLEMEN, FOR THE ***EMPRESS OF ESCAPE!*** THE ***PRINCESS*** OF ***PERIL!*** THE ***JUNGLE QUEEN*** THAT'S A ***DANGER MACHINE!*** THE BEAUTIFUL, THE TEMPESTUOUS...
I AM... ALIVE...BUT...
BUT THE QUESTION STILL REMAINS....
WHO ***AM*** I?
THE DEATH-DEFYING...
WINDRIDER!
I HEAR NOTHING BUT THE DEAFENING ROAR OF APPLAUSE.
AND SUDDENLY, AS IF BY MAGIC, ALL QUESTIONS... JUST SEEM TO...
...
TAKE A MINUTE TO CATCH YOUR BREATH, FOLKS, AND THEN FEAST YOUR EYES, IF YOU DARE, ON THE CENTER RING! WHERE A CAGE IS PACKED TO THE ROOF WITH THE MOST DANGEROUS ANIMALS KNOWN TO MAN!
WHO WOULD DARE ENTER SUCH A PLACE OF THEIR OWN ***FREE WILL***, I ASK YOU! WITH NOTHING BUT THEIR WITS TO SAVE THEM!

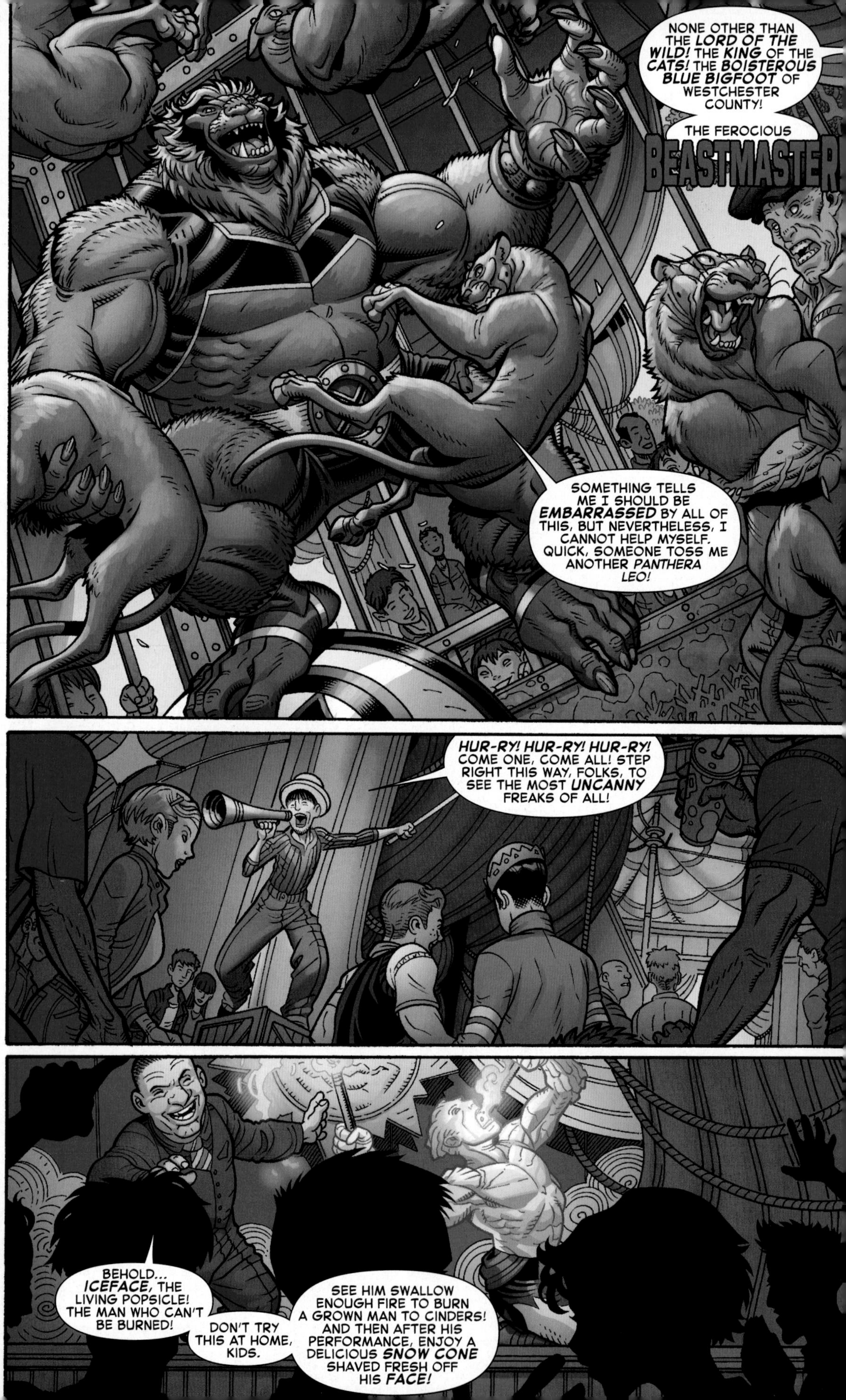

NONE OTHER THAN THE LORD OF THE WILD! THE KING OF THE CATS! THE BOISTEROUS BLUE BIGFOOT OF WESTCHESTER COUNTY!
THE FEROCIOUS
BEASTMASTER!
SOMETHING TELLS ME I SHOULD BE EMBARRASSED BY ALL OF THIS, BUT NEVERTHELESS, I CANNOT HELP MYSELF. QUICK, SOMEONE TOSS ME ANOTHER PANTHERA LEO!
HUR-RY! HUR-RY! HUR-RY! COME ONE, COME ALL! STEP RIGHT THIS WAY, FOLKS, TO SEE THE MOST UNCANNY FREAKS OF ALL!
BEHOLD... ICEFACE, THE LIVING POPSICLE! THE MAN WHO CAN'T BE BURNED!
DON'T TRY THIS AT HOME, KIDS.
SEE HIM SWALLOW ENOUGH FIRE TO BURN A GROWN MAN TO CINDERS! AND THEN AFTER HIS PERFORMANCE, ENJOY A DELICIOUS SNOW CONE SHAVED FRESH OFF HIS FACE!

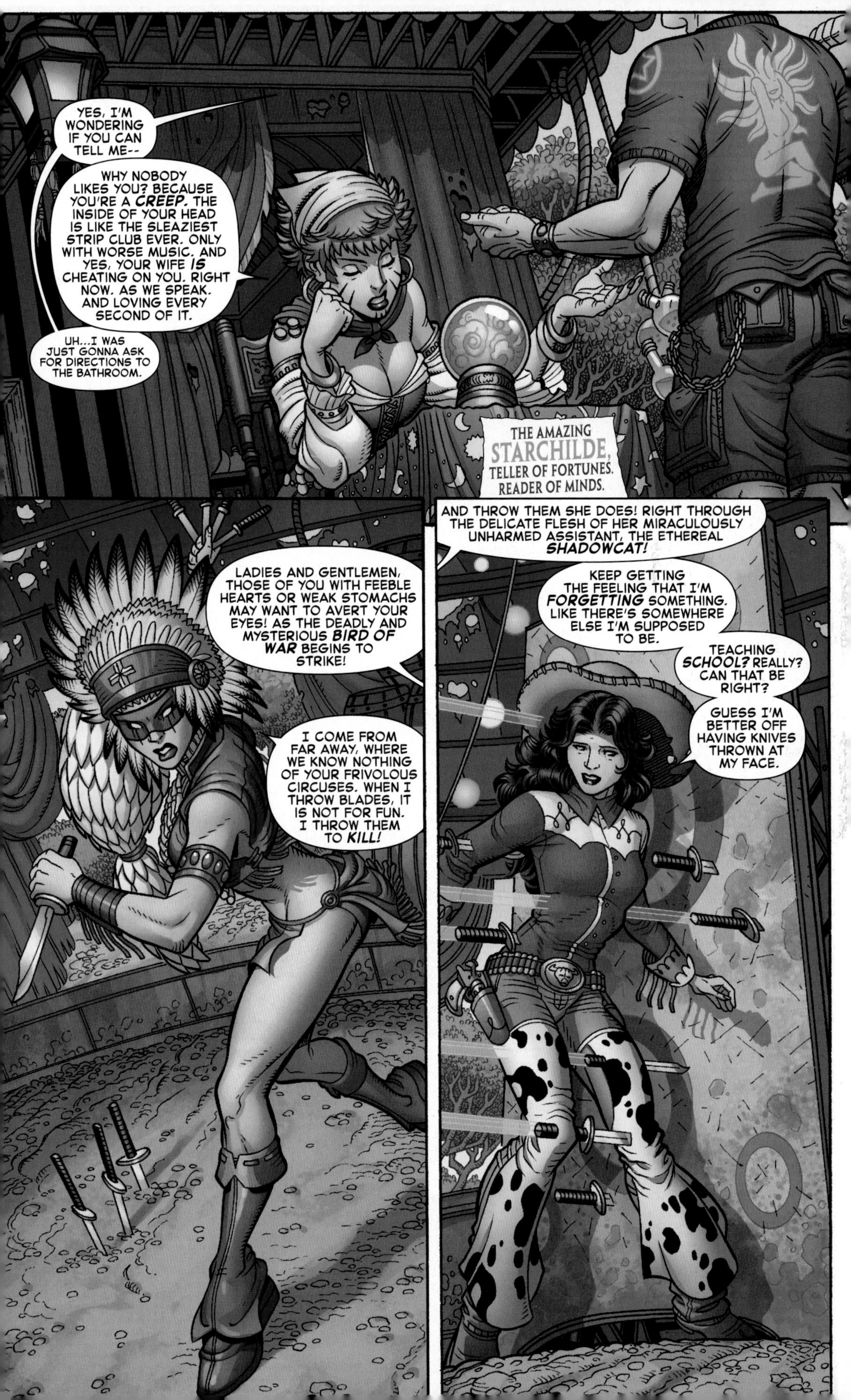
YES, I'M WONDERING IF YOU CAN TELL ME--
WHY NOBODY LIKES YOU? BECAUSE YOU'RE A CREEP. THE INSIDE OF YOUR HEAD IS LIKE THE SLEAZIEST STRIP CLUB EVER. ONLY WITH WORSE MUSIC. AND YES, YOUR WIFE IS CHEATING ON YOU. RIGHT NOW. AS WE SPEAK. AND LOVING EVERY SECOND OF IT.
UH...I WAS JUST GONNA ASK FOR DIRECTIONS TO THE BATHROOM.
THE AMAZING STARCHILDE, TELLER OF FORTUNES. READER OF MINDS.
LADIES AND GENTLEMEN, THOSE OF YOU WITH FEEBLE HEARTS OR WEAK STOMACHS MAY WANT TO AVERT YOUR EYES! AS THE DEADLY AND MYSTERIOUS BIRD OF WAR BEGINS TO STRIKE!
I COME FROM FAR AWAY, WHERE WE KNOW NOTHING OF YOUR FRIVOLOUS CIRCUSES. WHEN I THROW BLADES, IT IS NOT FOR FUN. I THROW THEM TO KILL!
AND THROW THEM SHE DOES! RIGHT THROUGH THE DELICATE FLESH OF HER MIRACULOUSLY UNHARMED ASSISTANT, THE ETHEREAL SHADOWCAT!
KEEP GETTING THE FEELING THAT I'M FORGETTING SOMETHING. LIKE THERE'S SOMEWHERE ELSE I'M SUPPOSED TO BE.
TEACHING SCHOOL? REALLY? CAN THAT BE RIGHT?
GUESS I'M BETTER OFF HAVING KNIVES THROWN AT MY FACE.

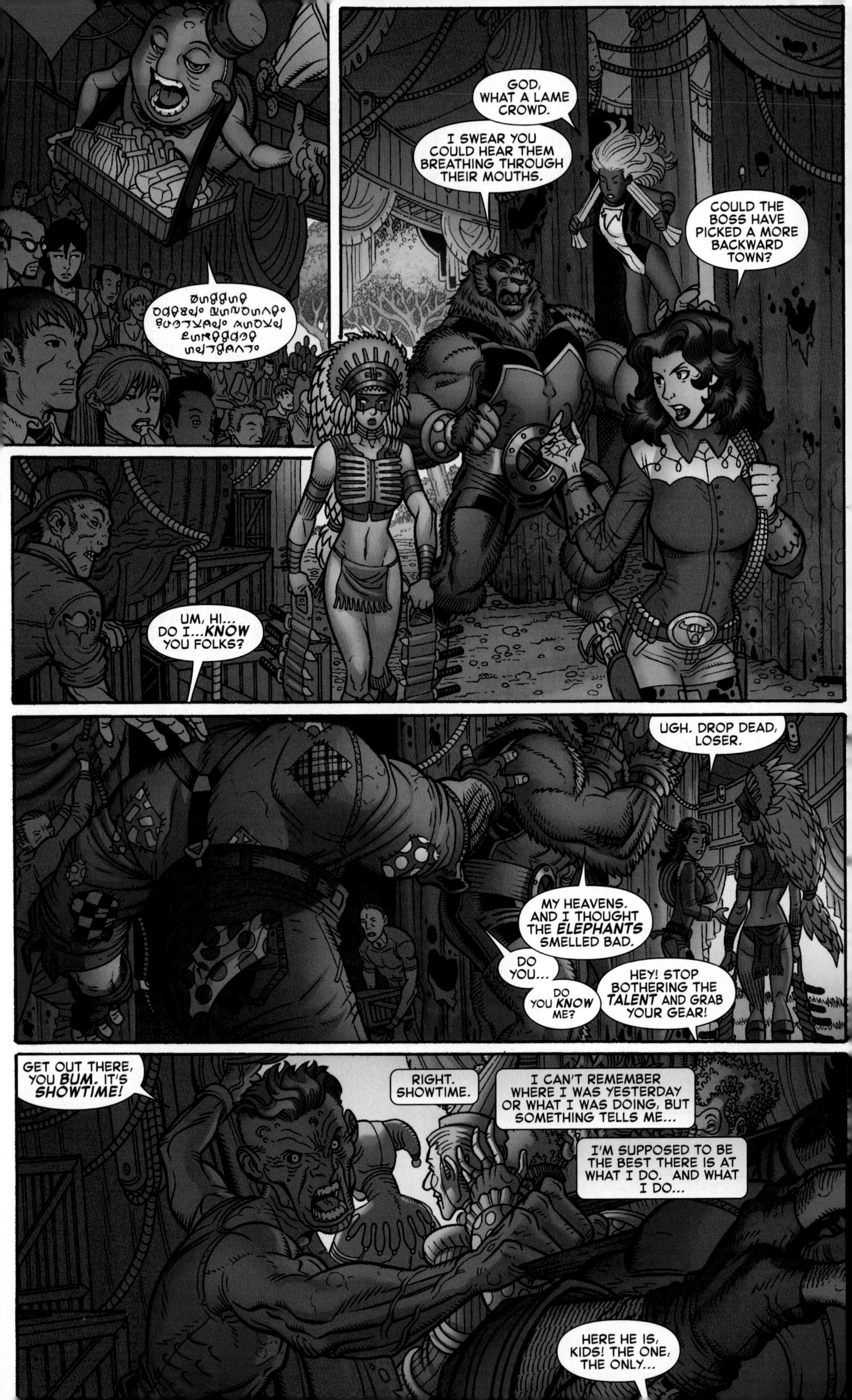
GOD, WHAT A LAME CROWD.
I SWEAR YOU COULD HEAR THEM BREATHING THROUGH THEIR MOUTHS.
COULD THE BOSS HAVE PICKED A MORE BACKWARD TOWN?
UM, HI... DO I...KNOW YOU FOLKS?
UGH. DROP DEAD, LOSER.
MY HEAVENS. AND I THOUGHT THE ELEPHANTS SMELLED BAD.
DO YOU...
DO YOU KNOW ME?
HEY! STOP BOTHERING THE TALENT AND GRAB YOUR GEAR!
GET OUT THERE, YOU BUM. IT'S SHOWTIME!
RIGHT. SHOWTIME.
I CAN'T REMEMBER WHERE I WAS YESTERDAY OR WHAT I WAS DOING, BUT SOMETHING TELLS ME...
I'M SUPPOSED TO BE THE BEST THERE IS AT WHAT I DO. AND WHAT I DO...
HERE HE IS, KIDS! THE ONE, THE ONLY...

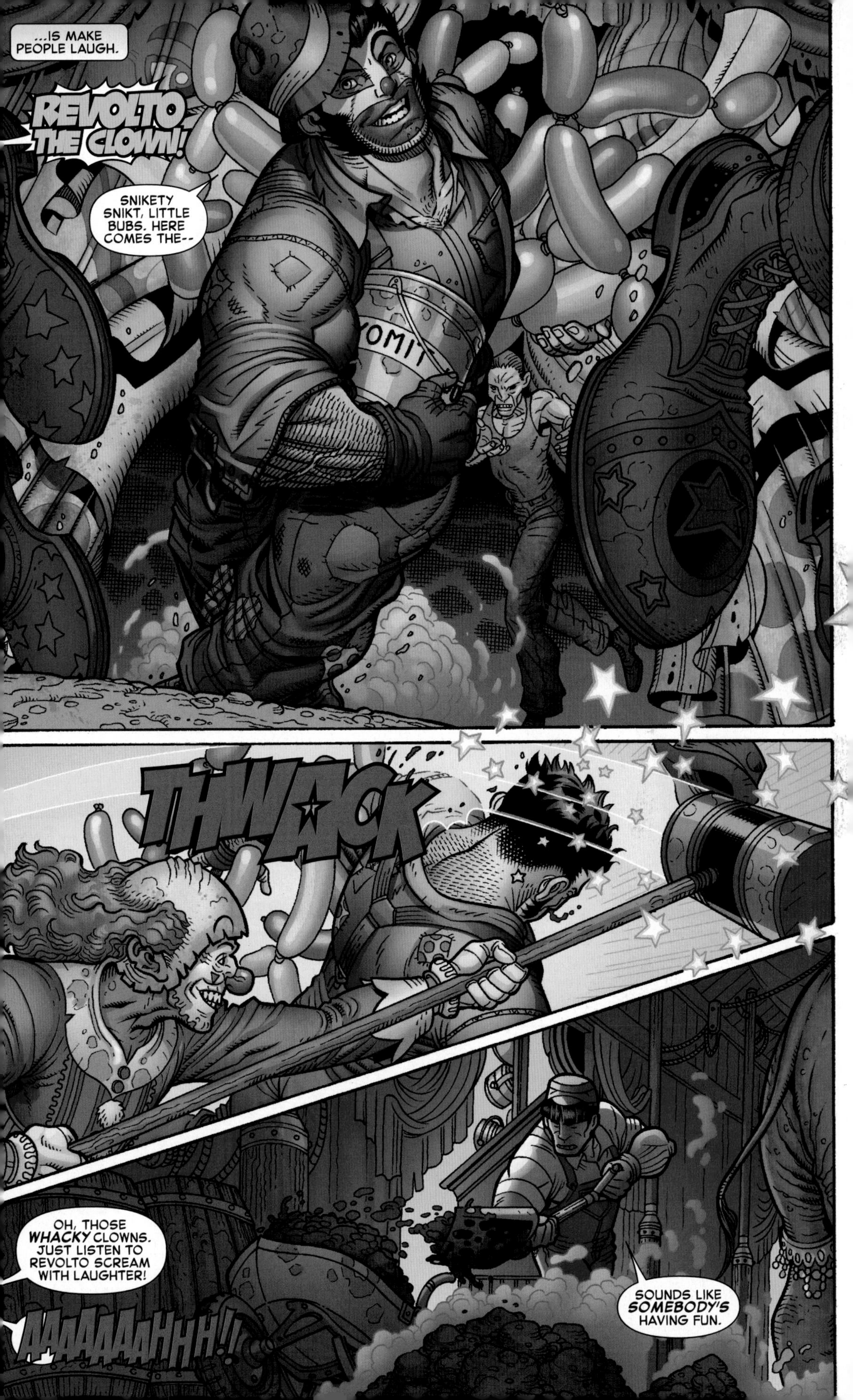
...IS MAKE PEOPLE LAUGH.
REVOLTO THE CLOWN!
SNIKETY SNIKT, LITTLE BUBS. HERE COMES THE--
VOMIT
THWACK
OH, THOSE WHACKY CLOWNS. JUST LISTEN TO REVOLTO SCREAM WITH LAUGHTER!
AAAAAAAHHH!!
SOUNDS LIKE SOMEBODY'S HAVING FUN.

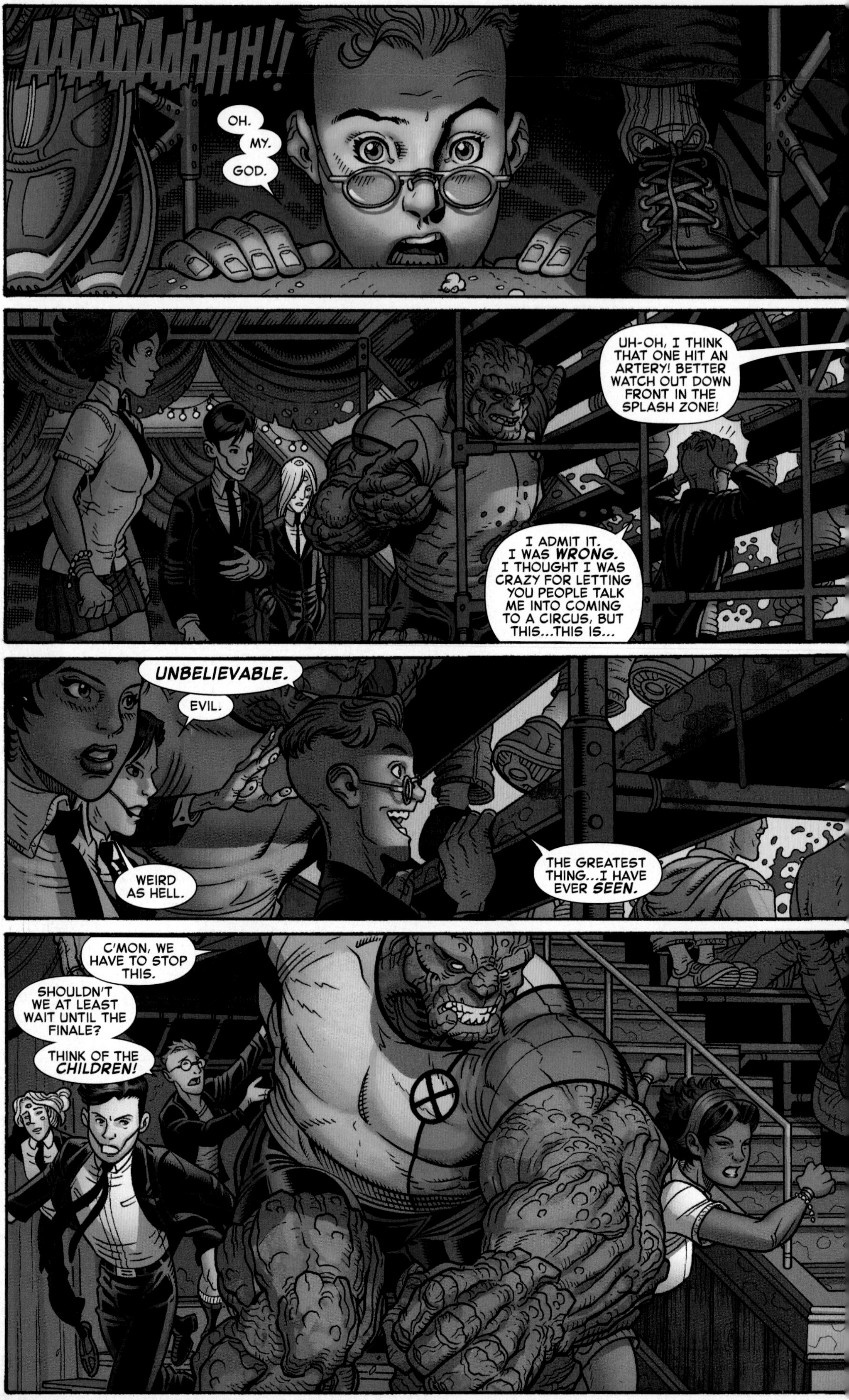
AAAAAAAHHH!!
OH.
MY.
GOD.
UH-OH, I THINK THAT ONE HIT AN ARTERY! BETTER WATCH OUT DOWN FRONT IN THE SPLASH ZONE!
I ADMIT IT. I WAS WRONG. I THOUGHT I WAS CRAZY FOR LETTING YOU PEOPLE TALK ME INTO COMING TO A CIRCUS, BUT THIS...THIS IS...
UNBELIEVABLE.
EVIL.
WEIRD AS HELL.
THE GREATEST THING...I HAVE EVER SEEN.
C'MON, WE HAVE TO STOP THIS.
SHOULDN'T WE AT LEAST WAIT UNTIL THE FINALE?
THINK OF THE CHILDREN!

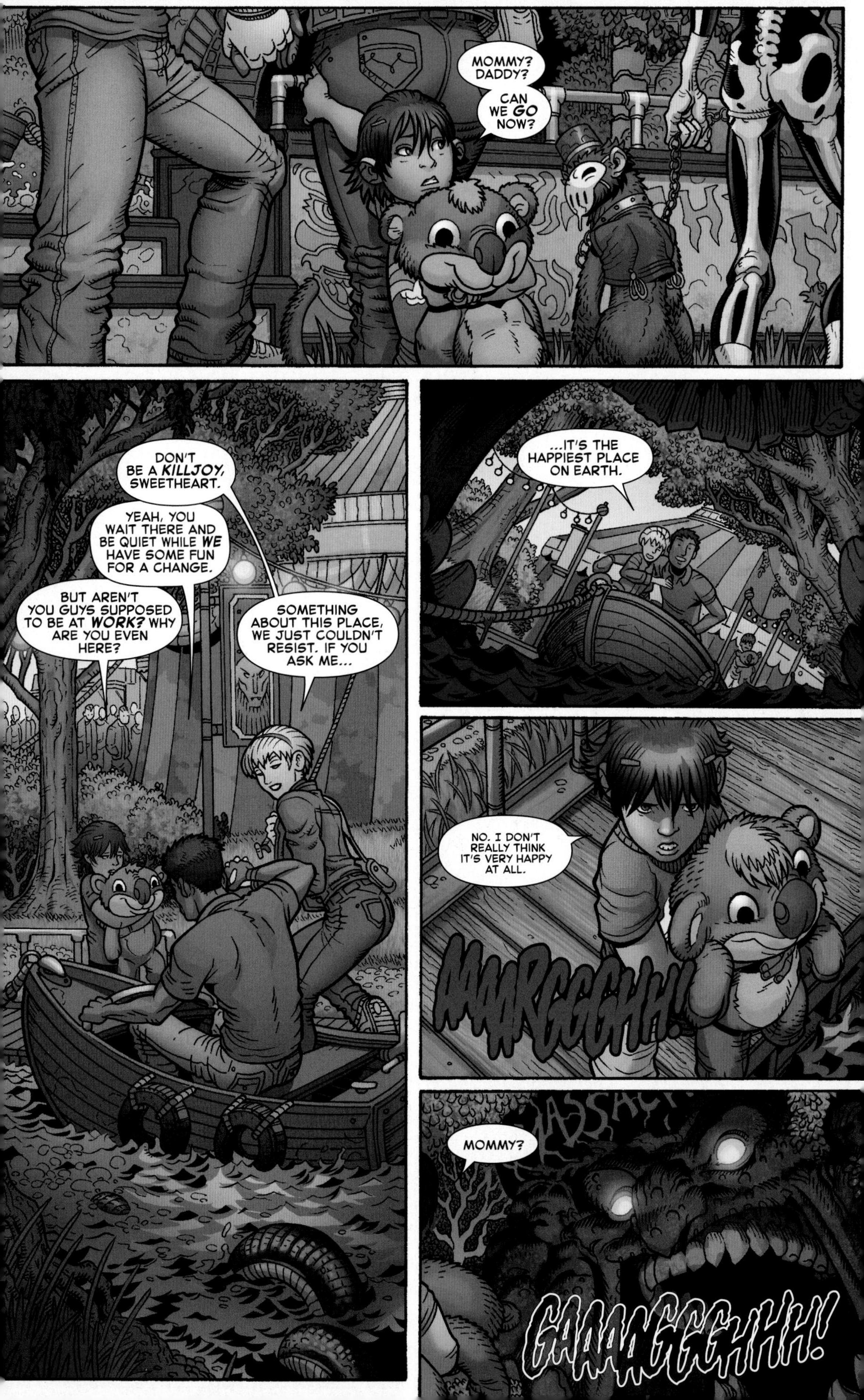
MOMMY? DADDY?
CAN WE GO NOW?
DON'T BE A KILLJOY, SWEETHEART.
YEAH, YOU WAIT THERE AND BE QUIET WHILE WE HAVE SOME FUN FOR A CHANGE.
BUT AREN'T YOU GUYS SUPPOSED TO BE AT WORK? WHY ARE YOU EVEN HERE?
SOMETHING ABOUT THIS PLACE, WE JUST COULDN'T RESIST. IF YOU ASK ME...
...IT'S THE HAPPIEST PLACE ON EARTH.
NO. I DON'T REALLY THINK IT'S VERY HAPPY AT ALL.
AAAARGGGHH!
MOMMY?
GAAAAGGGHHH!

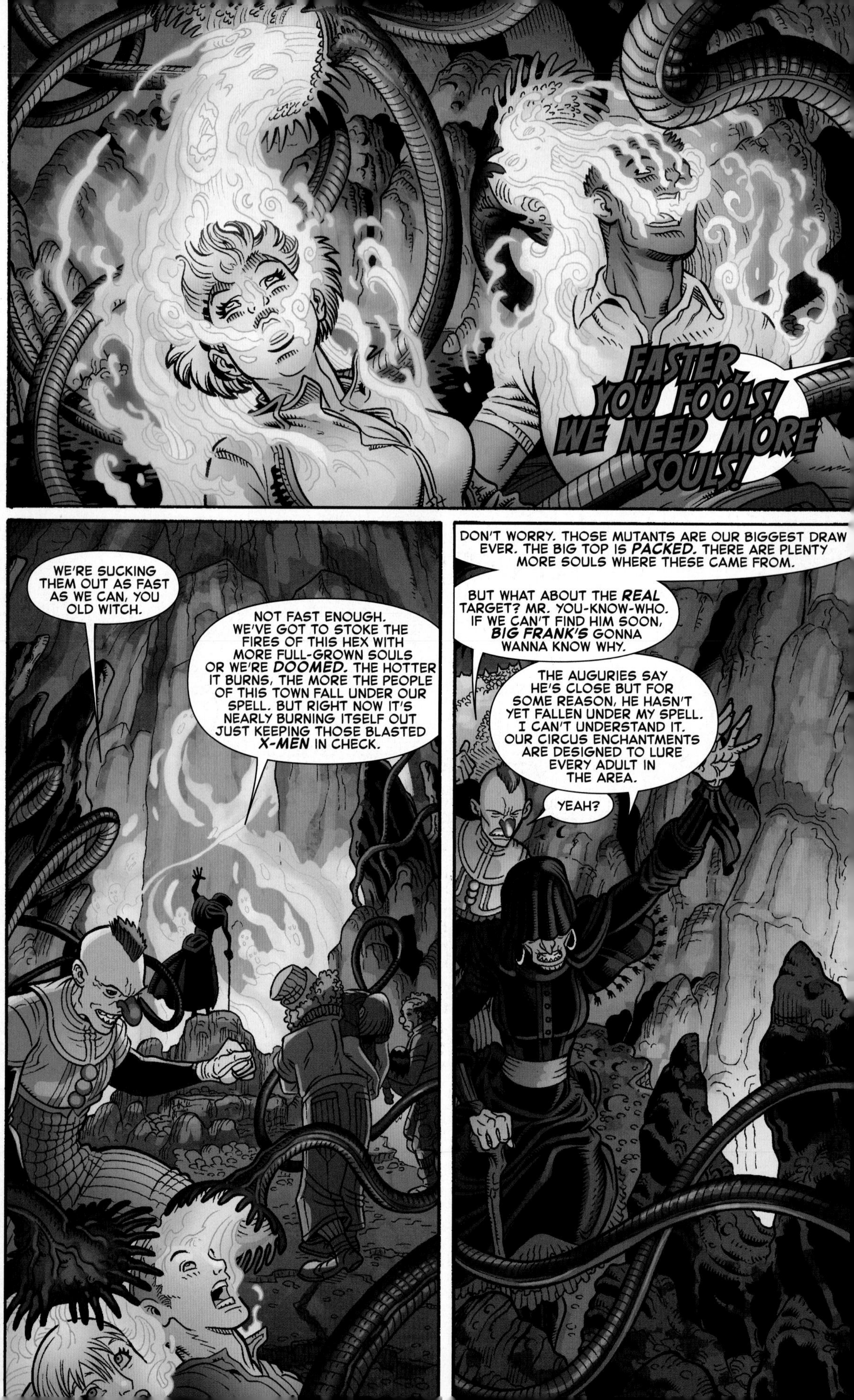

FASTER, YOU FOOLS! WE NEED MORE SOULS!
WE'RE SUCKING THEM OUT AS FAST AS WE CAN, YOU OLD WITCH.
NOT FAST ENOUGH. WE'VE GOT TO STOKE THE FIRES OF THIS HEX WITH MORE FULL-GROWN SOULS OR WE'RE DOOMED. THE HOTTER IT BURNS, THE MORE THE PEOPLE OF THIS TOWN FALL UNDER OUR SPELL. BUT RIGHT NOW IT'S NEARLY BURNING ITSELF OUT JUST KEEPING THOSE BLASTED X-MEN IN CHECK.
DON'T WORRY. THOSE MUTANTS ARE OUR BIGGEST DRAW EVER. THE BIG TOP IS PACKED. THERE ARE PLENTY MORE SOULS WHERE THESE CAME FROM.
BUT WHAT ABOUT THE REAL TARGET? MR. YOU-KNOW-WHO. IF WE CAN'T FIND HIM SOON, BIG FRANK'S GONNA WANNA KNOW WHY.
THE AUGURIES SAY HE'S CLOSE BUT FOR SOME REASON, HE HASN'T YET FALLEN UNDER MY SPELL. I CAN'T UNDERSTAND IT. OUR CIRCUS ENCHANTMENTS ARE DESIGNED TO LURE EVERY ADULT IN THE AREA.
YEAH?

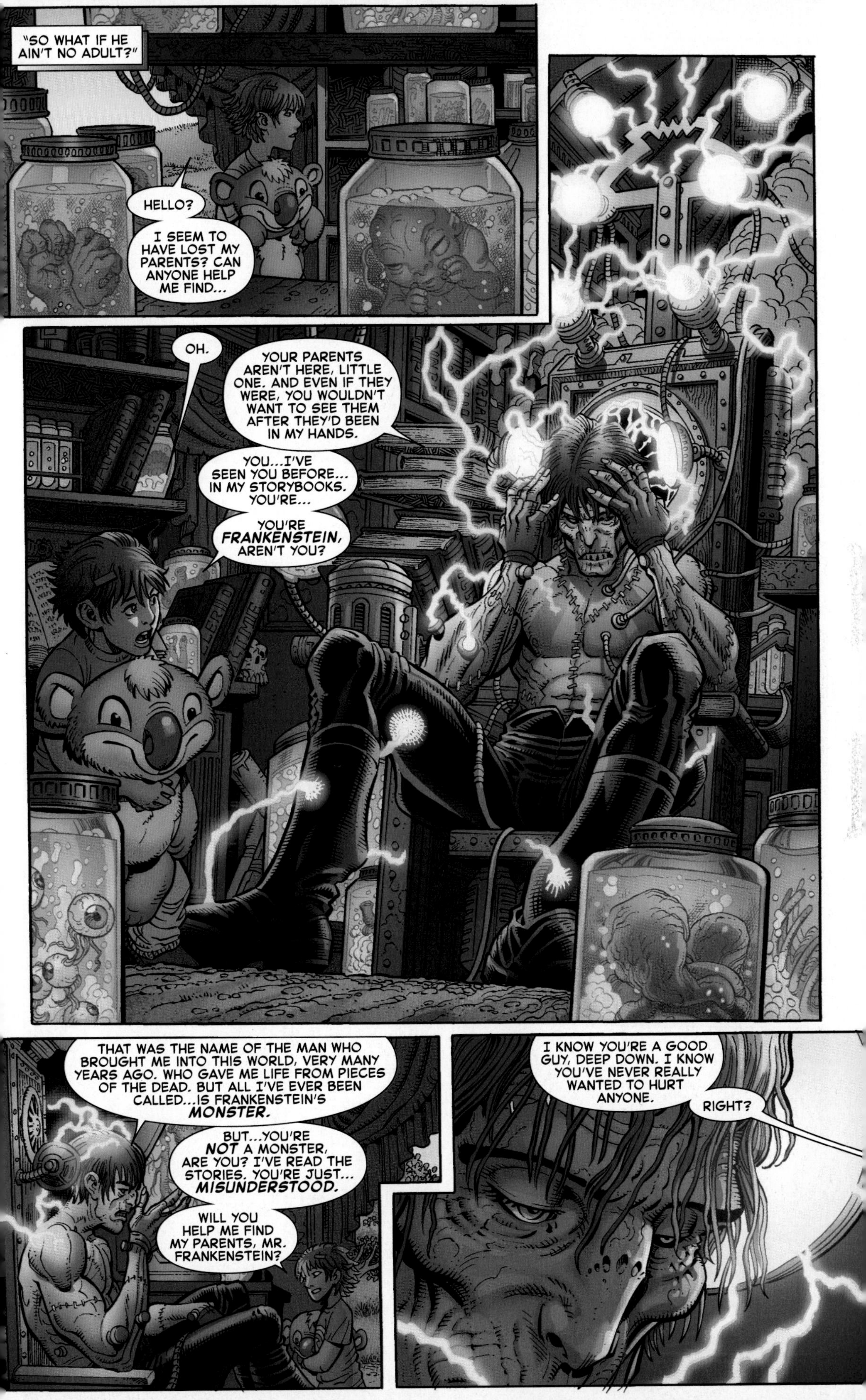
"SO WHAT IF HE AIN'T NO ADULT?"
HELLO?
I SEEM TO HAVE LOST MY PARENTS? CAN ANYONE HELP ME FIND...
OH.
YOUR PARENTS AREN'T HERE, LITTLE ONE. AND EVEN IF THEY WERE, YOU WOULDN'T WANT TO SEE THEM AFTER THEY'D BEEN IN MY HANDS.
YOU...I'VE SEEN YOU BEFORE... IN MY STORYBOOKS. YOU'RE...
YOU'RE FRANKENSTEIN, AREN'T YOU?
THAT WAS THE NAME OF THE MAN WHO BROUGHT ME INTO THIS WORLD, VERY MANY YEARS AGO. WHO GAVE ME LIFE FROM PIECES OF THE DEAD. BUT ALL I'VE EVER BEEN CALLED...IS FRANKENSTEIN'S MONSTER.
BUT...YOU'RE NOT A MONSTER, ARE YOU? I'VE READ THE STORIES. YOU'RE JUST... MISUNDERSTOOD.
WILL YOU HELP ME FIND MY PARENTS, MR. FRANKENSTEIN?
I KNOW YOU'RE A GOOD GUY, DEEP DOWN. I KNOW YOU'VE NEVER REALLY WANTED TO HURT ANYONE.
RIGHT?

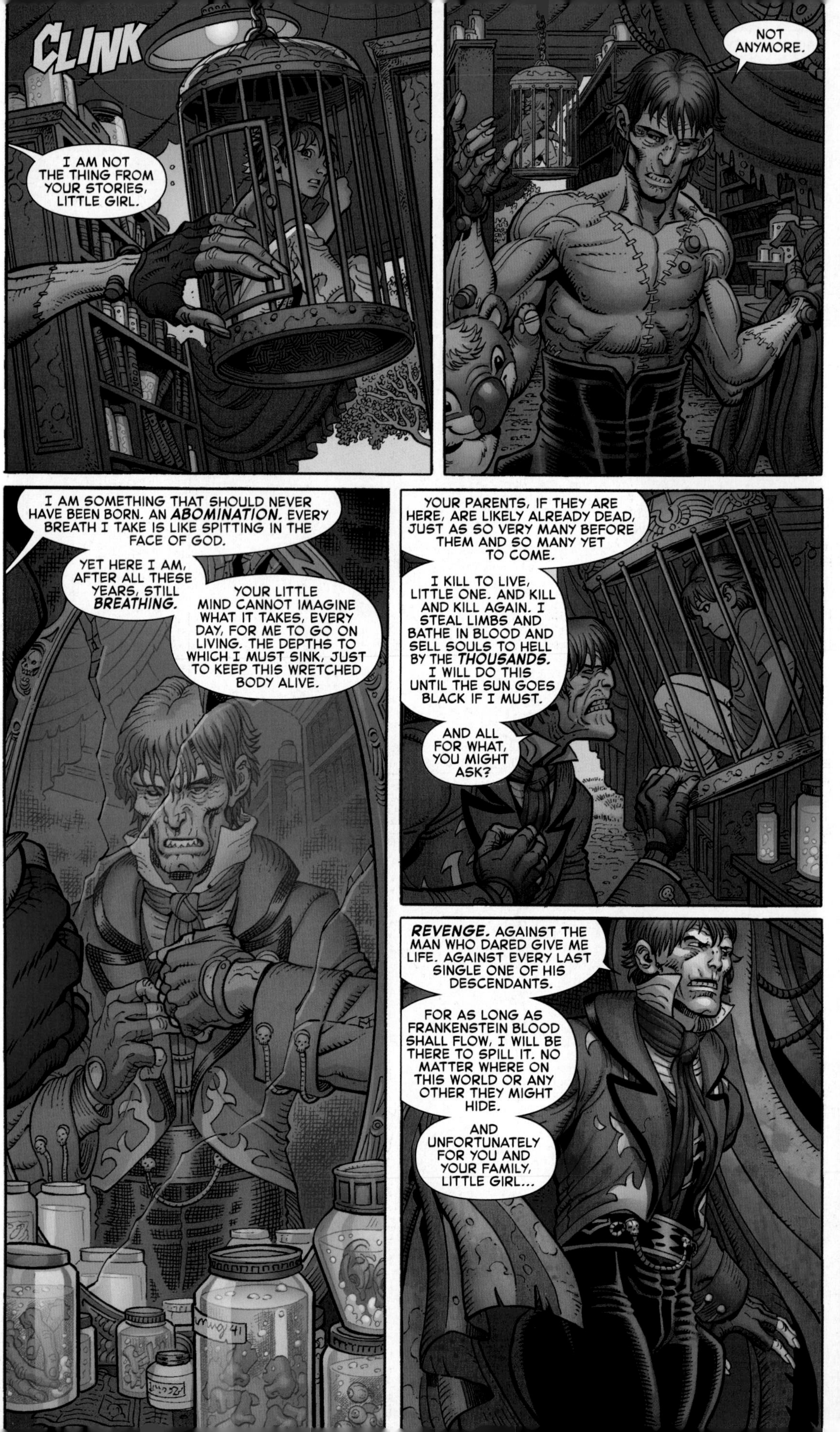
CLINK
I AM NOT THE THING FROM YOUR STORIES, LITTLE GIRL.
NOT ANYMORE.
I AM SOMETHING THAT SHOULD NEVER HAVE BEEN BORN. AN ABOMINATION. EVERY BREATH I TAKE IS LIKE SPITTING IN THE FACE OF GOD.
YET HERE I AM, AFTER ALL THESE YEARS, STILL BREATHING.
YOUR LITTLE MIND CANNOT IMAGINE WHAT IT TAKES, EVERY DAY, FOR ME TO GO ON LIVING. THE DEPTHS TO WHICH I MUST SINK, JUST TO KEEP THIS WRETCHED BODY ALIVE.
YOUR PARENTS, IF THEY ARE HERE, ARE LIKELY ALREADY DEAD, JUST AS SO VERY MANY BEFORE THEM AND SO MANY YET TO COME.
I KILL TO LIVE, LITTLE ONE. AND KILL AND KILL AGAIN. I STEAL LIMBS AND BATHE IN BLOOD AND SELL SOULS TO HELL BY THE THOUSANDS. I WILL DO THIS UNTIL THE SUN GOES BLACK IF I MUST.
AND ALL FOR WHAT, YOU MIGHT ASK?
REVENGE. AGAINST THE MAN WHO DARED GIVE ME LIFE. AGAINST EVERY LAST SINGLE ONE OF HIS DESCENDANTS.
FOR AS LONG AS FRANKENSTEIN BLOOD SHALL FLOW, I WILL BE THERE TO SPILL IT. NO MATTER WHERE ON THIS WORLD OR ANY OTHER THEY MIGHT HIDE.
AND UNFORTUNATELY FOR YOU AND YOUR FAMILY, LITTLE GIRL...

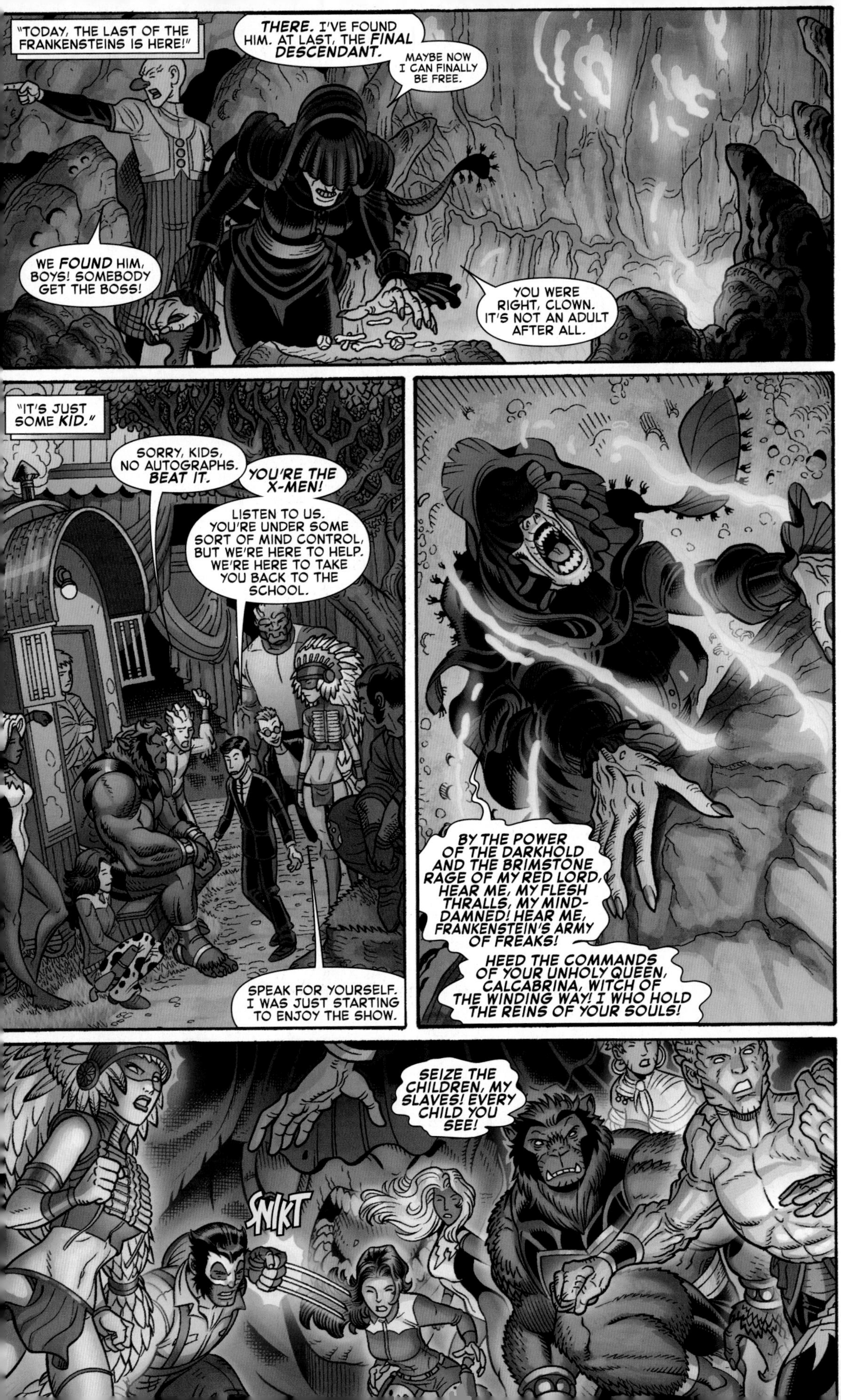
"TODAY, THE LAST OF THE FRANKENSTEINS IS HERE!"
THERE. I'VE FOUND HIM. AT LAST, THE FINAL DESCENDANT.
MAYBE NOW I CAN FINALLY BE FREE.
WE FOUND HIM, BOYS! SOMEBODY GET THE BOSS!
YOU WERE RIGHT, CLOWN. IT'S NOT AN ADULT AFTER ALL.
"IT'S JUST SOME KID."
SORRY, KIDS, NO AUTOGRAPHS. BEAT IT.
YOU'RE THE X-MEN!
LISTEN TO US. YOU'RE UNDER SOME SORT OF MIND CONTROL, BUT WE'RE HERE TO HELP. WE'RE HERE TO TAKE YOU BACK TO THE SCHOOL.
SPEAK FOR YOURSELF. I WAS JUST STARTING TO ENJOY THE SHOW.
BY THE POWER OF THE DARKHOLD AND THE BRIMSTONE RAGE OF MY RED LORD, HEAR ME, MY FLESH THRALLS, MY MIND-DAMNED! HEAR ME, FRANKENSTEIN'S ARMY OF FREAKS!
HEED THE COMMANDS OF YOUR UNHOLY QUEEN, CALCABRINA, WITCH OF THE WINDING WAY! I WHO HOLD THE REINS OF YOUR SOULS!
SEIZE THE CHILDREN, MY SLAVES! EVERY CHILD YOU SEE!
SNIKT

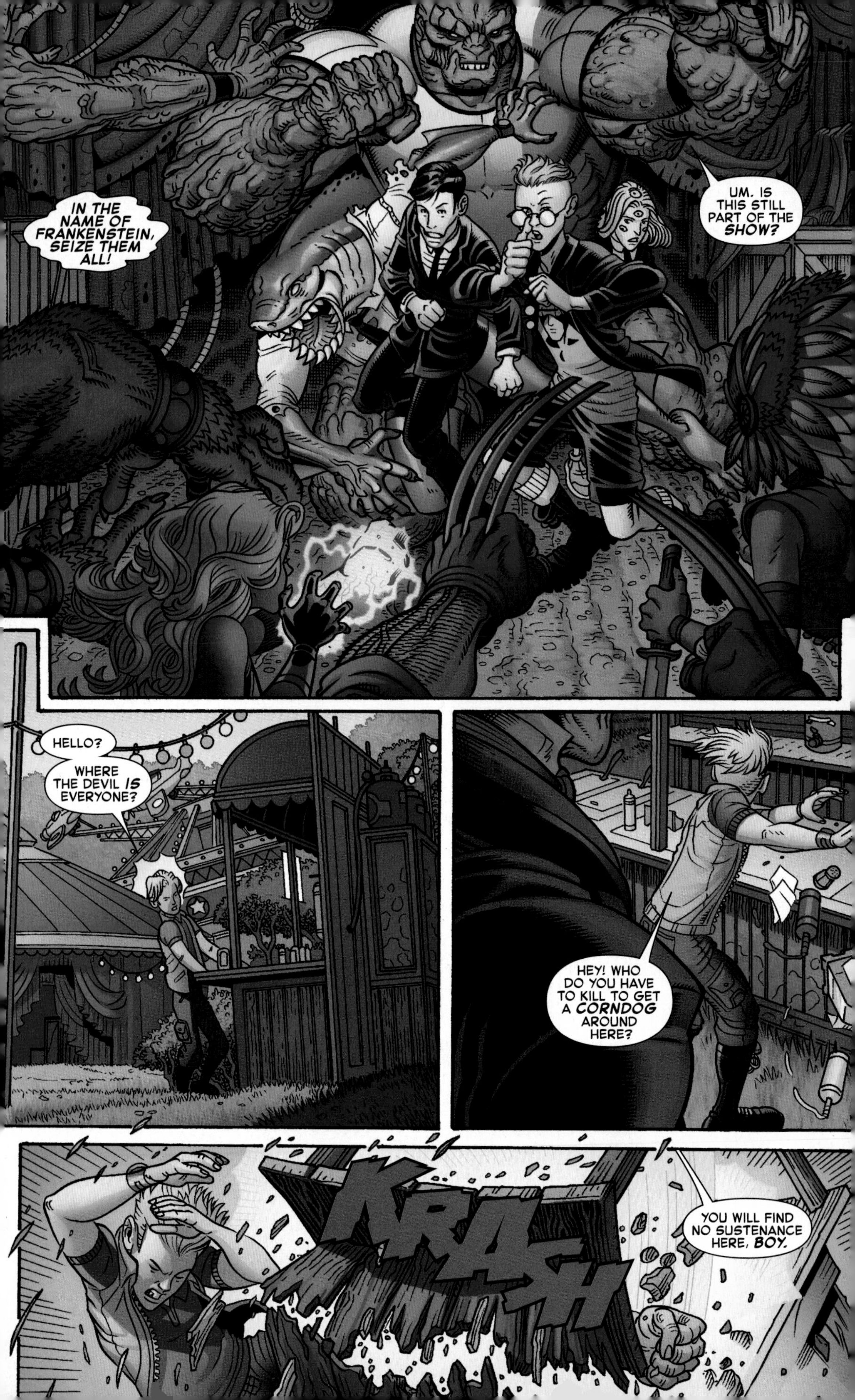
IN THE NAME OF FRANKENSTEIN, SEIZE THEM ALL!
UM. IS THIS STILL PART OF THE SHOW?
HELLO?
WHERE THE DEVIL IS EVERYONE?
HEY! WHO DO YOU HAVE TO KILL TO GET A CORNDOG AROUND HERE?
KRASH
YOU WILL FIND NO SUSTENANCE HERE, BOY.

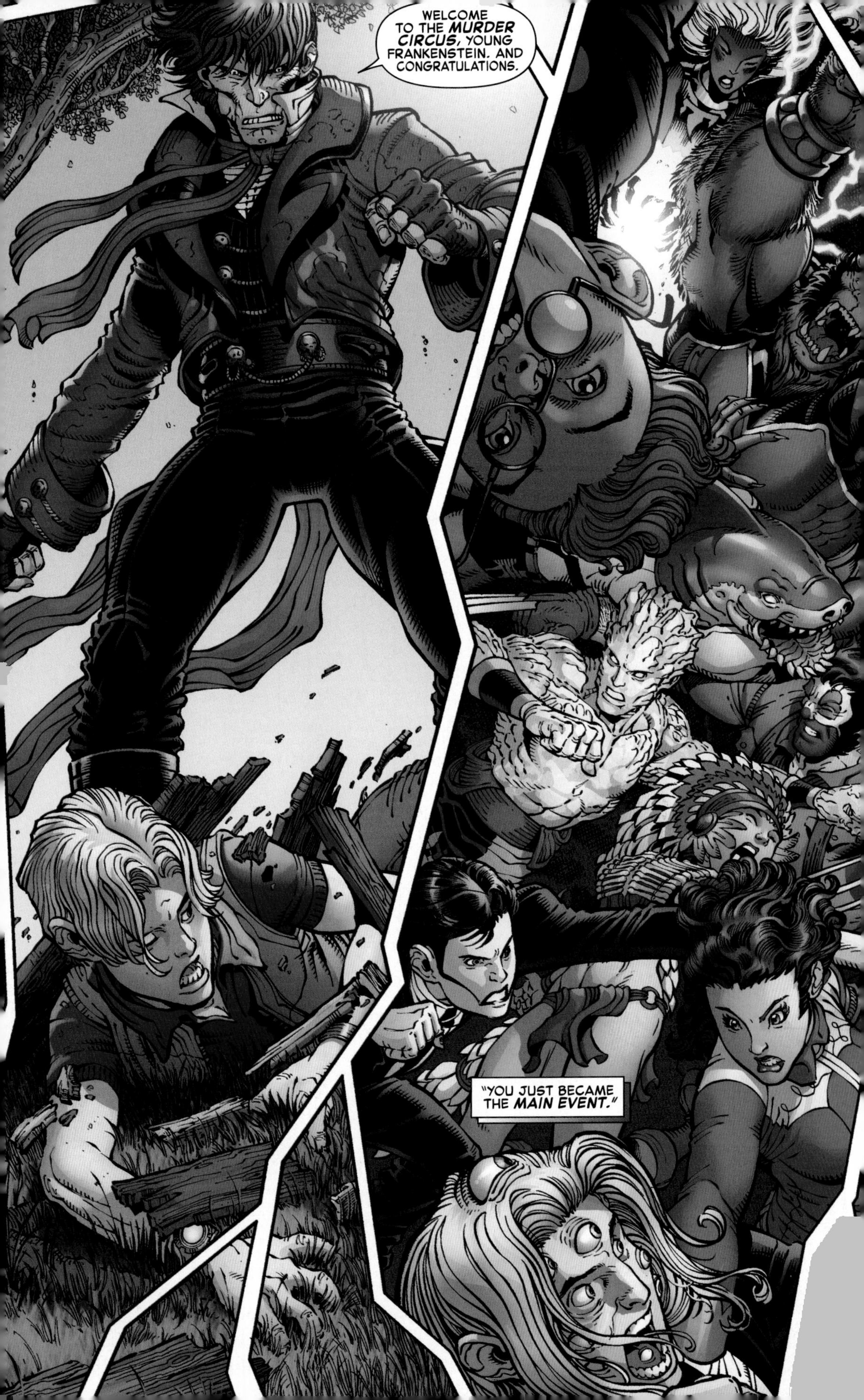
WELCOME TO THE MURDER CIRCUS, YOUNG FRANKENSTEIN. AND CONGRATULATIONS.
"YOU JUST BECAME THE MAIN EVENT."

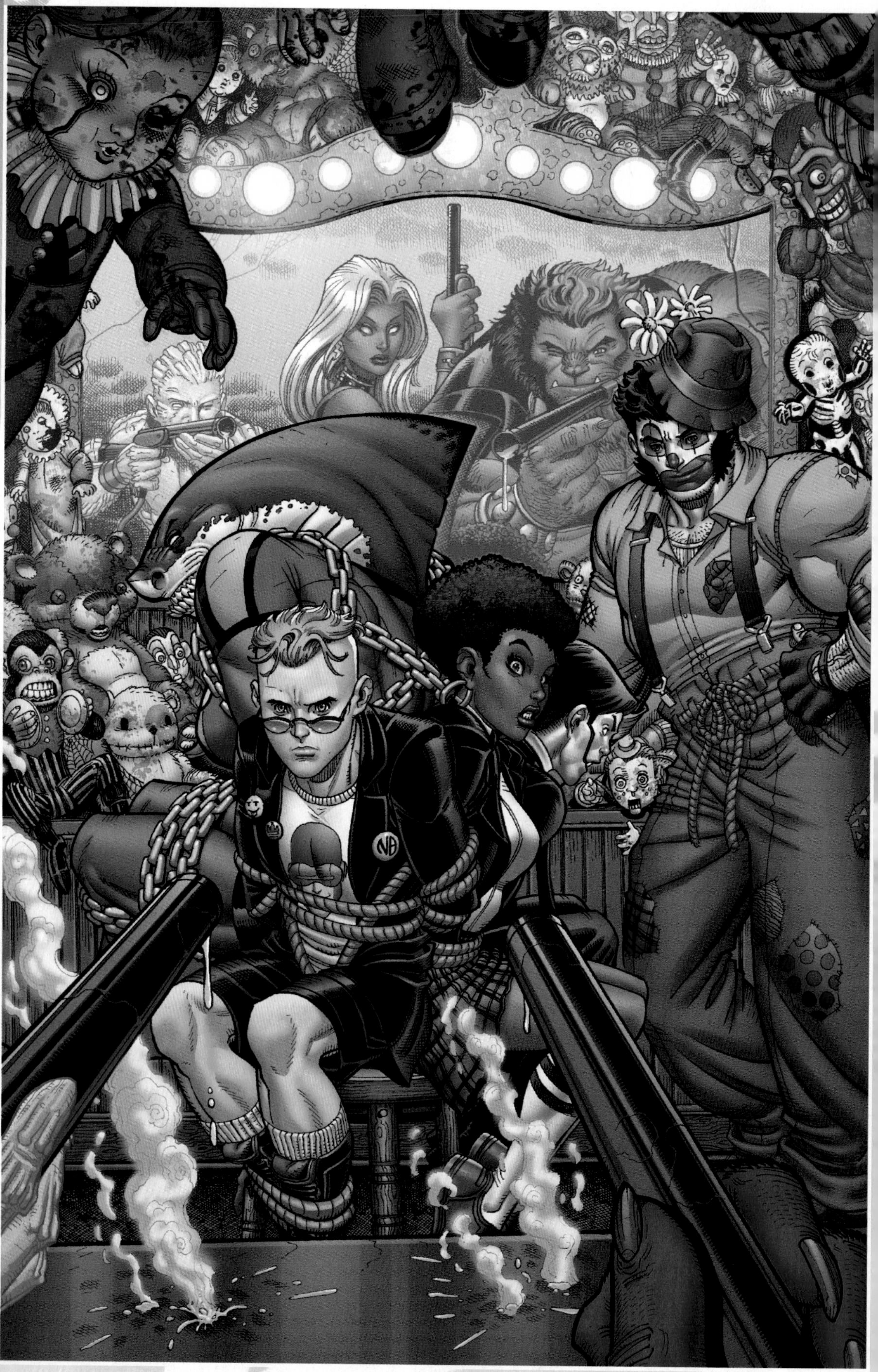

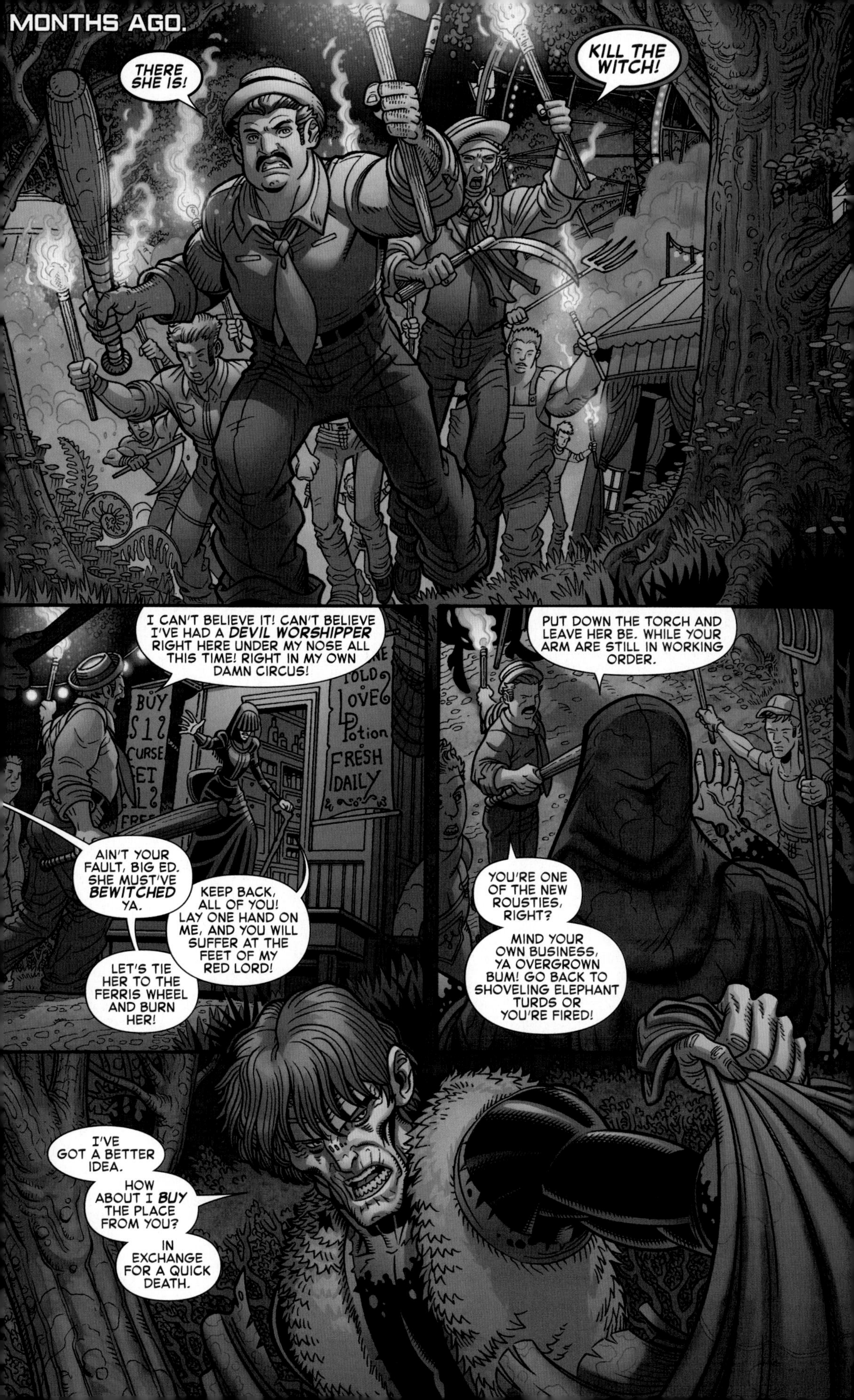
MONTHS AGO.
THERE SHE IS!
KILL THE WITCH!
I CAN'T BELIEVE IT! CAN'T BELIEVE I'VE HAD A DEVIL WORSHIPPER RIGHT HERE UNDER MY NOSE ALL THIS TIME! RIGHT IN MY OWN DAMN CIRCUS!
BUY
CURSE
TOLD
LOVE
Potion
FRESH
DAILY
AIN'T YOUR FAULT, BIG ED. SHE MUST'VE BEWITCHED YA.
KEEP BACK, ALL OF YOU! LAY ONE HAND ON ME, AND YOU WILL SUFFER AT THE FEET OF MY RED LORD!
LET'S TIE HER TO THE FERRIS WHEEL AND BURN HER!
PUT DOWN THE TORCH AND LEAVE HER BE. WHILE YOUR ARM ARE STILL IN WORKING ORDER.
YOU'RE ONE OF THE NEW ROUSTIES, RIGHT?
MIND YOUR OWN BUSINESS, YA OVERGROWN BUM! GO BACK TO SHOVELING ELEPHANT TURDS OR YOU'RE FIRED!
I'VE GOT A BETTER IDEA.
HOW ABOUT I BUY THE PLACE FROM YOU?
IN EXCHANGE FOR A QUICK DEATH.

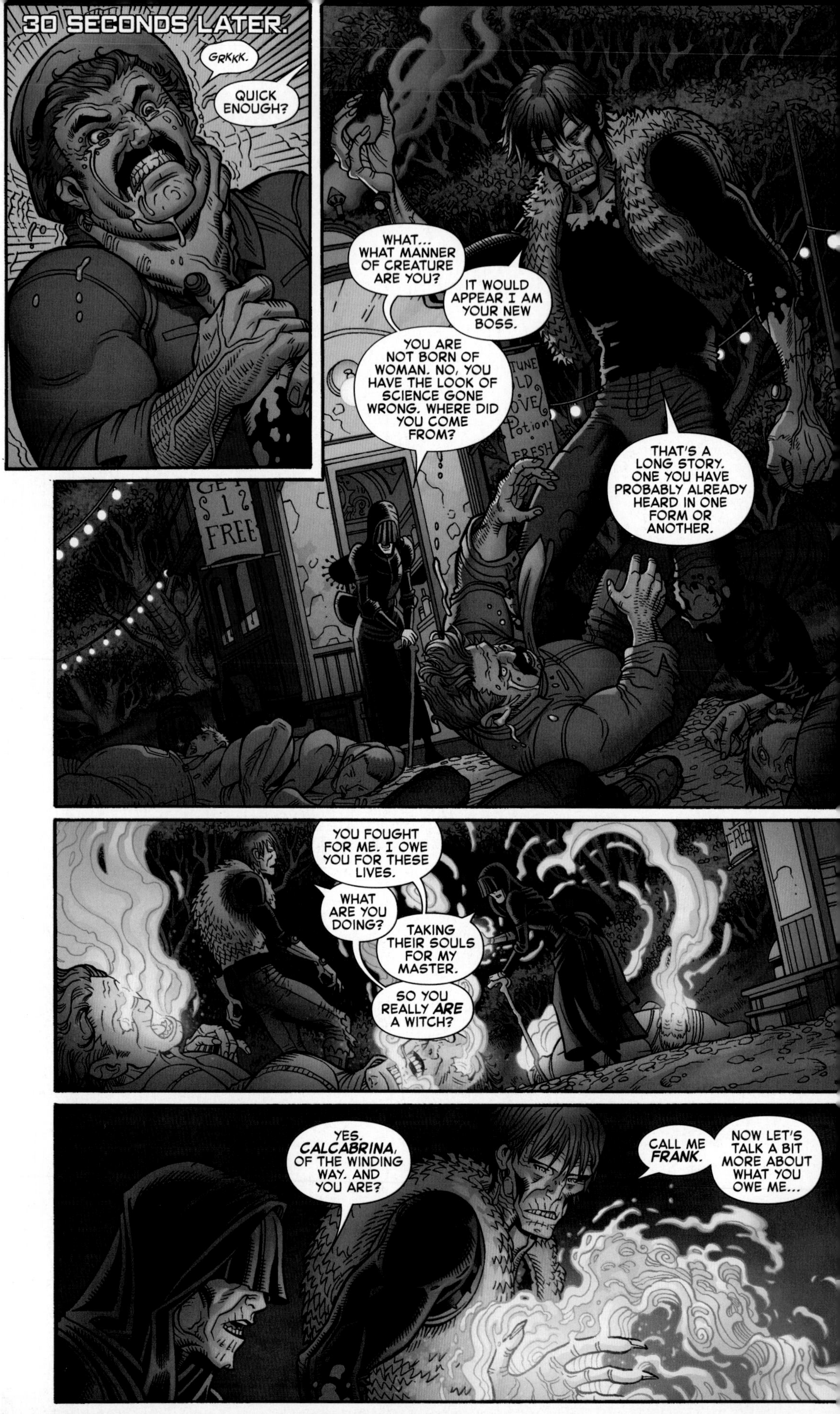
30 SECONDS LATER.
GRKKK.
QUICK ENOUGH?
WHAT... WHAT MANNER OF CREATURE ARE YOU?
IT WOULD APPEAR I AM YOUR NEW BOSS.
YOU ARE NOT BORN OF WOMAN. NO, YOU HAVE THE LOOK OF SCIENCE GONE WRONG. WHERE DID YOU COME FROM?
THAT'S A LONG STORY. ONE YOU HAVE PROBABLY ALREADY HEARD IN ONE FORM OR ANOTHER.
YOU FOUGHT FOR ME. I OWE YOU FOR THESE LIVES.
WHAT ARE YOU DOING?
TAKING THEIR SOULS FOR MY MASTER.
SO YOU REALLY ARE A WITCH?
YES. CALCABRINA, OF THE WINDING WAY. AND YOU ARE?
CALL ME FRANK.
NOW LET'S TALK A BIT MORE ABOUT WHAT YOU OWE ME...

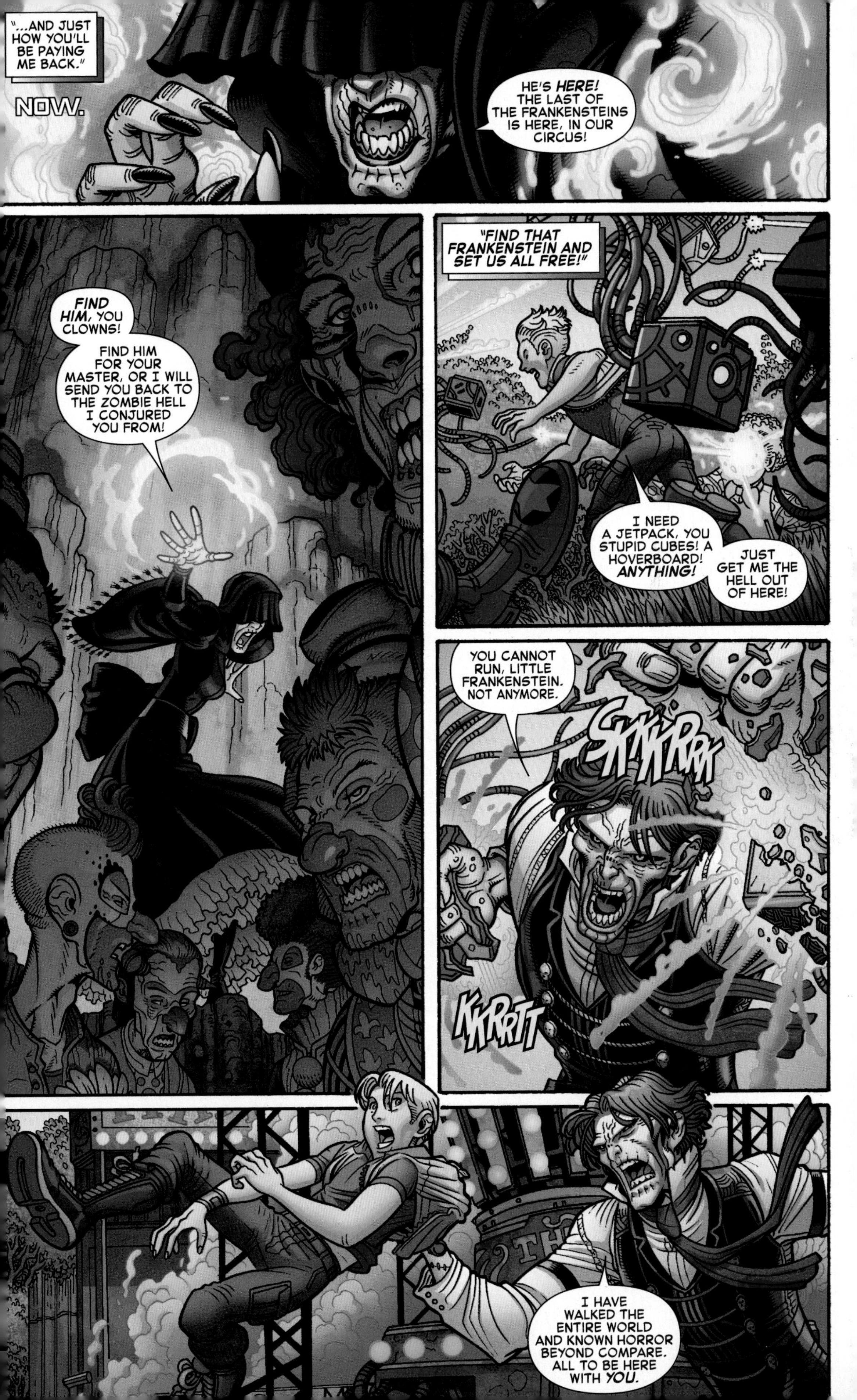
"...AND JUST HOW YOU'LL BE PAYING ME BACK."
NOW.
HE'S HERE! THE LAST OF THE FRANKENSTEINS IS HERE, IN OUR CIRCUS!
FIND HIM, YOU CLOWNS!
FIND HIM FOR YOUR MASTER, OR I WILL SEND YOU BACK TO THE ZOMBIE HELL I CONJURED YOU FROM!
"FIND THAT FRANKENSTEIN AND SET US ALL FREE!"
I NEED A JETPACK, YOU STUPID CUBES! A HOVERBOARD! ANYTHING!
JUST GET ME THE HELL OUT OF HERE!
YOU CANNOT RUN, LITTLE FRANKENSTEIN. NOT ANYMORE.
SKKKRRRK
KKRRRTT
I HAVE WALKED THE ENTIRE WORLD AND KNOWN HORROR BEYOND COMPARE. ALL TO BE HERE WITH YOU.

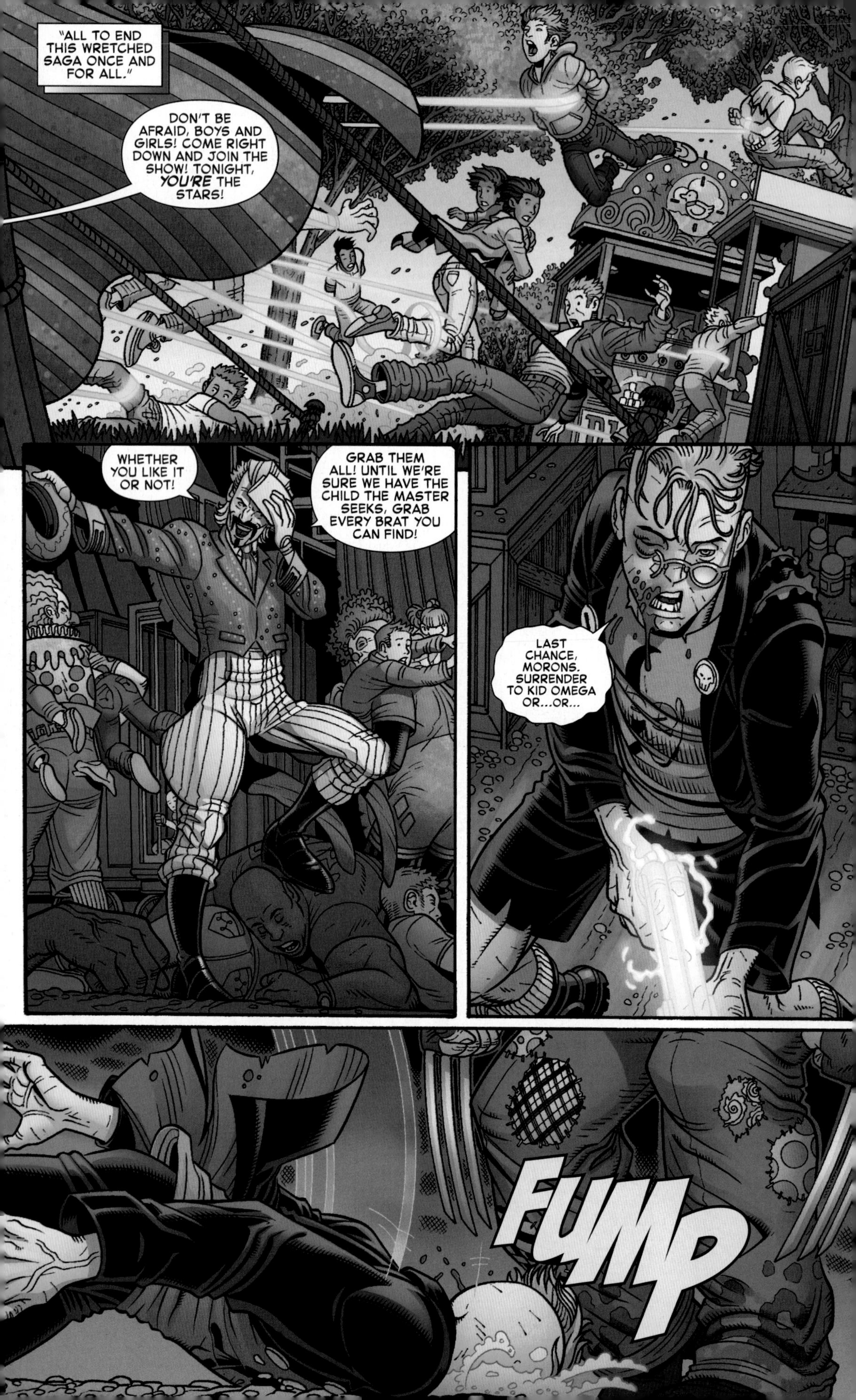
"ALL TO END THIS WRETCHED SAGA ONCE AND FOR ALL."
DON'T BE AFRAID, BOYS AND GIRLS! COME RIGHT DOWN AND JOIN THE SHOW! TONIGHT, *YOU'RE* THE STARS!
WHETHER YOU LIKE IT OR NOT!
GRAB THEM ALL! UNTIL WE'RE SURE WE HAVE THE CHILD THE MASTER SEEKS, GRAB EVERY BRAT YOU CAN FIND!
LAST CHANCE, MORONS. SURRENDER TO KID OMEGA OR...OR...
FUMP

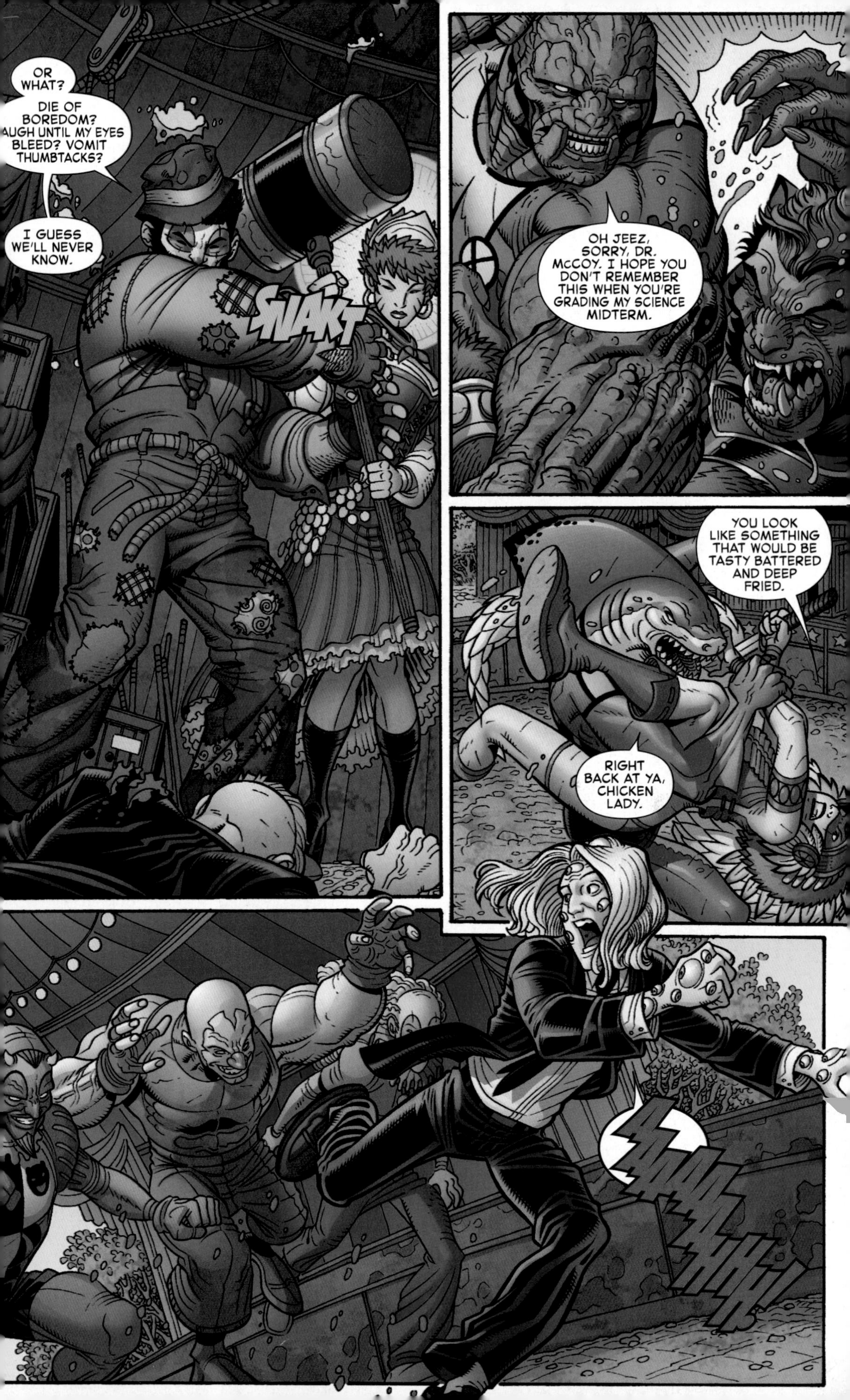
OR WHAT?
DIE OF BOREDOM? LAUGH UNTIL MY EYES BLEED? VOMIT THUMBTACKS?
I GUESS WE'LL NEVER KNOW.
SNAKT
OH JEEZ, SORRY, DR. McCOY. I HOPE YOU DON'T REMEMBER THIS WHEN YOU'RE GRADING MY SCIENCE MIDTERM.
YOU LOOK LIKE SOMETHING THAT WOULD BE TASTY BATTERED AND DEEP FRIED.
RIGHT BACK AT YA, CHICKEN LADY.

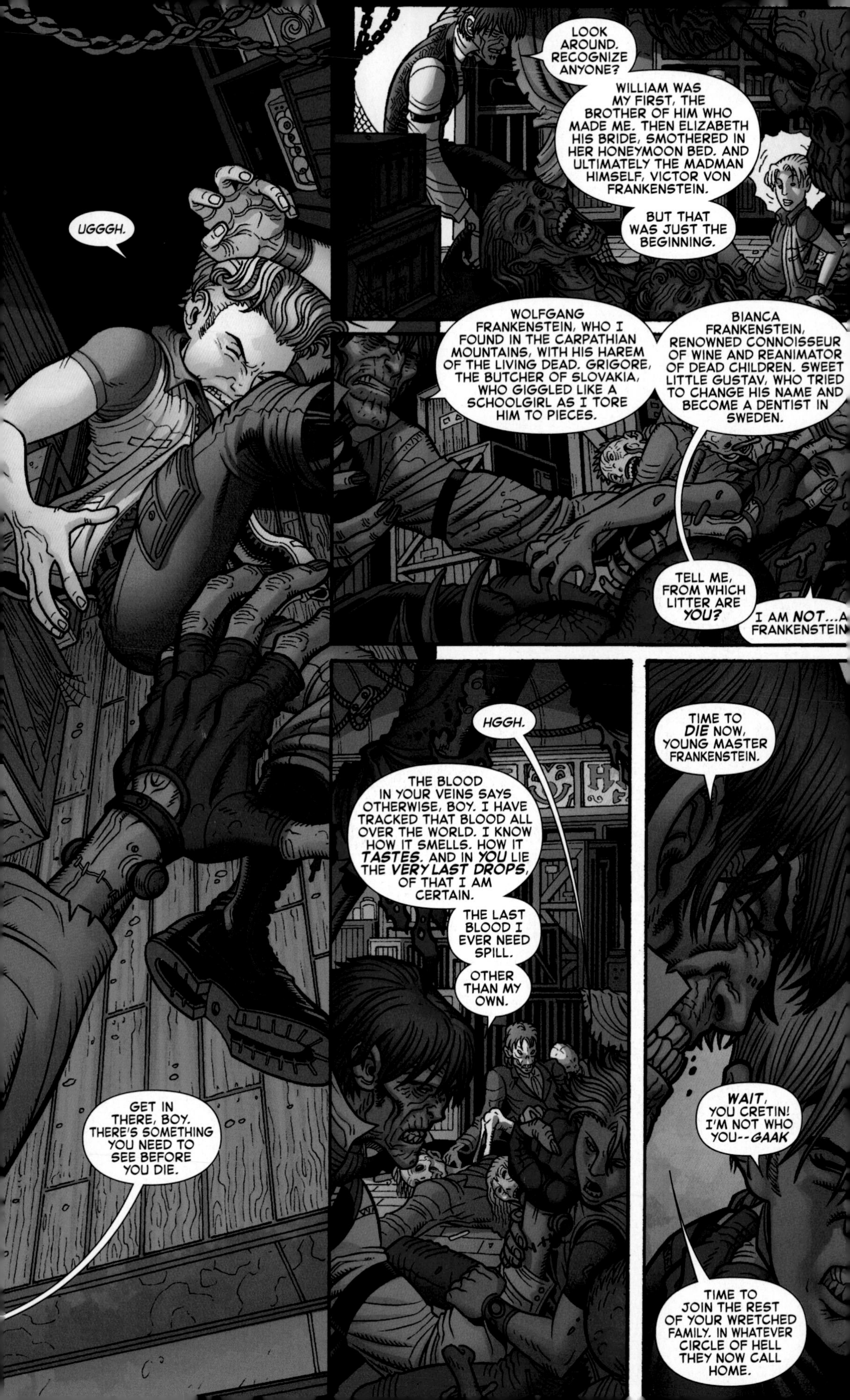
UGGGH.
GET IN THERE, BOY. THERE'S SOMETHING YOU NEED TO SEE BEFORE YOU DIE.
LOOK AROUND. RECOGNIZE ANYONE?
WILLIAM WAS MY FIRST, THE BROTHER OF HIM WHO MADE ME. THEN ELIZABETH HIS BRIDE, SMOTHERED IN HER HONEYMOON BED. AND ULTIMATELY THE MADMAN HIMSELF, VICTOR VON FRANKENSTEIN.
BUT THAT WAS JUST THE BEGINNING.
WOLFGANG FRANKENSTEIN, WHO I FOUND IN THE CARPATHIAN MOUNTAINS, WITH HIS HAREM OF THE LIVING DEAD. GRIGORE, THE BUTCHER OF SLOVAKIA, WHO GIGGLED LIKE A SCHOOLGIRL AS I TORE HIM TO PIECES.
BIANCA FRANKENSTEIN, RENOWNED CONNOISSEUR OF WINE AND REANIMATOR OF DEAD CHILDREN. SWEET LITTLE GUSTAV, WHO TRIED TO CHANGE HIS NAME AND BECOME A DENTIST IN SWEDEN.
TELL ME, FROM WHICH LITTER ARE *YOU?*
I AM **NOT**...A FRANKENSTEIN
HGGH.
THE BLOOD IN YOUR VEINS SAYS OTHERWISE, BOY. I HAVE TRACKED THAT BLOOD ALL OVER THE WORLD. I KNOW HOW IT SMELLS. HOW IT ***TASTES.*** AND IN ***YOU*** LIE THE ***VERY LAST DROPS,*** OF THAT I AM CERTAIN.
THE LAST BLOOD I EVER NEED SPILL.
OTHER THAN MY OWN.
TIME TO ***DIE*** NOW, YOUNG MASTER FRANKENSTEIN.
WAIT, YOU CRETIN! I'M NOT WHO YOU--***GAAK***
TIME TO JOIN THE REST OF YOUR WRETCHED FAMILY. IN WHATEVER CIRCLE OF HELL THEY NOW CALL HOME.

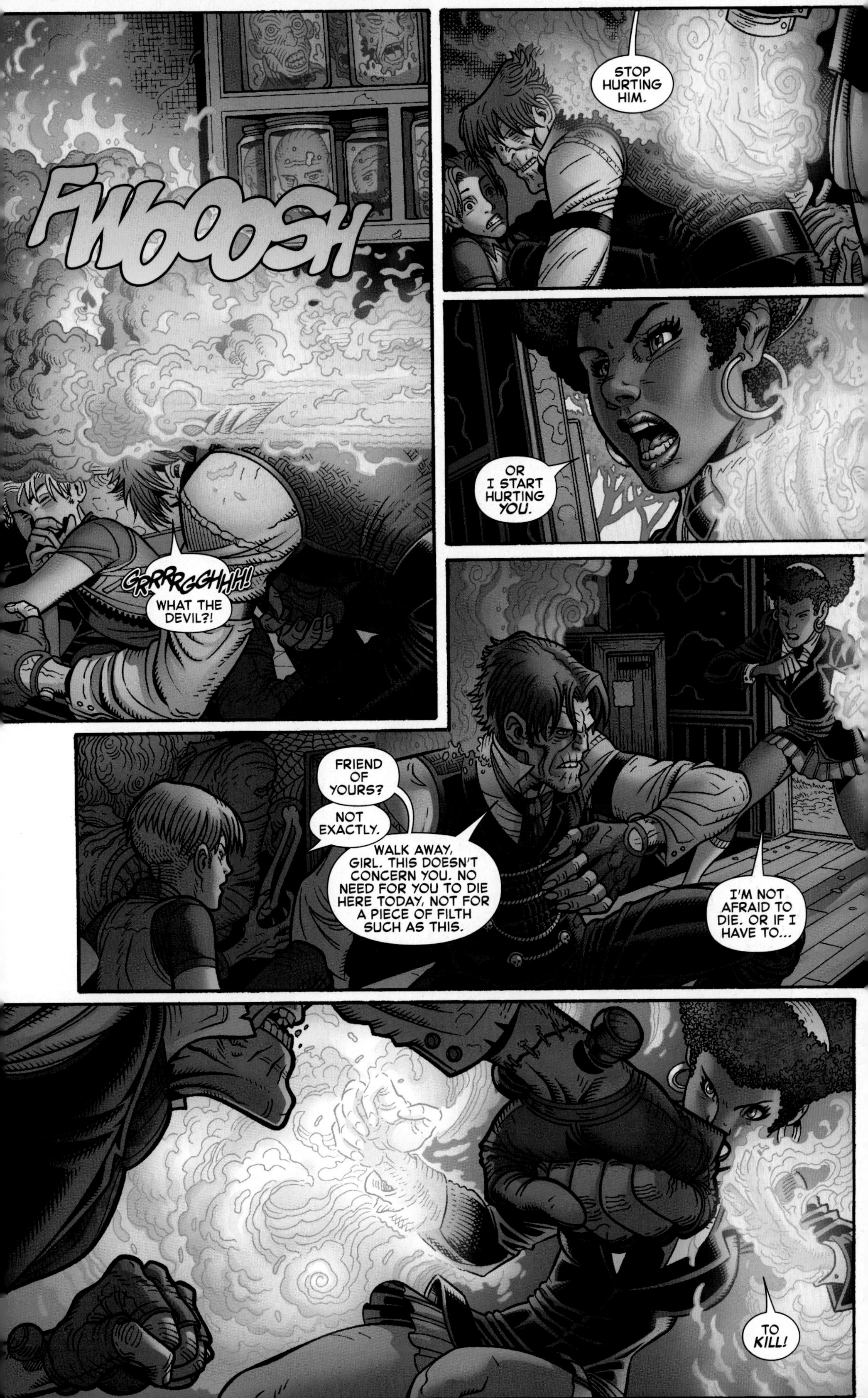
FWOOOSH
GRRRRGGHHH! WHAT THE DEVIL?!
STOP HURTING HIM.
OR I START HURTING YOU.
FRIEND OF YOURS?
NOT EXACTLY.
WALK AWAY, GIRL. THIS DOESN'T CONCERN YOU. NO NEED FOR YOU TO DIE HERE TODAY, NOT FOR A PIECE OF FILTH SUCH AS THIS.
I'M NOT AFRAID TO DIE. OR IF I HAVE TO...
TO KILL!

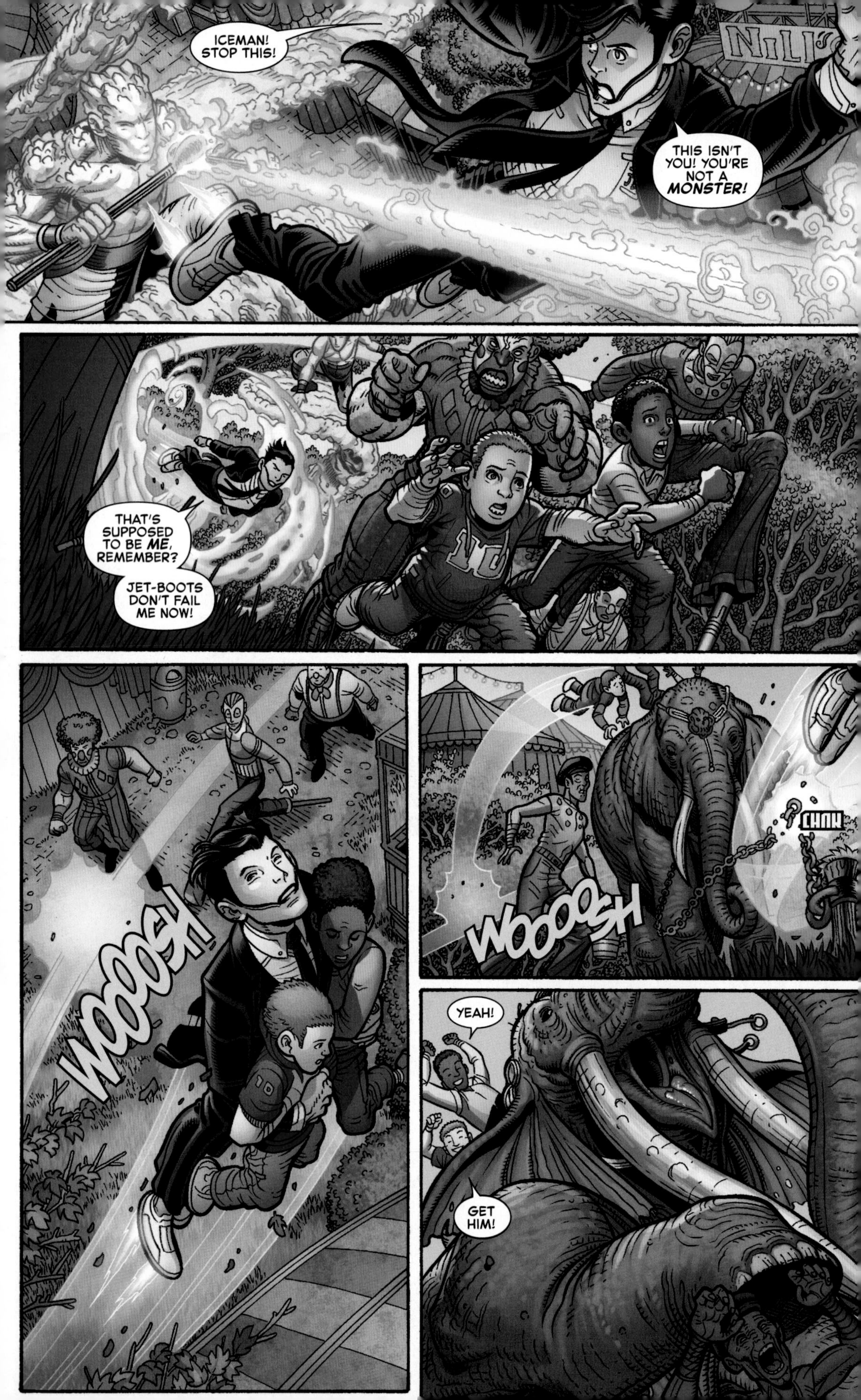

ICEMAN! STOP THIS!
THIS ISN'T YOU! YOU'RE NOT A *MONSTER!*
THAT'S SUPPOSED TO BE *ME*, REMEMBER?
JET-BOOTS DON'T FAIL ME NOW!
WOOOOSH
WOOOOSH
CHNK
YEAH!
GET HIM!

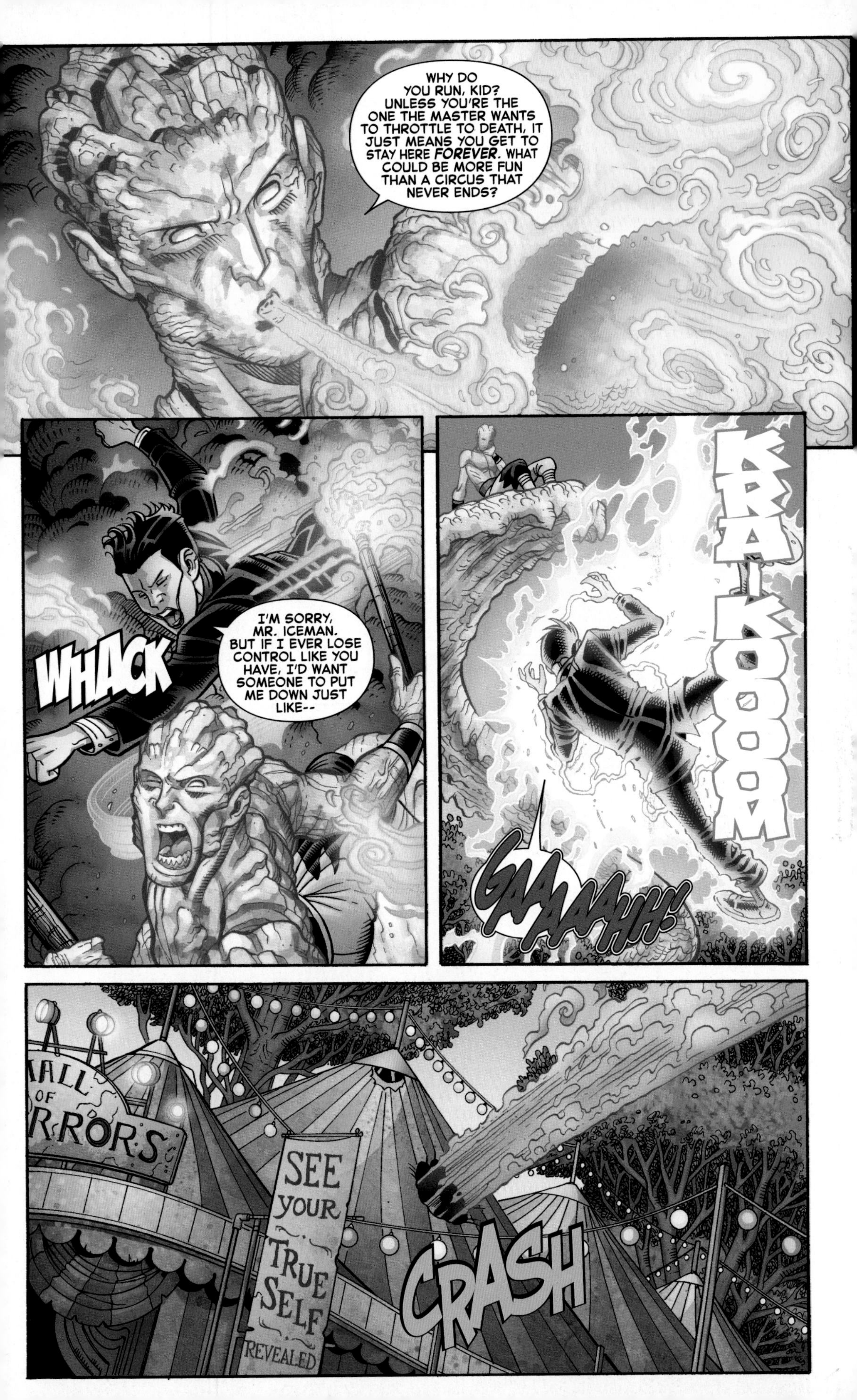
WHY DO YOU RUN, KID? UNLESS YOU'RE THE ONE THE MASTER WANTS TO THROTTLE TO DEATH, IT JUST MEANS YOU GET TO STAY HERE *FOREVER*. WHAT COULD BE MORE FUN THAN A CIRCUS THAT NEVER ENDS?
WHACK
I'M SORRY, MR. ICEMAN. BUT IF I EVER LOSE CONTROL LIKE YOU HAVE, I'D WANT SOMEONE TO PUT ME DOWN JUST LIKE--
KRA-KOOOOM
GAAAAAHH!
HALL OF MIRRORS
SEE YOUR TRUE SELF REVEALED
CRASH

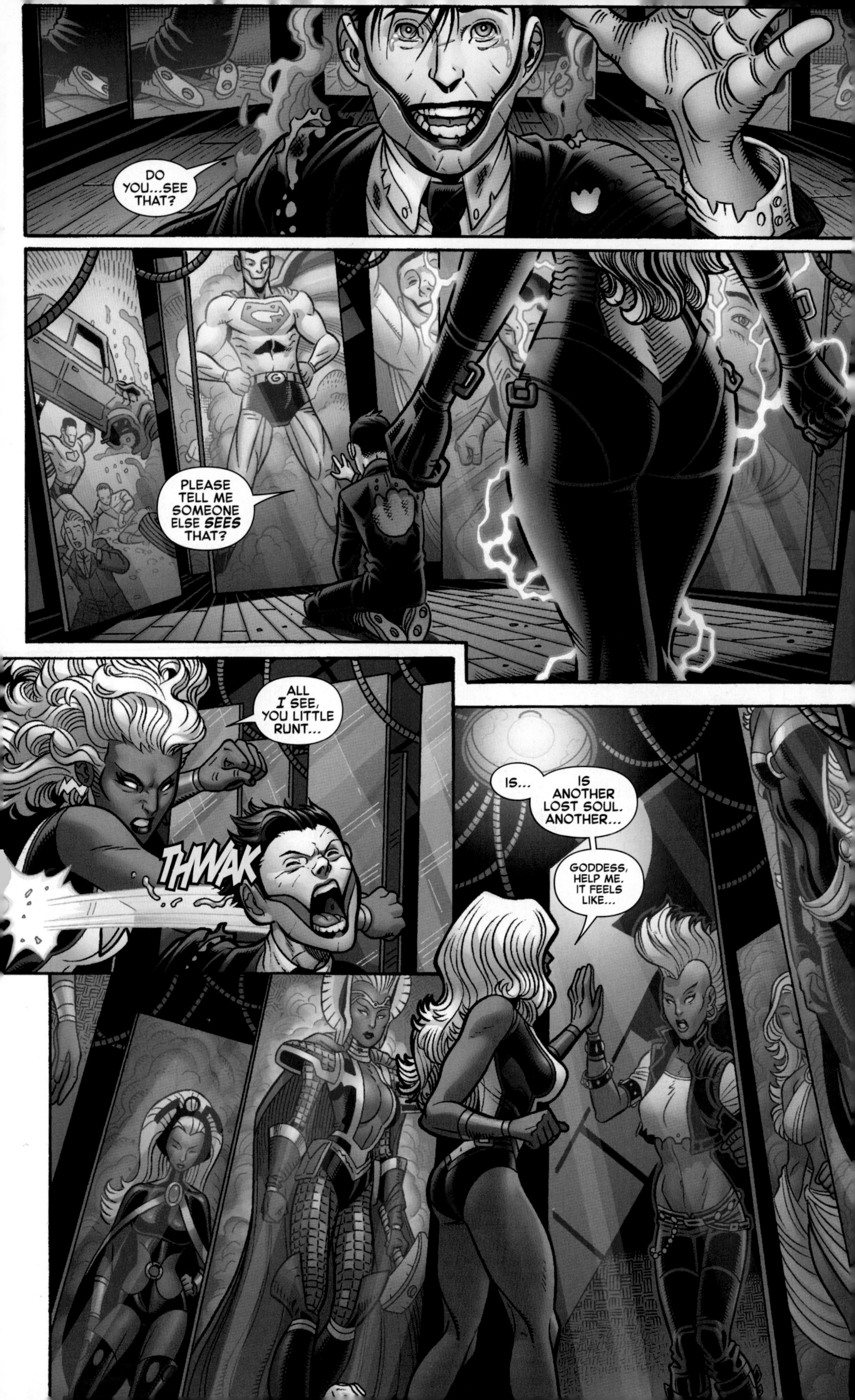
DO YOU...SEE THAT?
PLEASE TELL ME SOMEONE ELSE SEES THAT?
ALL I SEE, YOU LITTLE RUNT...
THWAK
IS...
IS ANOTHER LOST SOUL. ANOTHER...
GODDESS, HELP ME. IT FEELS LIKE...

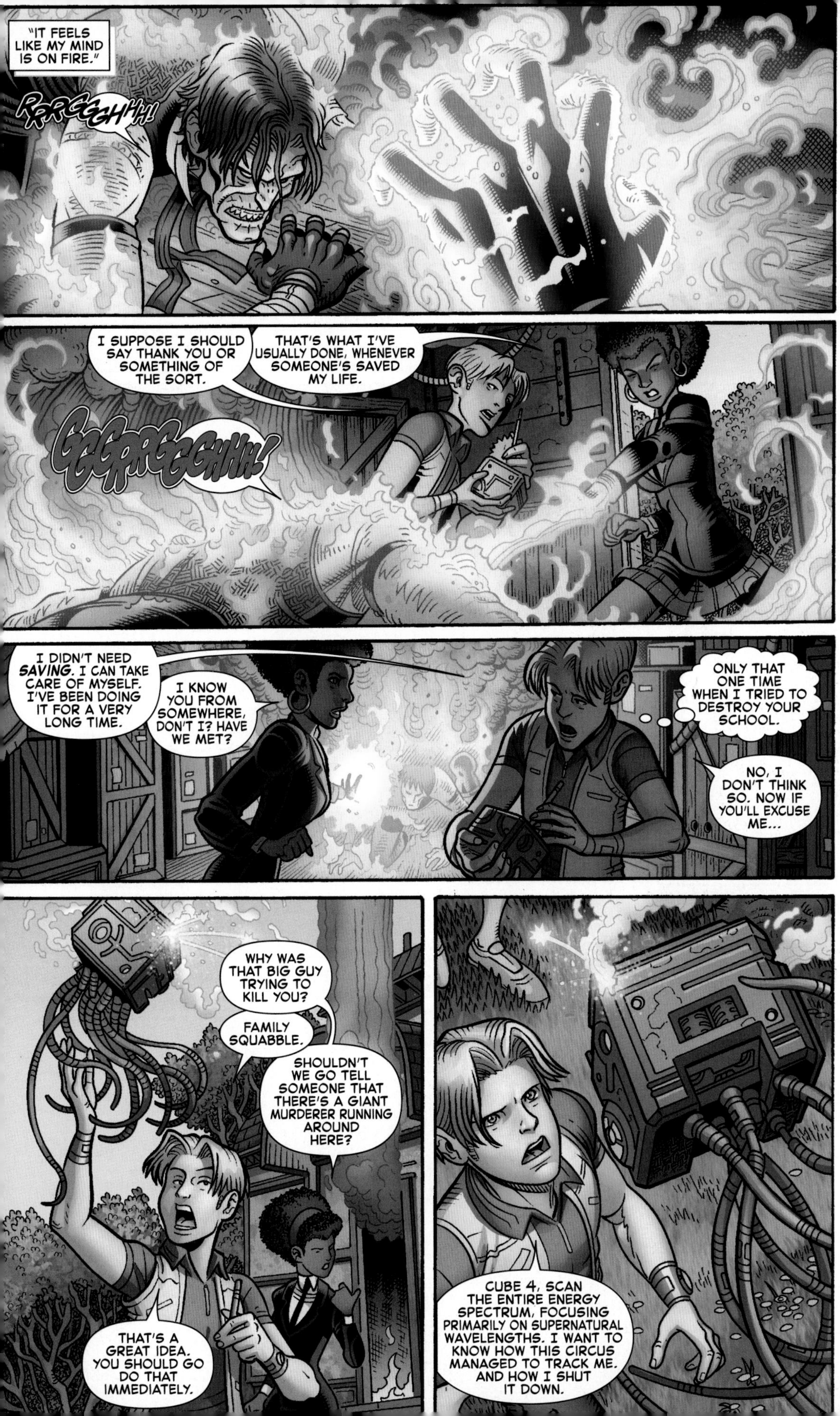
"IT FEELS LIKE MY MIND IS ON FIRE."
RRRGGGHHH!
I SUPPOSE I SHOULD SAY THANK YOU OR SOMETHING OF THE SORT.
THAT'S WHAT I'VE USUALLY DONE, WHENEVER SOMEONE'S SAVED MY LIFE.
GGGRRGGGHHH!
I DIDN'T NEED *SAVING*. I CAN TAKE CARE OF MYSELF. I'VE BEEN DOING IT FOR A VERY LONG TIME.
I KNOW YOU FROM SOMEWHERE, DON'T I? HAVE WE MET?
ONLY THAT ONE TIME WHEN I TRIED TO DESTROY YOUR SCHOOL.
NO, I DON'T THINK SO. NOW IF YOU'LL EXCUSE ME...
WHY WAS THAT BIG GUY TRYING TO KILL YOU?
FAMILY SQUABBLE.
SHOULDN'T WE GO TELL SOMEONE THAT THERE'S A GIANT MURDERER RUNNING AROUND HERE?
THAT'S A GREAT IDEA. YOU SHOULD GO DO THAT IMMEDIATELY.
CUBE 4, SCAN THE ENTIRE ENERGY SPECTRUM, FOCUSING PRIMARILY ON SUPERNATURAL WAVELENGTHS. I WANT TO KNOW HOW THIS CIRCUS MANAGED TO TRACK ME. AND HOW I SHUT IT DOWN.

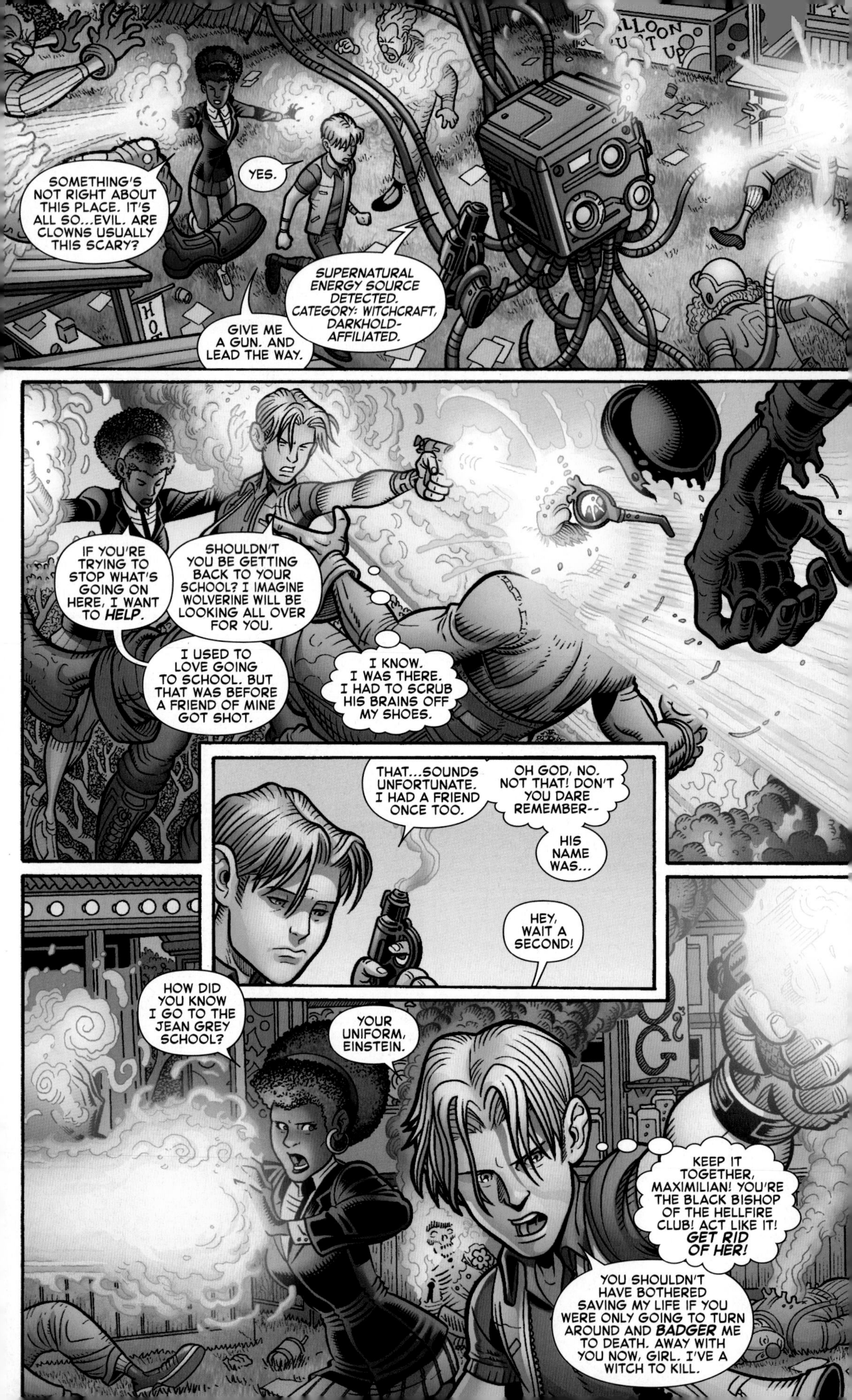
SOMETHING'S NOT RIGHT ABOUT THIS PLACE. IT'S ALL SO...EVIL. ARE CLOWNS USUALLY THIS SCARY?
YES.
SUPERNATURAL ENERGY SOURCE DETECTED. CATEGORY: WITCHCRAFT, DARKHOLD-AFFILIATED.
GIVE ME A GUN. AND LEAD THE WAY.
IF YOU'RE TRYING TO STOP WHAT'S GOING ON HERE, I WANT TO HELP.
SHOULDN'T YOU BE GETTING BACK TO YOUR SCHOOL? I IMAGINE WOLVERINE WILL BE LOOKING ALL OVER FOR YOU.
I USED TO LOVE GOING TO SCHOOL. BUT THAT WAS BEFORE A FRIEND OF MINE GOT SHOT.
I KNOW. I WAS THERE. I HAD TO SCRUB HIS BRAINS OFF MY SHOES.
THAT...SOUNDS UNFORTUNATE. I HAD A FRIEND ONCE TOO.
OH GOD, NO. NOT THAT! DON'T YOU DARE REMEMBER--
HIS NAME WAS...
HEY, WAIT A SECOND!
HOW DID YOU KNOW I GO TO THE JEAN GREY SCHOOL?
YOUR UNIFORM, EINSTEIN.
KEEP IT TOGETHER, MAXIMILIAN! YOU'RE THE BLACK BISHOP OF THE HELLFIRE CLUB! ACT LIKE IT! GET RID OF HER!
YOU SHOULDN'T HAVE BOTHERED SAVING MY LIFE IF YOU WERE ONLY GOING TO TURN AROUND AND BADGER ME TO DEATH. AWAY WITH YOU NOW, GIRL. I'VE A WITCH TO KILL.

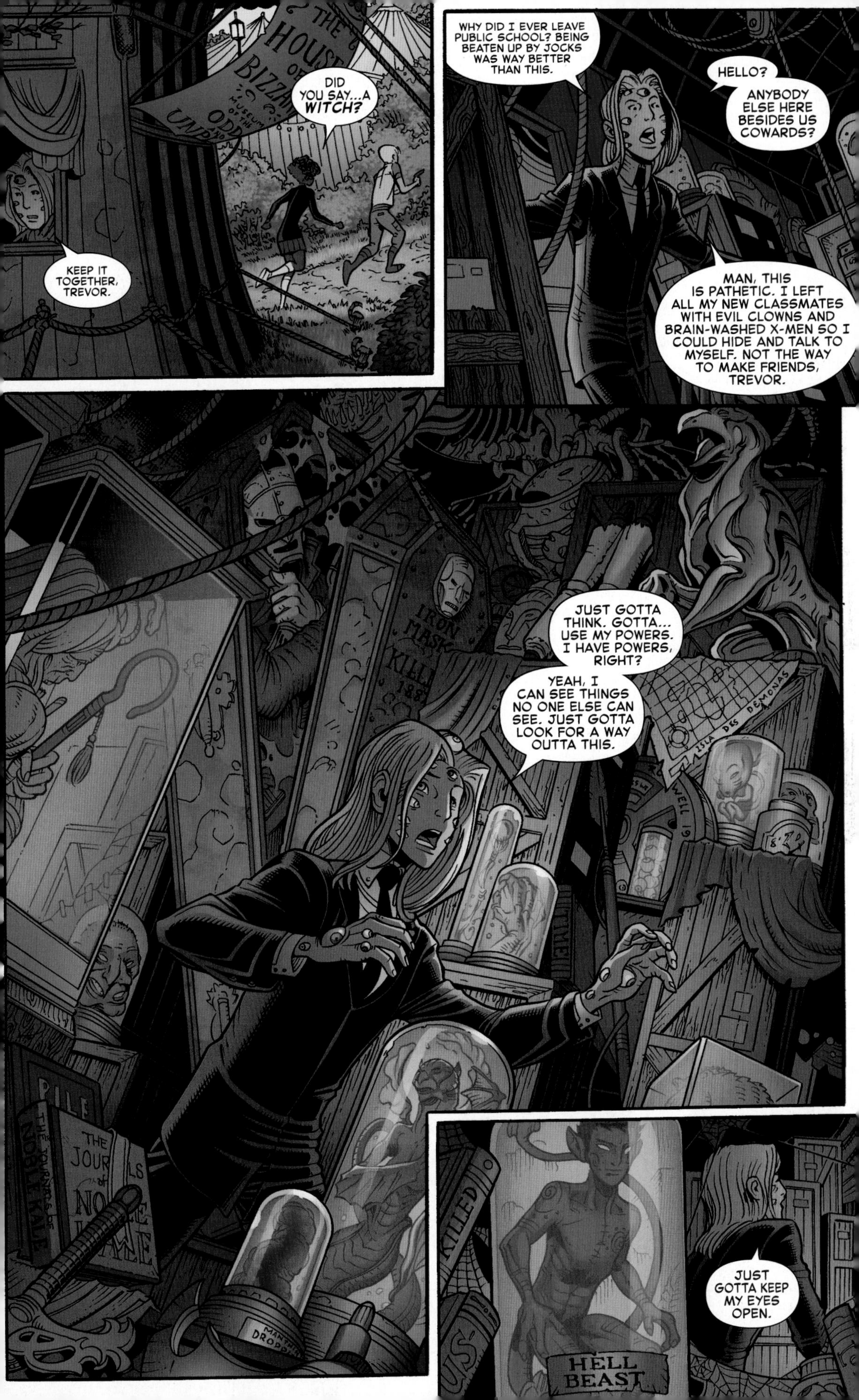
DID YOU SAY...A *WITCH?*
KEEP IT TOGETHER, TREVOR.
WHY DID I EVER LEAVE PUBLIC SCHOOL? BEING BEATEN UP BY JOCKS WAS WAY BETTER THAN THIS.
HELLO?
ANYBODY ELSE HERE BESIDES US COWARDS?
MAN, THIS IS PATHETIC. I LEFT ALL MY NEW CLASSMATES WITH EVIL CLOWNS AND BRAIN-WASHED X-MEN SO I COULD HIDE AND TALK TO MYSELF. NOT THE WAY TO MAKE FRIENDS, TREVOR.
IRON MASK
ISLA DES DEMONAS
JUST GOTTA THINK. GOTTA... USE MY POWERS. I HAVE POWERS, RIGHT?
YEAH, I CAN SEE THINGS NO ONE ELSE CAN SEE. JUST GOTTA LOOK FOR A WAY OUTTA THIS.
HELL BEAST
JUST GOTTA KEEP MY EYES OPEN.

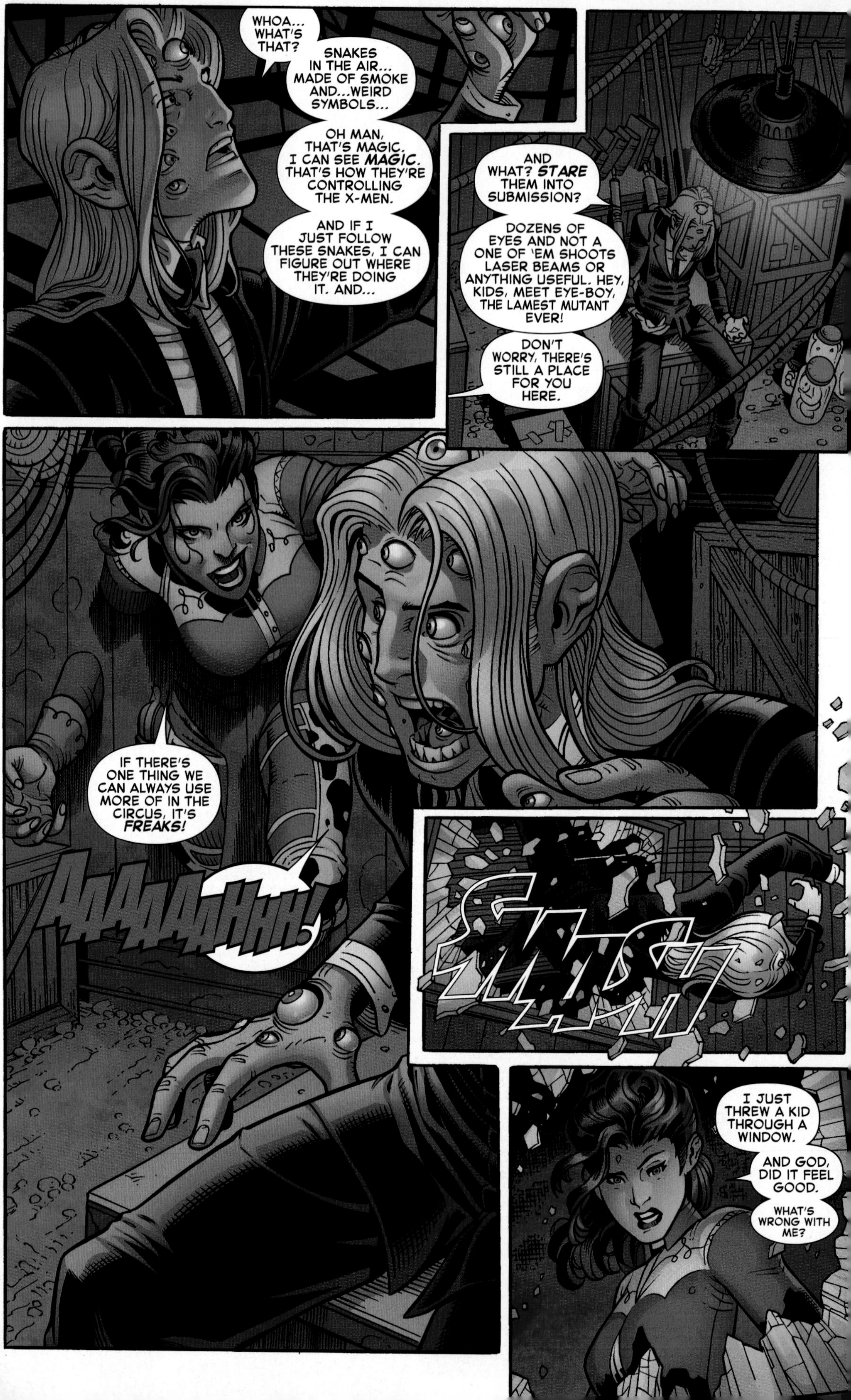
WHOA... WHAT'S THAT?
SNAKES IN THE AIR... MADE OF SMOKE AND...WEIRD SYMBOLS...
OH MAN, THAT'S MAGIC. I CAN SEE *MAGIC*. THAT'S HOW THEY'RE CONTROLLING THE X-MEN.
AND IF I JUST FOLLOW THESE SNAKES, I CAN FIGURE OUT WHERE THEY'RE DOING IT. AND...
AND WHAT? *STARE* THEM INTO SUBMISSION?
DOZENS OF EYES AND NOT A ONE OF 'EM SHOOTS LASER BEAMS OR ANYTHING USEFUL. HEY, KIDS, MEET EYE-BOY, THE LAMEST MUTANT EVER!
DON'T WORRY, THERE'S STILL A PLACE FOR YOU HERE.
IF THERE'S ONE THING WE CAN ALWAYS USE MORE OF IN THE CIRCUS, IT'S *FREAKS!*
AAAAAAHHH!
SMASH
I JUST THREW A KID THROUGH A WINDOW.
AND GOD, DID IT FEEL GOOD.
WHAT'S WRONG WITH ME?

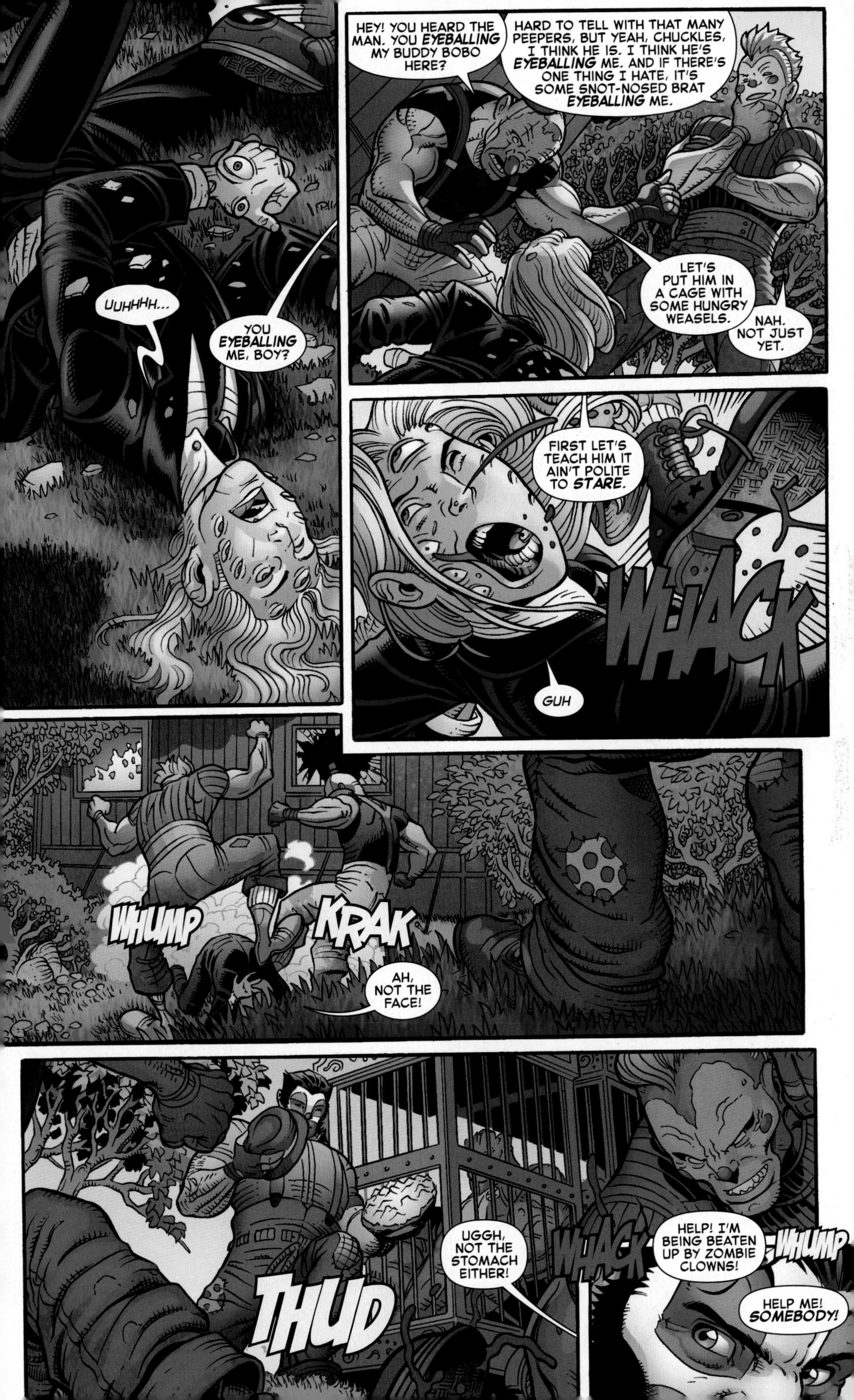

UUHHHH...
YOU EYEBALLING ME, BOY?
HEY! YOU HEARD THE MAN. YOU EYEBALLING MY BUDDY BOBO HERE?
HARD TO TELL WITH THAT MANY PEEPERS, BUT YEAH, CHUCKLES, I THINK HE IS. I THINK HE'S EYEBALLING ME. AND IF THERE'S ONE THING I HATE, IT'S SOME SNOT-NOSED BRAT EYEBALLING ME.
LET'S PUT HIM IN A CAGE WITH SOME HUNGRY WEASELS.
NAH. NOT JUST YET.
FIRST LET'S TEACH HIM IT AIN'T POLITE TO STARE.
WHACK
GUH
WHUMP
KRAK
AH, NOT THE FACE!
THUD
UGGH, NOT THE STOMACH EITHER!
WHACK
HELP! I'M BEING BEATEN UP BY ZOMBIE CLOWNS!
WHUMP
HELP ME! SOMEBODY!

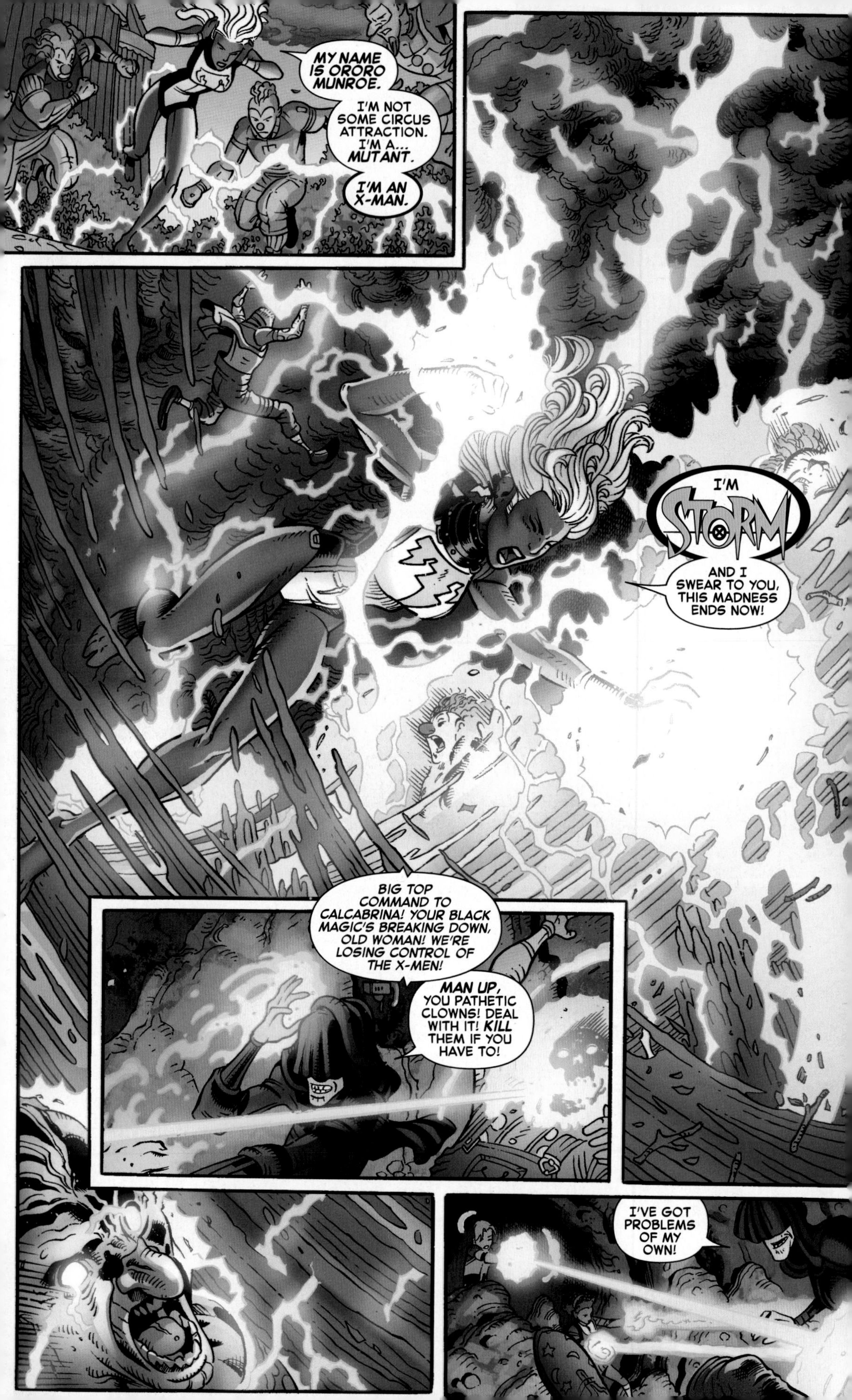

MY NAME IS ORORO MUNROE.
I'M NOT SOME CIRCUS ATTRACTION. I'M A... MUTANT.
I'M AN X-MAN.
I'M STORM
AND I SWEAR TO YOU, THIS MADNESS ENDS NOW!
BIG TOP COMMAND TO CALCABRINA! YOUR BLACK MAGIC'S BREAKING DOWN, OLD WOMAN! WE'RE LOSING CONTROL OF THE X-MEN!
MAN UP, YOU PATHETIC CLOWNS! DEAL WITH IT! KILL THEM IF YOU HAVE TO!
I'VE GOT PROBLEMS OF MY OWN!

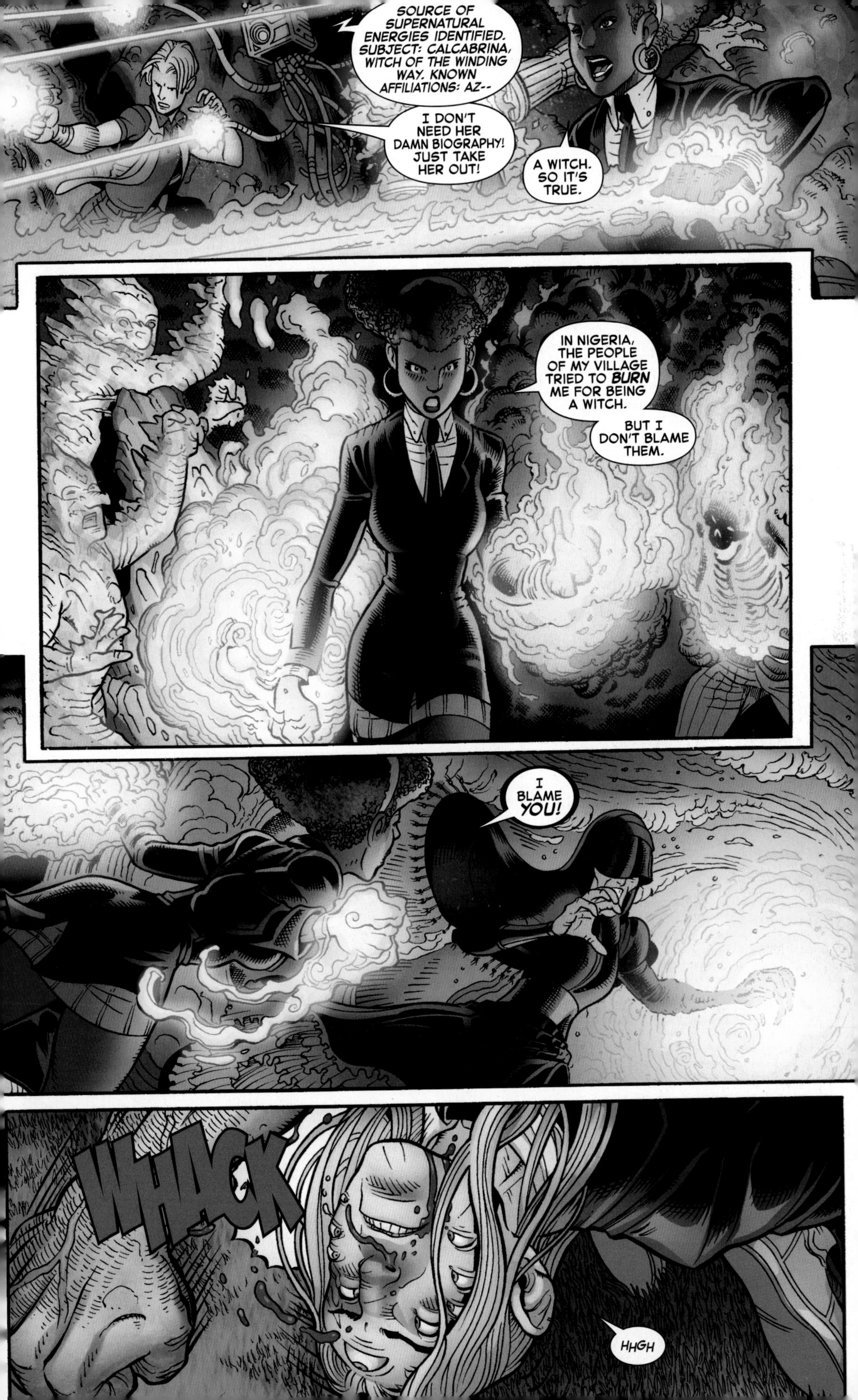

SOURCE OF SUPERNATURAL ENERGIES IDENTIFIED. SUBJECT: CALCABRINA, WITCH OF THE WINDING WAY. KNOWN AFFILIATIONS: AZ--
I DON'T NEED HER DAMN BIOGRAPHY! JUST TAKE HER OUT!
A WITCH. SO IT'S TRUE.
IN NIGERIA, THE PEOPLE OF MY VILLAGE TRIED TO BURN ME FOR BEING A WITCH.
BUT I DON'T BLAME THEM.
I BLAME YOU!
WHACK
HHGH

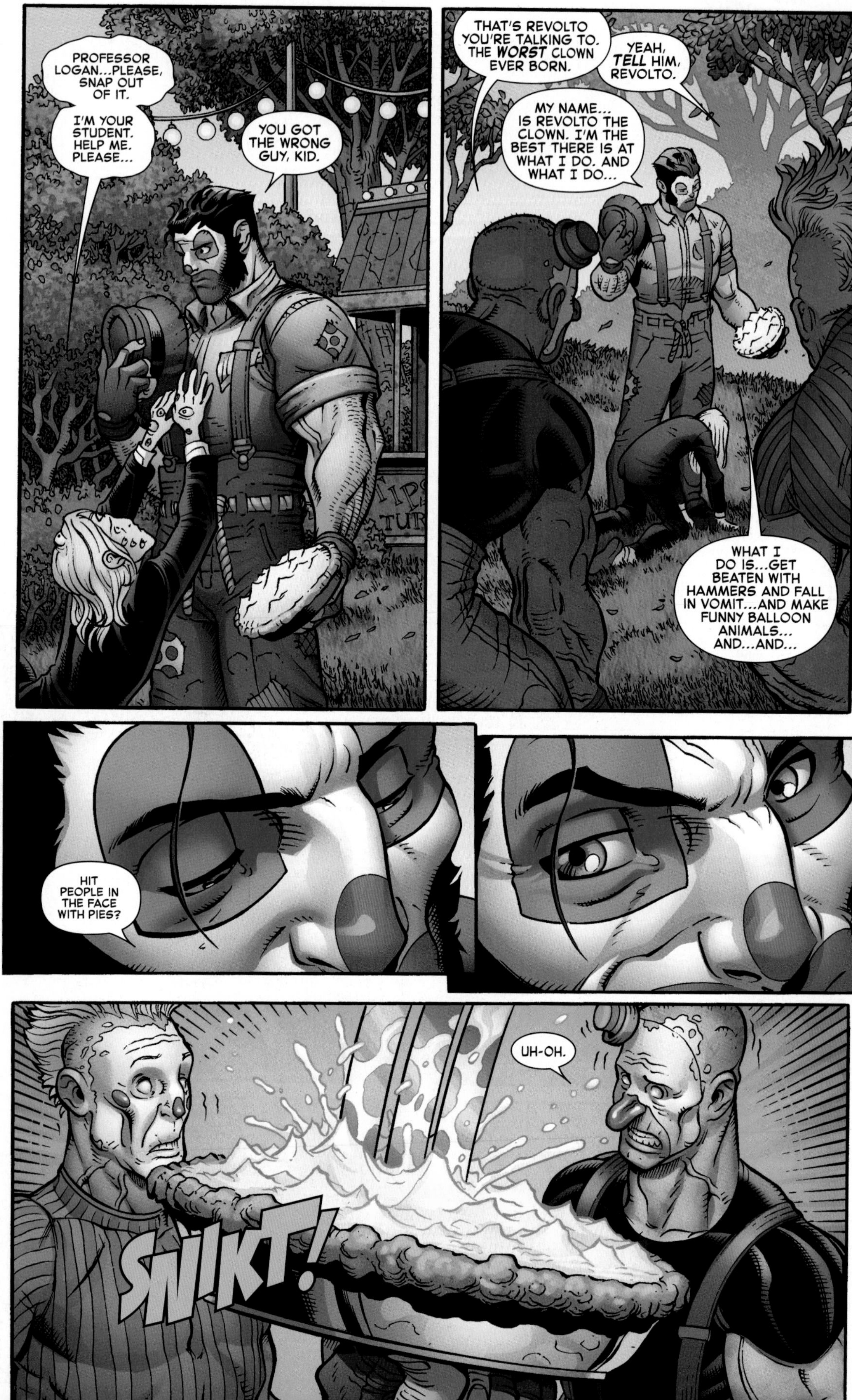
PROFESSOR LOGAN...PLEASE, SNAP OUT OF IT.
I'M YOUR STUDENT. HELP ME. PLEASE...
YOU GOT THE WRONG GUY, KID.
THAT'S REVOLTO YOU'RE TALKING TO. THE WORST CLOWN EVER BORN.
YEAH, TELL HIM, REVOLTO.
MY NAME... IS REVOLTO THE CLOWN. I'M THE BEST THERE IS AT WHAT I DO. AND WHAT I DO...
WHAT I DO IS...GET BEATEN WITH HAMMERS AND FALL IN VOMIT...AND MAKE FUNNY BALLOON ANIMALS... AND...AND...
HIT PEOPLE IN THE FACE WITH PIES?
UH-OH.
SNIKT!

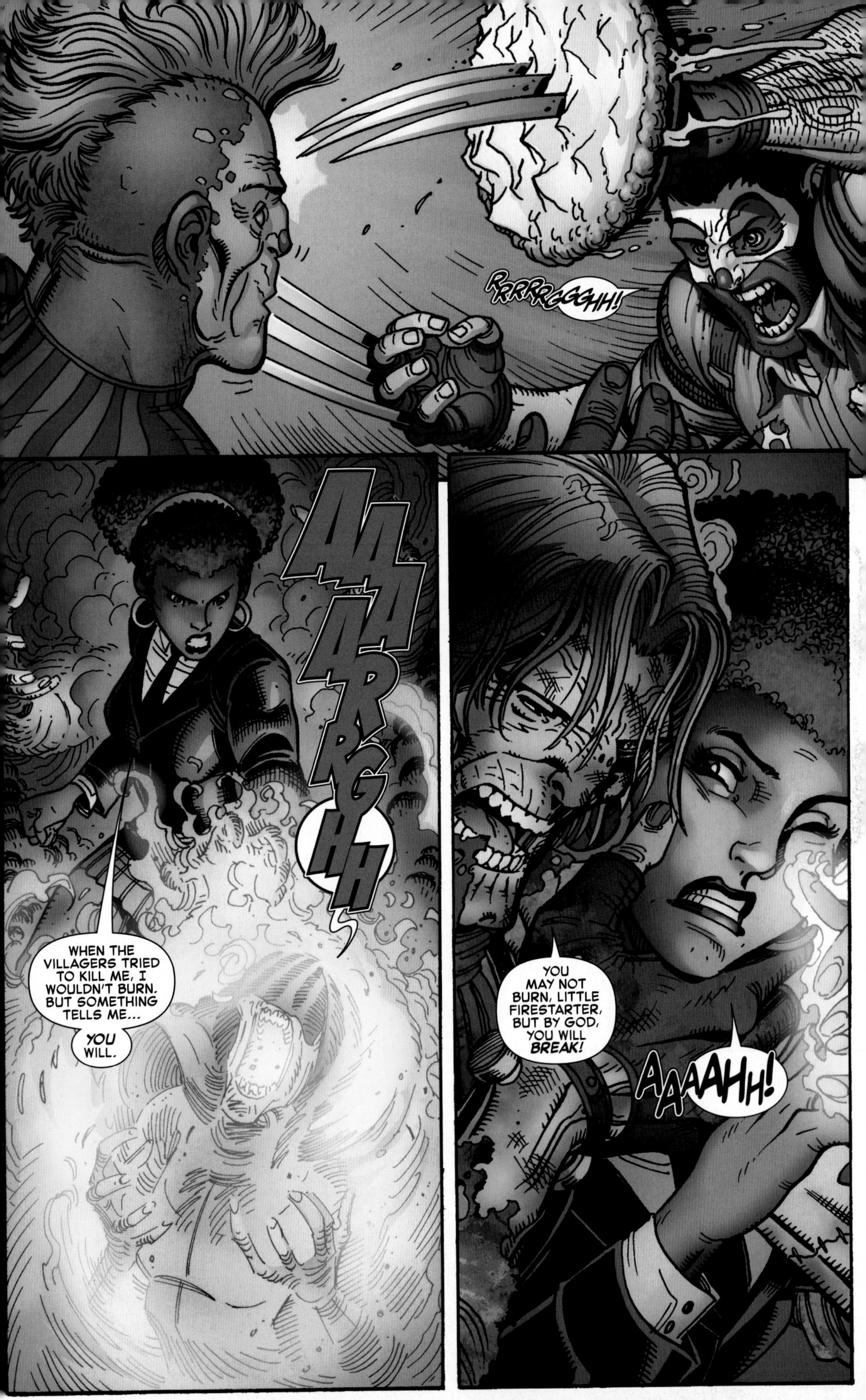
RRRRRGGGHH!
AAARRGHH
WHEN THE VILLAGERS TRIED TO KILL ME, I WOULDN'T BURN. BUT SOMETHING TELLS ME...
YOU WILL.
YOU MAY NOT BURN, LITTLE FIRESTARTER, BUT BY GOD, YOU WILL *BREAK!*
AAAAHH!

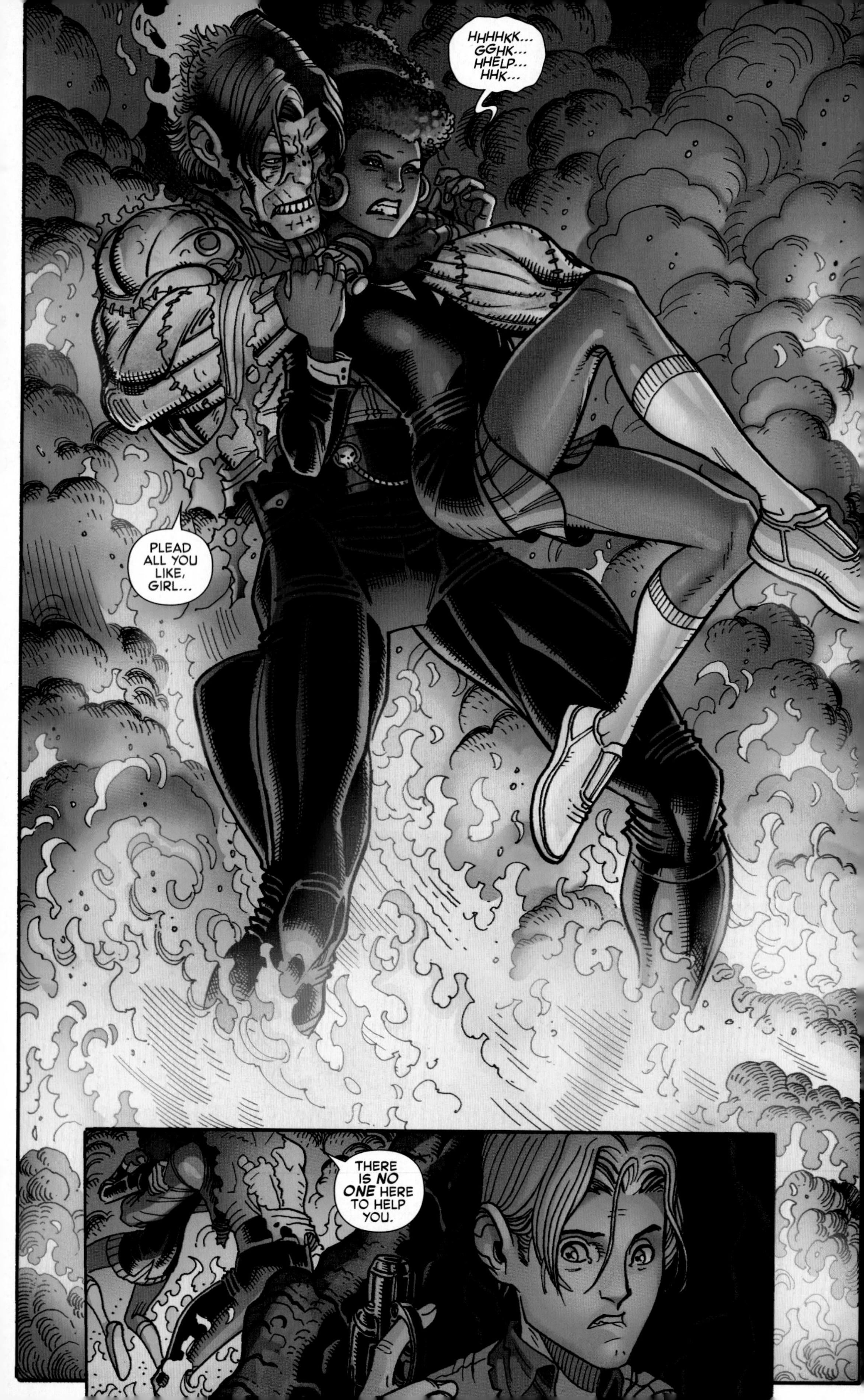
HHHHKK... GGHK... HHELP... HHK...
PLEAD ALL YOU LIKE, GIRL...
THERE IS NO ONE HERE TO HELP YOU.

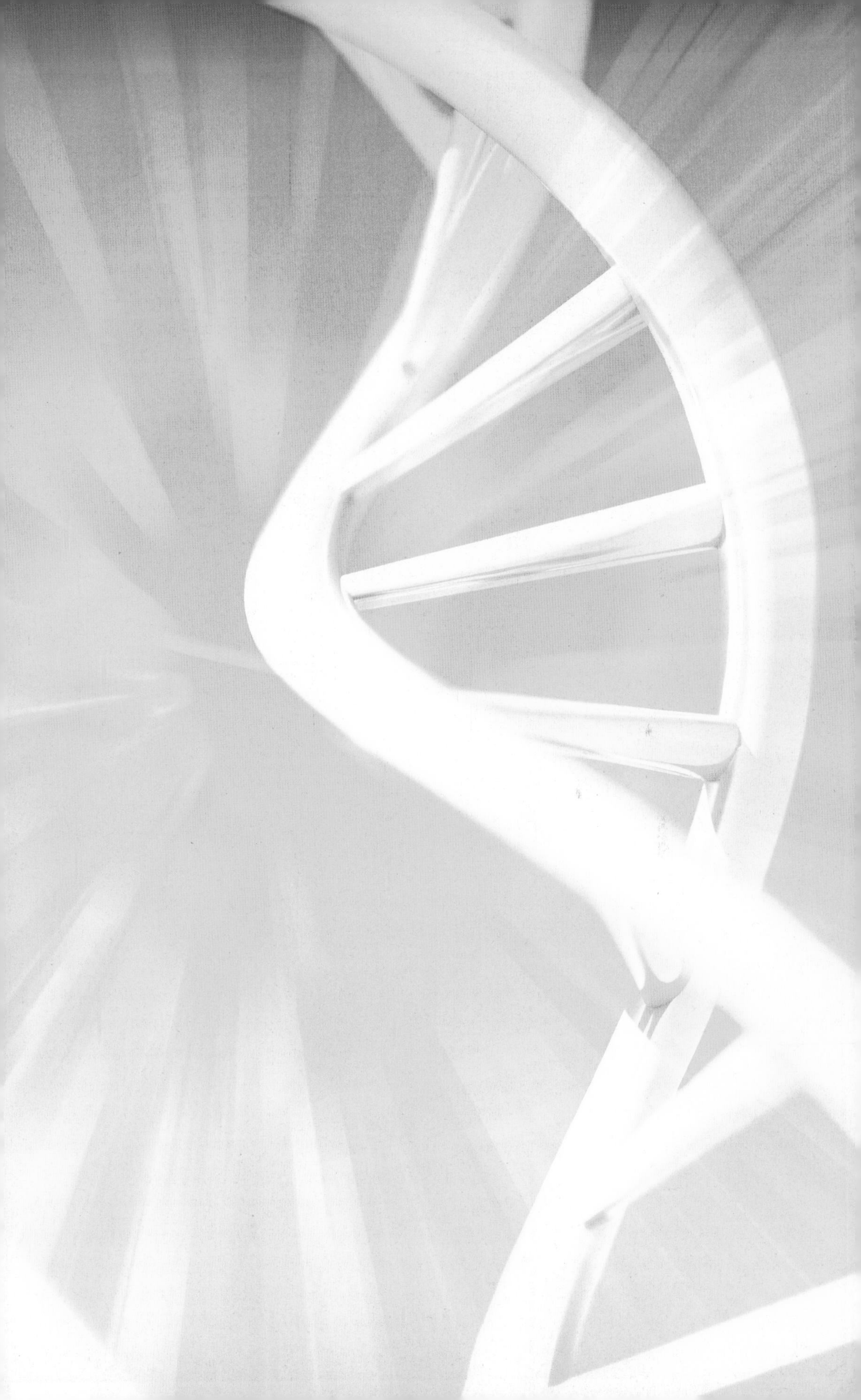

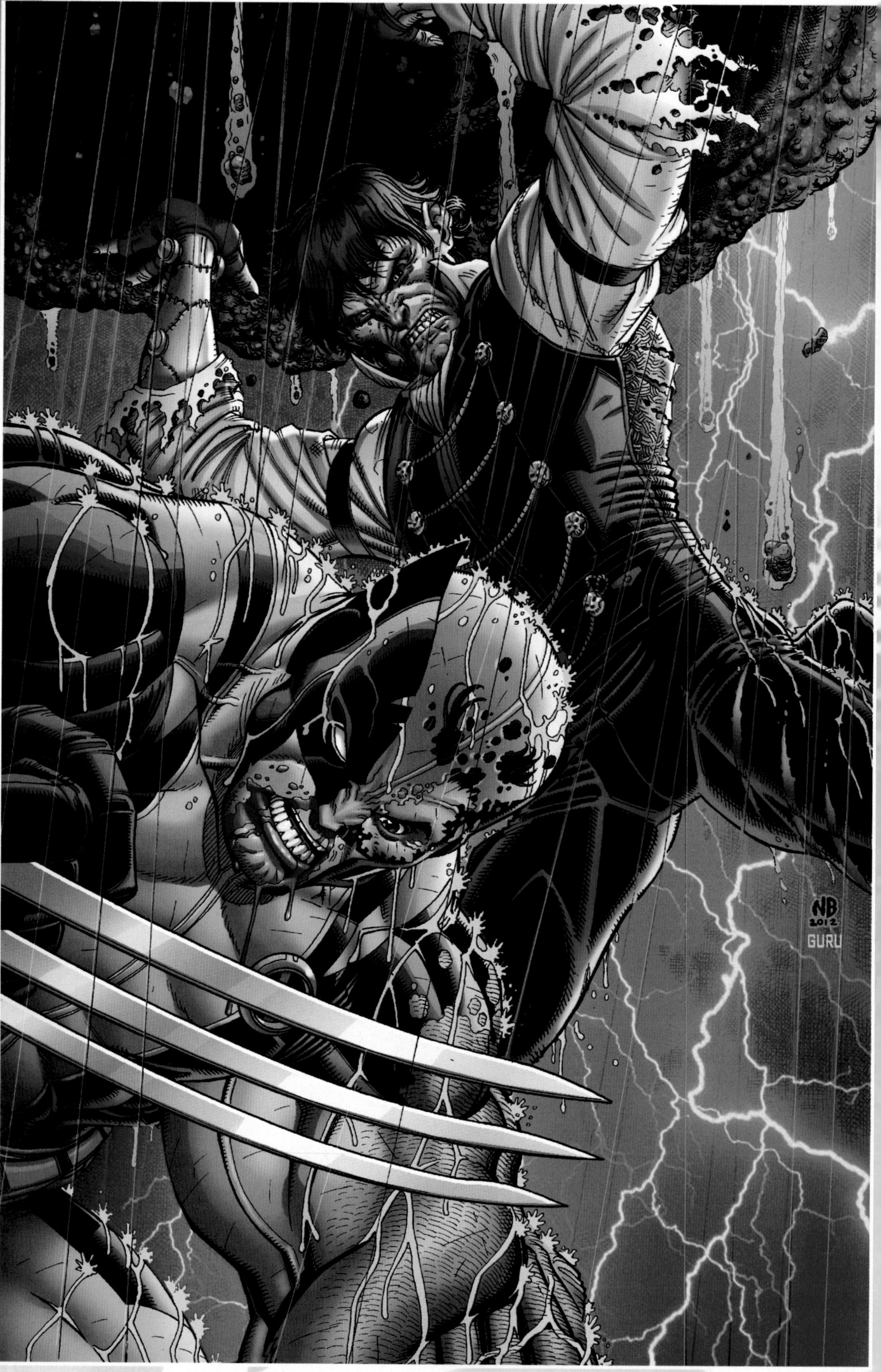
NB
2012
GURU

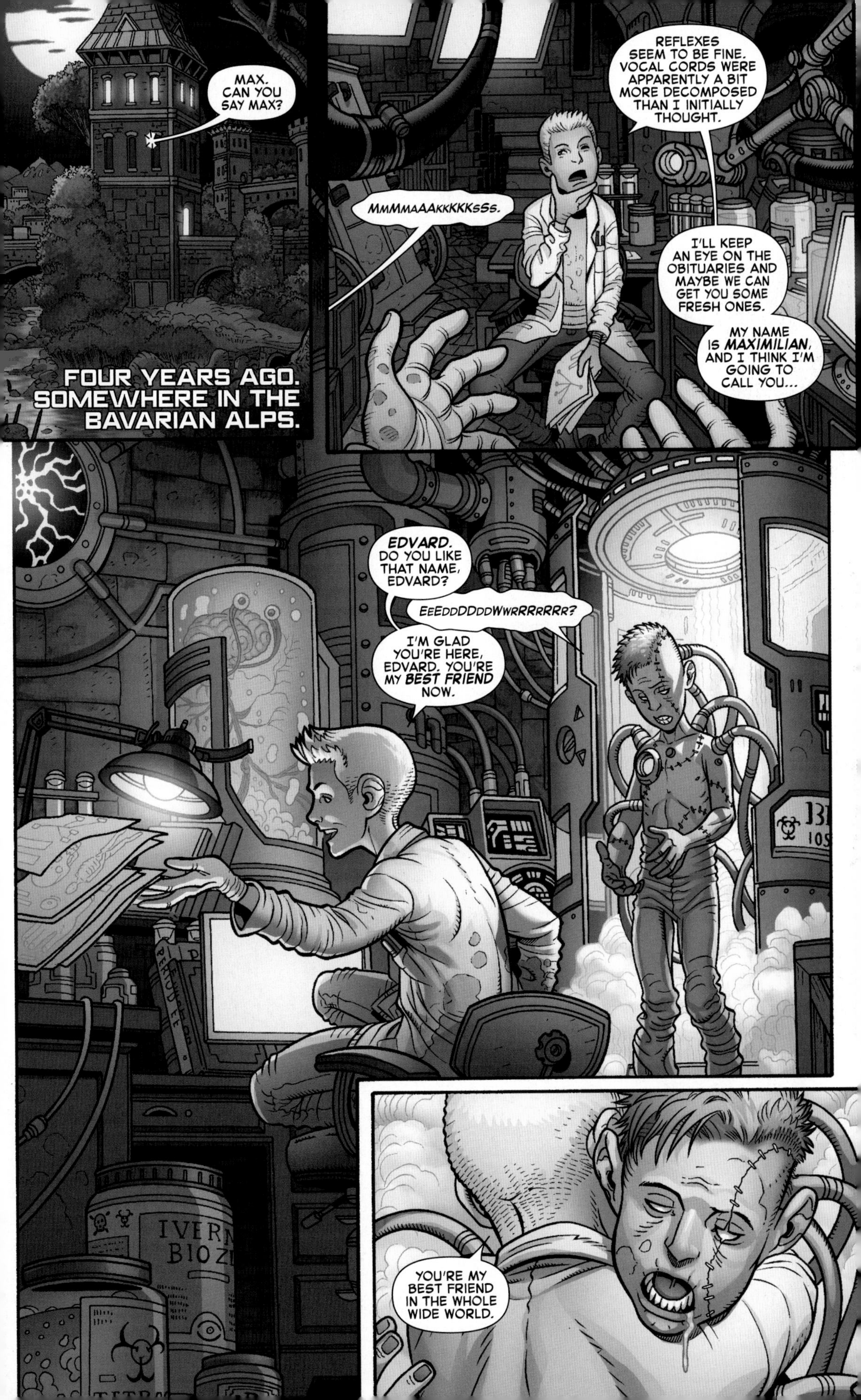
FOUR YEARS AGO. SOMEWHERE IN THE BAVARIAN ALPS.
MAX. CAN YOU SAY MAX?
MMMMAAAKKKKKSSS.
REFLEXES SEEM TO BE FINE. VOCAL CORDS WERE APPARENTLY A BIT MORE DECOMPOSED THAN I INITIALLY THOUGHT.
I'LL KEEP AN EYE ON THE OBITUARIES AND MAYBE WE CAN GET YOU SOME FRESH ONES.
MY NAME IS MAXIMILIAN, AND I THINK I'M GOING TO CALL YOU...
EDVARD. DO YOU LIKE THAT NAME, EDVARD?
EEEDDDDDDWWRRRRRRR?
I'M GLAD YOU'RE HERE, EDVARD. YOU'RE MY BEST FRIEND NOW.
YOU'RE MY BEST FRIEND IN THE WHOLE WIDE WORLD.

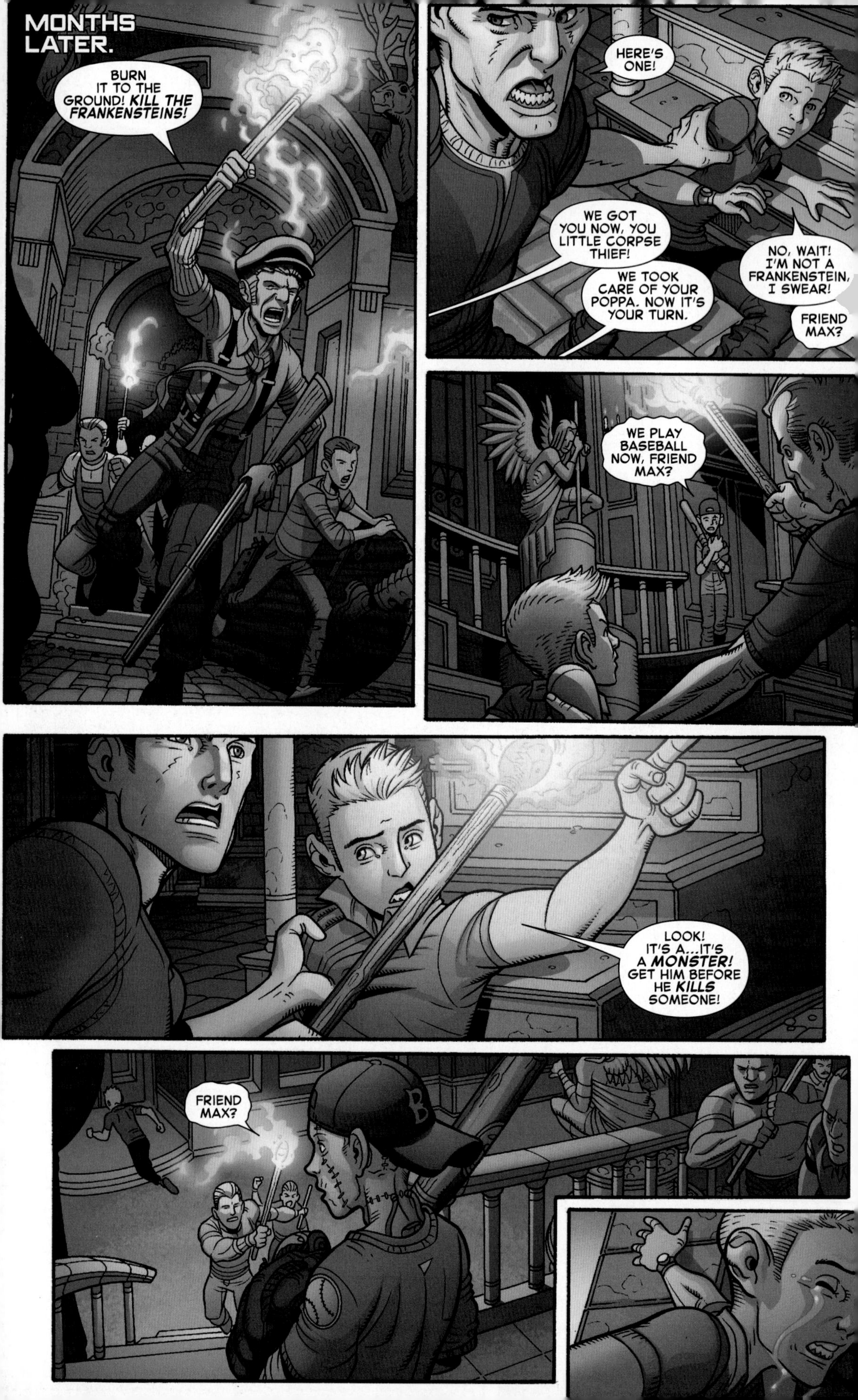
MONTHS LATER.
BURN IT TO THE GROUND! KILL THE FRANKENSTEINS!
HERE'S ONE!
WE GOT YOU NOW, YOU LITTLE CORPSE THIEF!
WE TOOK CARE OF YOUR POPPA. NOW IT'S YOUR TURN.
NO, WAIT! I'M NOT A FRANKENSTEIN, I SWEAR!
FRIEND MAX?
WE PLAY BASEBALL NOW, FRIEND MAX?
LOOK! IT'S A...IT'S A MONSTER! GET HIM BEFORE HE KILLS SOMEONE!
FRIEND MAX?

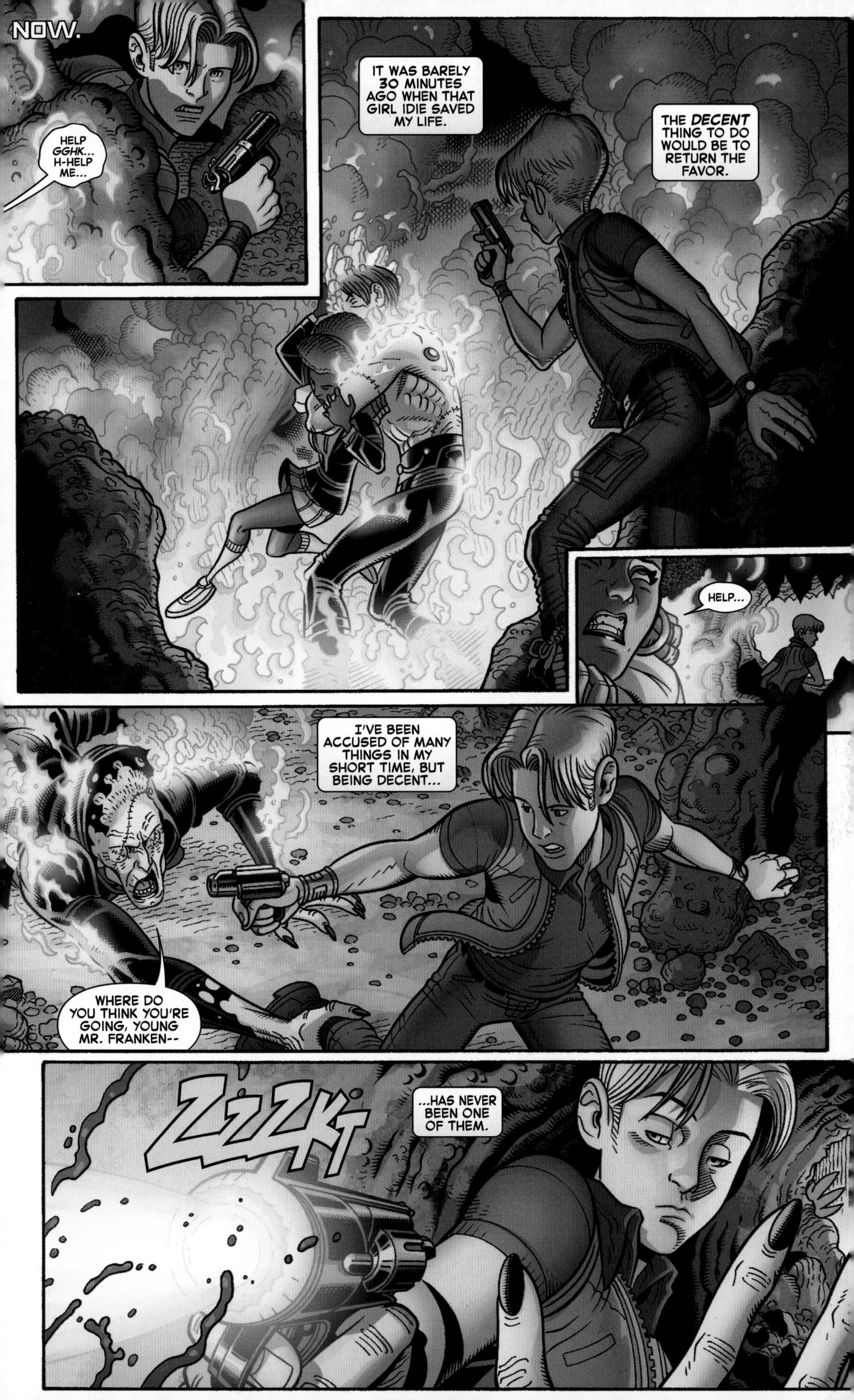
NOW.
HELP GGHK... H-HELP ME...
IT WAS BARELY 30 MINUTES AGO WHEN THAT GIRL IDIE SAVED MY LIFE.
THE *DECENT* THING TO DO WOULD BE TO RETURN THE FAVOR.
HELP...
I'VE BEEN ACCUSED OF MANY THINGS IN MY SHORT TIME, BUT BEING DECENT...
WHERE DO YOU THINK YOU'RE GOING, YOUNG MR. FRANKEN--
ZZZKT
...HAS NEVER BEEN ONE OF THEM.

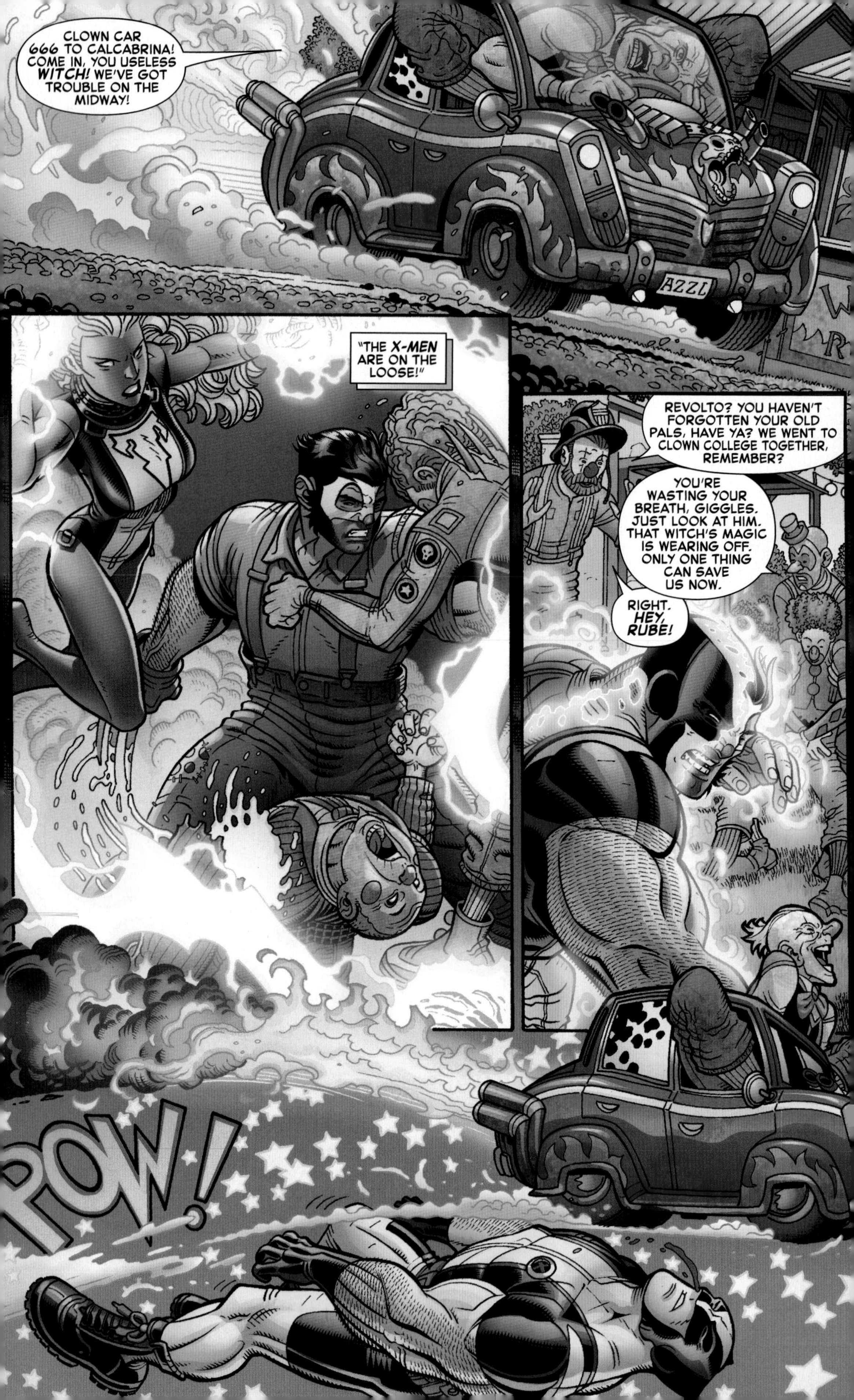
CLOWN CAR 666 TO CALCABRINA! COME IN, YOU USELESS WITCH! WE'VE GOT TROUBLE ON THE MIDWAY!
AZZL
"THE X-MEN ARE ON THE LOOSE!"
REVOLTO? YOU HAVEN'T FORGOTTEN YOUR OLD PALS, HAVE YA? WE WENT TO CLOWN COLLEGE TOGETHER, REMEMBER?
YOU'RE WASTING YOUR BREATH, GIGGLES. JUST LOOK AT HIM. THAT WITCH'S MAGIC IS WEARING OFF. ONLY ONE THING CAN SAVE US NOW.
RIGHT. HEY, RUBE!
POW!

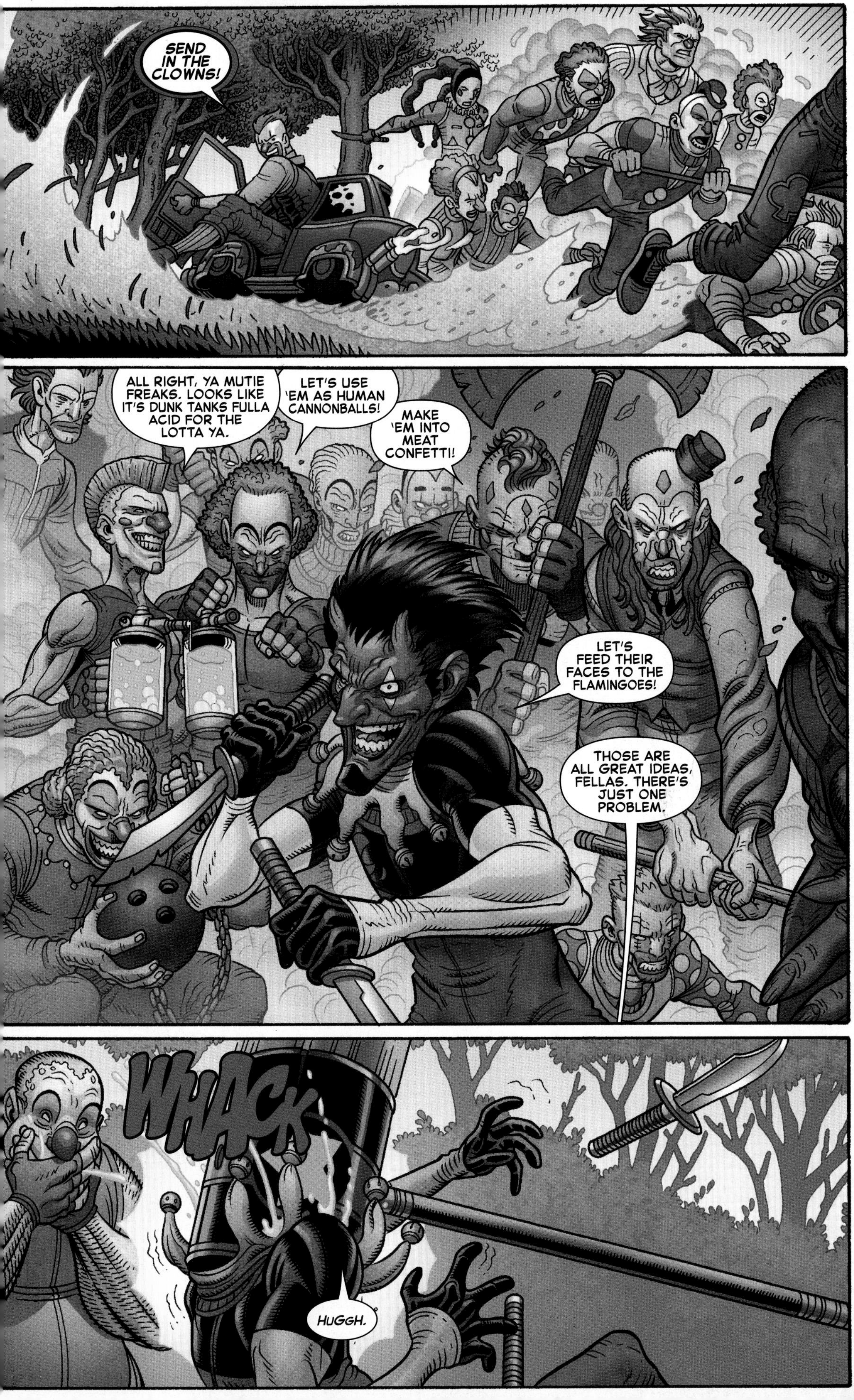
SEND IN THE CLOWNS!
ALL RIGHT, YA MUTIE FREAKS. LOOKS LIKE IT'S DUNK TANKS FULLA ACID FOR THE LOTTA YA.
LET'S USE 'EM AS HUMAN CANNONBALLS!
MAKE 'EM INTO MEAT CONFETTI!
LET'S FEED THEIR FACES TO THE FLAMINGOES!
THOSE ARE ALL GREAT IDEAS, FELLAS. THERE'S JUST ONE PROBLEM.
WHACK
HUGGH.

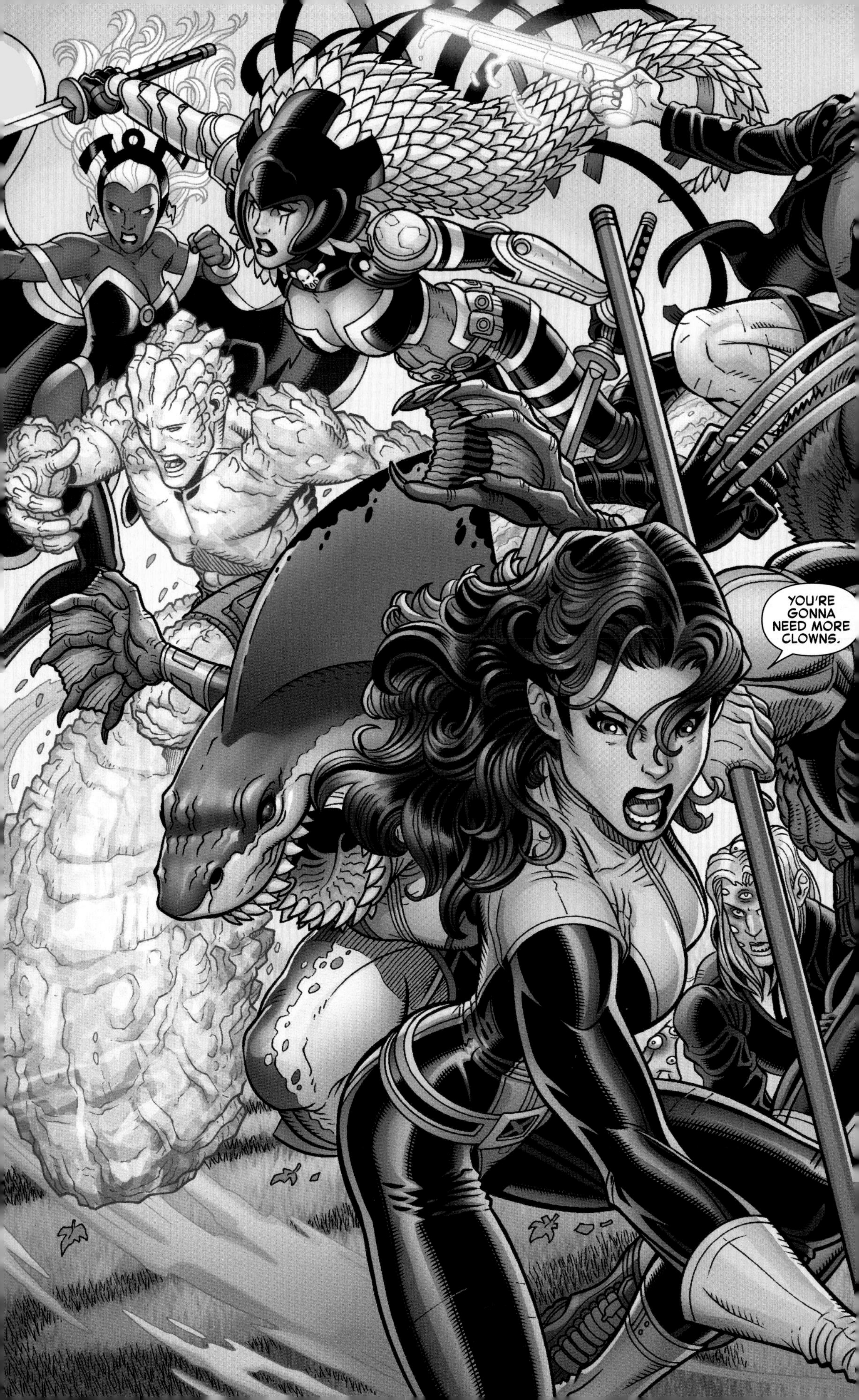
YOU'RE
GONNA
NEED MORE
CLOWNS.

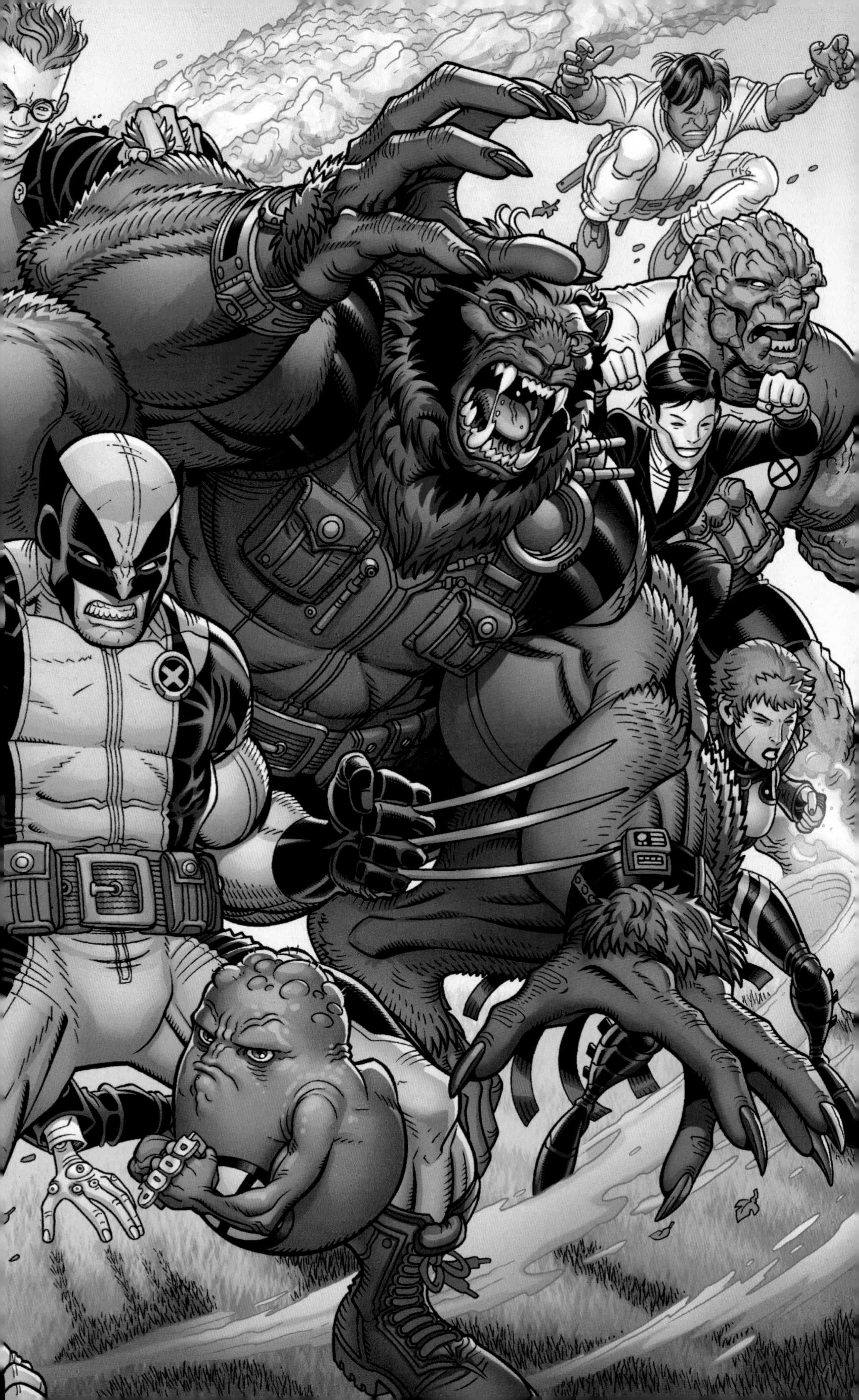

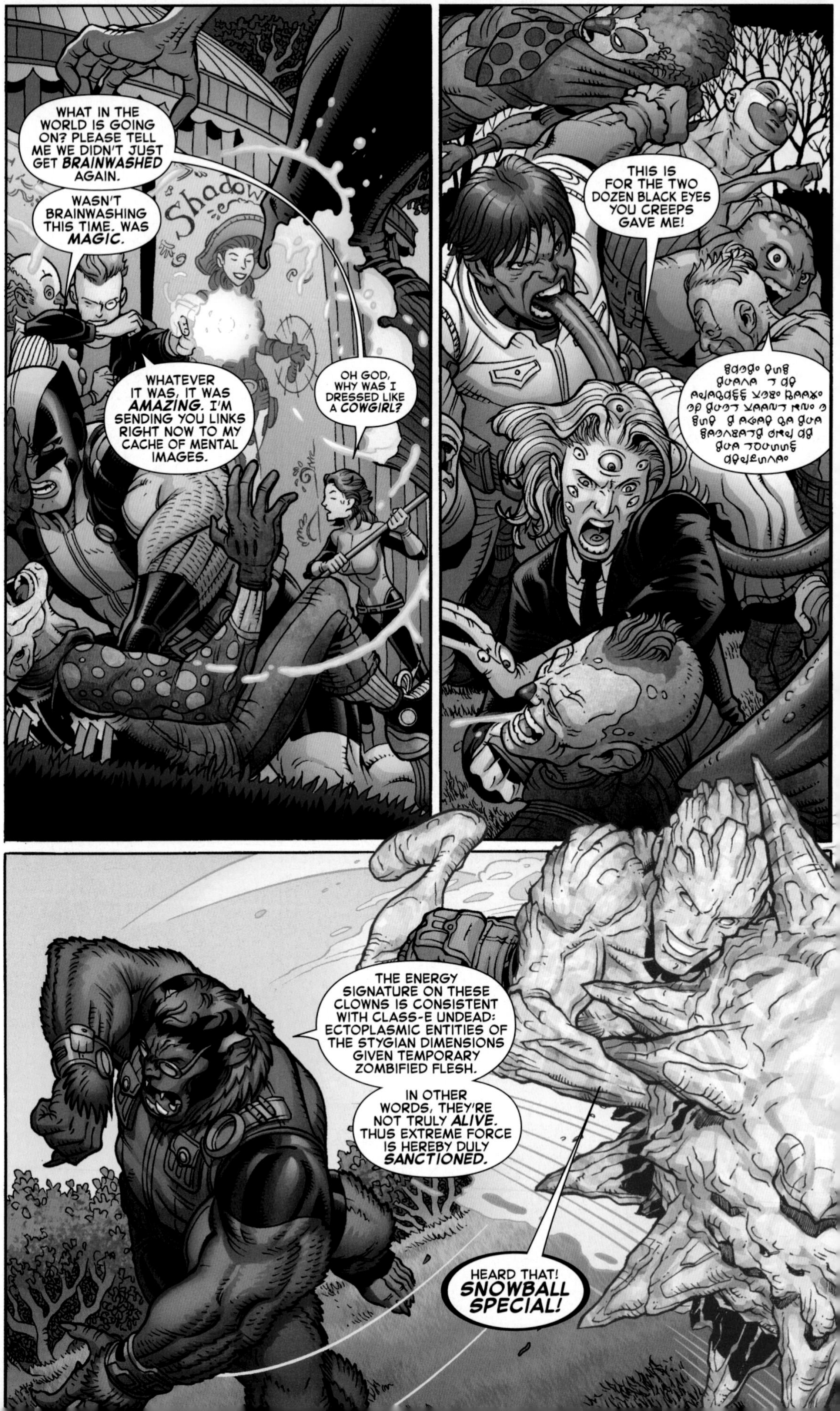
WHAT IN THE WORLD IS GOING ON? PLEASE TELL ME WE DIDN'T JUST GET BRAINWASHED AGAIN.
WASN'T BRAINWASHING THIS TIME. WAS MAGIC.
Shadow
WHATEVER IT WAS, IT WAS AMAZING. I'M SENDING YOU LINKS RIGHT NOW TO MY CACHE OF MENTAL IMAGES.
OH GOD, WHY WAS I DRESSED LIKE A COWGIRL?
THIS IS FOR THE TWO DOZEN BLACK EYES YOU CREEPS GAVE ME!
THE ENERGY SIGNATURE ON THESE CLOWNS IS CONSISTENT WITH CLASS-E UNDEAD: ECTOPLASMIC ENTITIES OF THE STYGIAN DIMENSIONS GIVEN TEMPORARY ZOMBIFIED FLESH.
IN OTHER WORDS, THEY'RE NOT TRULY ALIVE. THUS EXTREME FORCE IS HEREBY DULY SANCTIONED.
HEARD THAT! SNOWBALL SPECIAL!

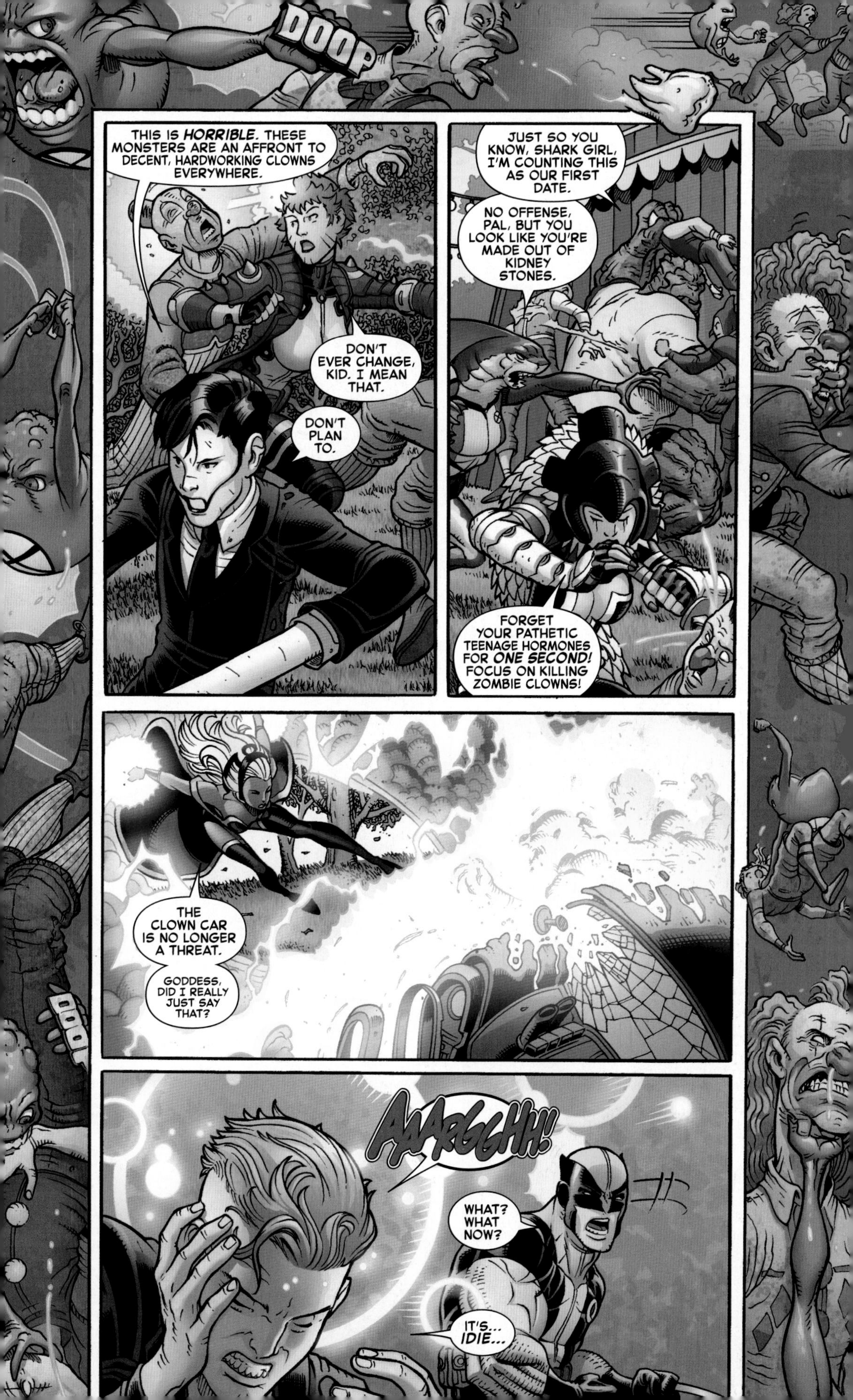
DOOP
THIS IS HORRIBLE. THESE MONSTERS ARE AN AFFRONT TO DECENT, HARDWORKING CLOWNS EVERYWHERE.
DON'T EVER CHANGE, KID. I MEAN THAT.
DON'T PLAN TO.
JUST SO YOU KNOW, SHARK GIRL, I'M COUNTING THIS AS OUR FIRST DATE.
NO OFFENSE, PAL, BUT YOU LOOK LIKE YOU'RE MADE OUT OF KIDNEY STONES.
FORGET YOUR PATHETIC TEENAGE HORMONES FOR ONE SECOND! FOCUS ON KILLING ZOMBIE CLOWNS!
THE CLOWN CAR IS NO LONGER A THREAT.
GODDESS, DID I REALLY JUST SAY THAT?
AAARGGHH!
WHAT? WHAT NOW?
IT'S... IDIE...

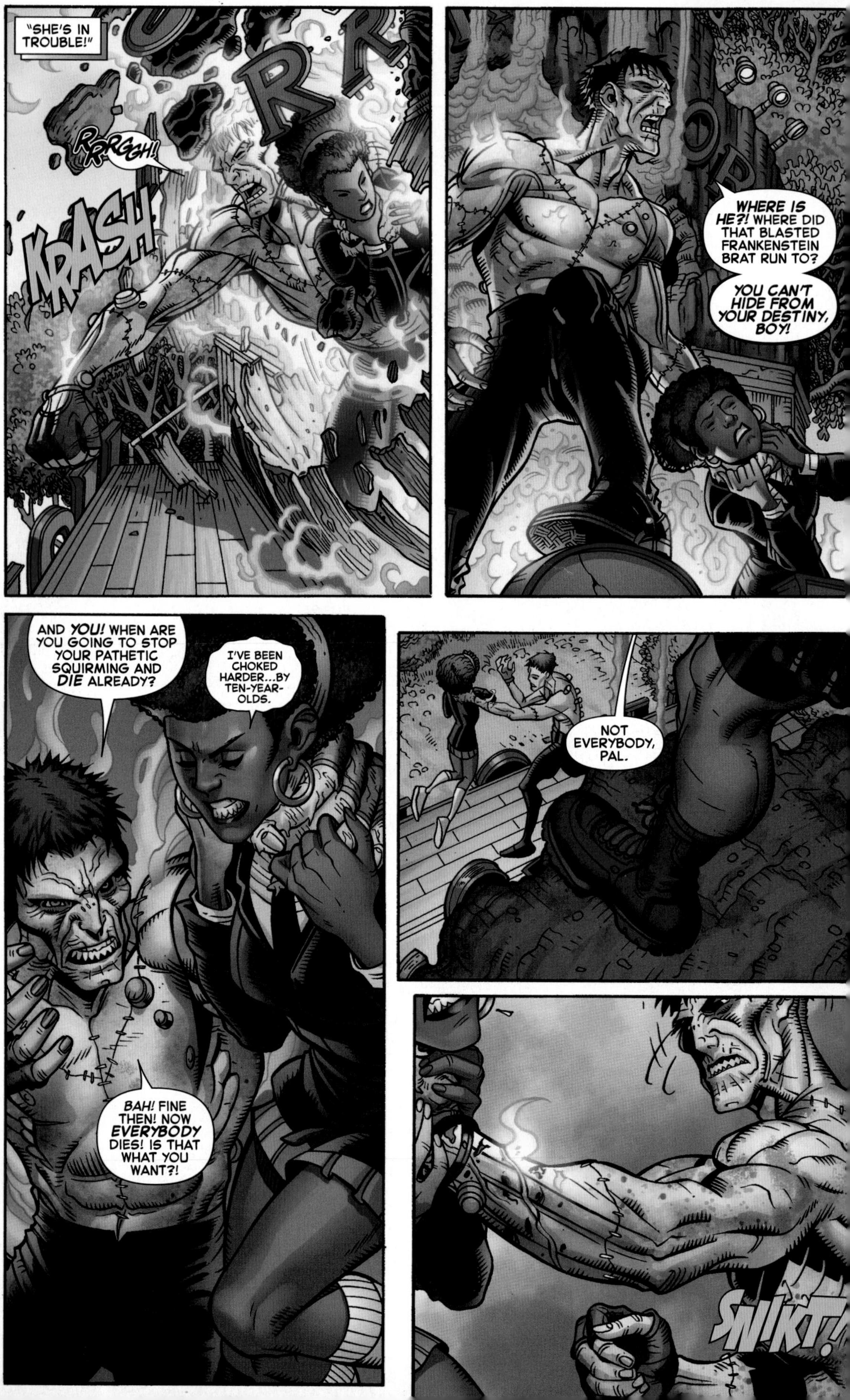
"SHE'S IN TROUBLE!"
RRRRGGH!
KRASH
WHERE IS HE?! WHERE DID THAT BLASTED FRANKENSTEIN BRAT RUN TO?
YOU CAN'T HIDE FROM YOUR DESTINY, BOY!
AND YOU! WHEN ARE YOU GOING TO STOP YOUR PATHETIC SQUIRMING AND DIE ALREADY?
I'VE BEEN CHOKED HARDER...BY TEN-YEAR-OLDS.
BAH! FINE THEN! NOW EVERYBODY DIES! IS THAT WHAT YOU WANT?!
NOT EVERYBODY, PAL.
SNIKT!

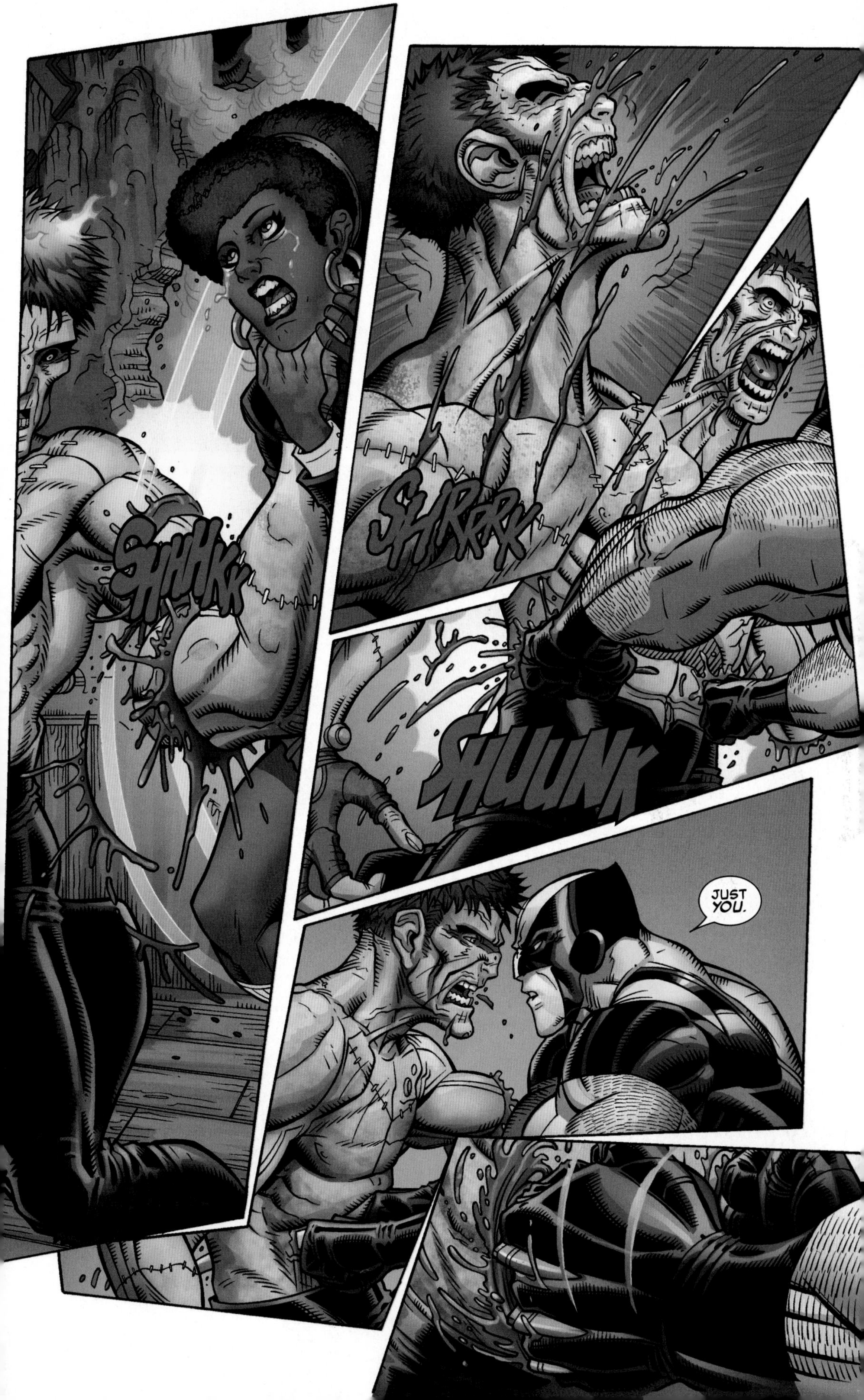
SHHKK
SHRRRK
SHUUNK
JUST YOU.

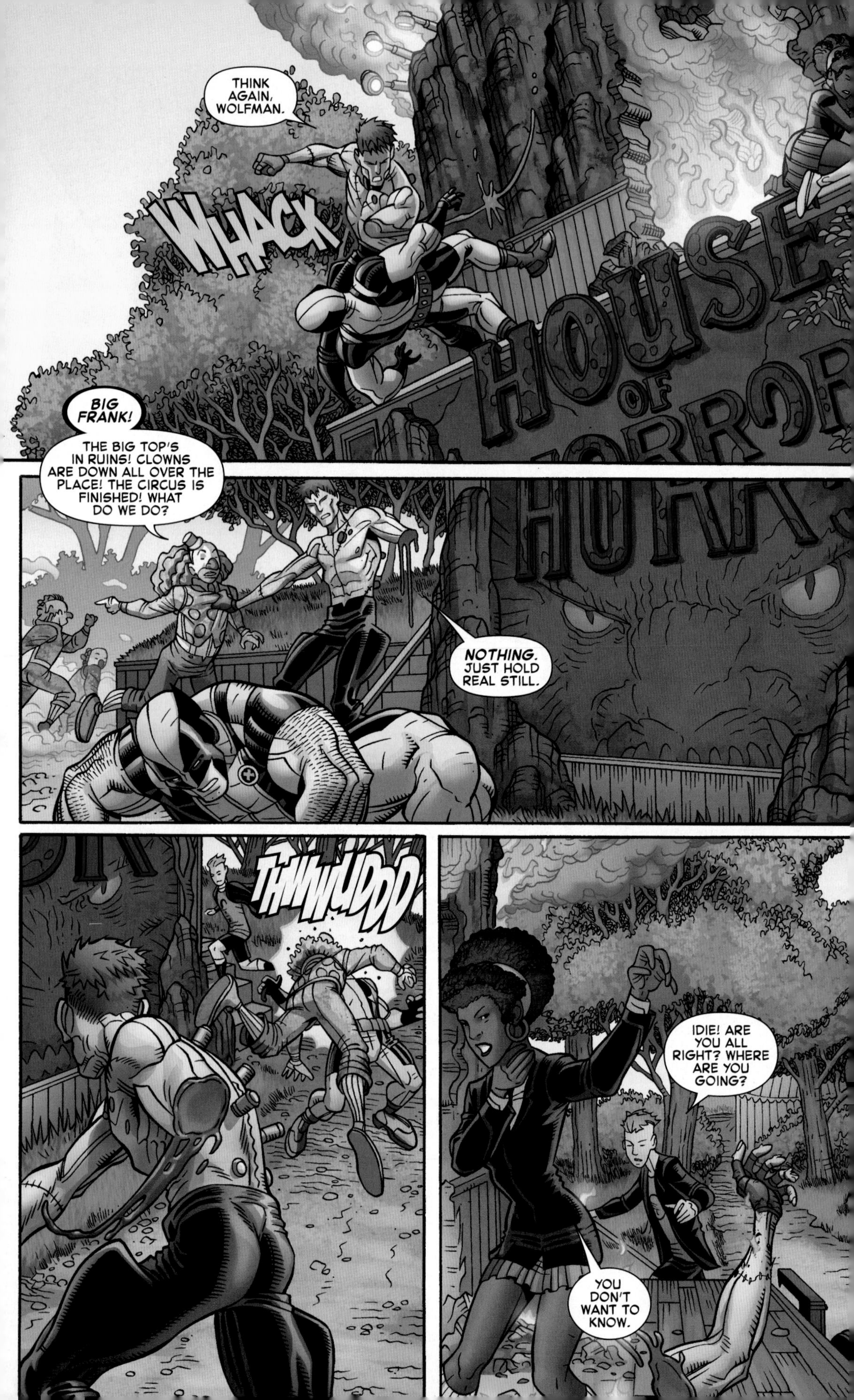
THINK AGAIN, WOLFMAN.
WHACK
HOUSE OF HORRORS
BIG FRANK!
THE BIG TOP'S IN RUINS! CLOWNS ARE DOWN ALL OVER THE PLACE! THE CIRCUS IS FINISHED! WHAT DO WE DO?
NOTHING. JUST HOLD REAL STILL.
THWWUDDD
IDIE! ARE YOU ALL RIGHT? WHERE ARE YOU GOING?
YOU DON'T WANT TO KNOW.

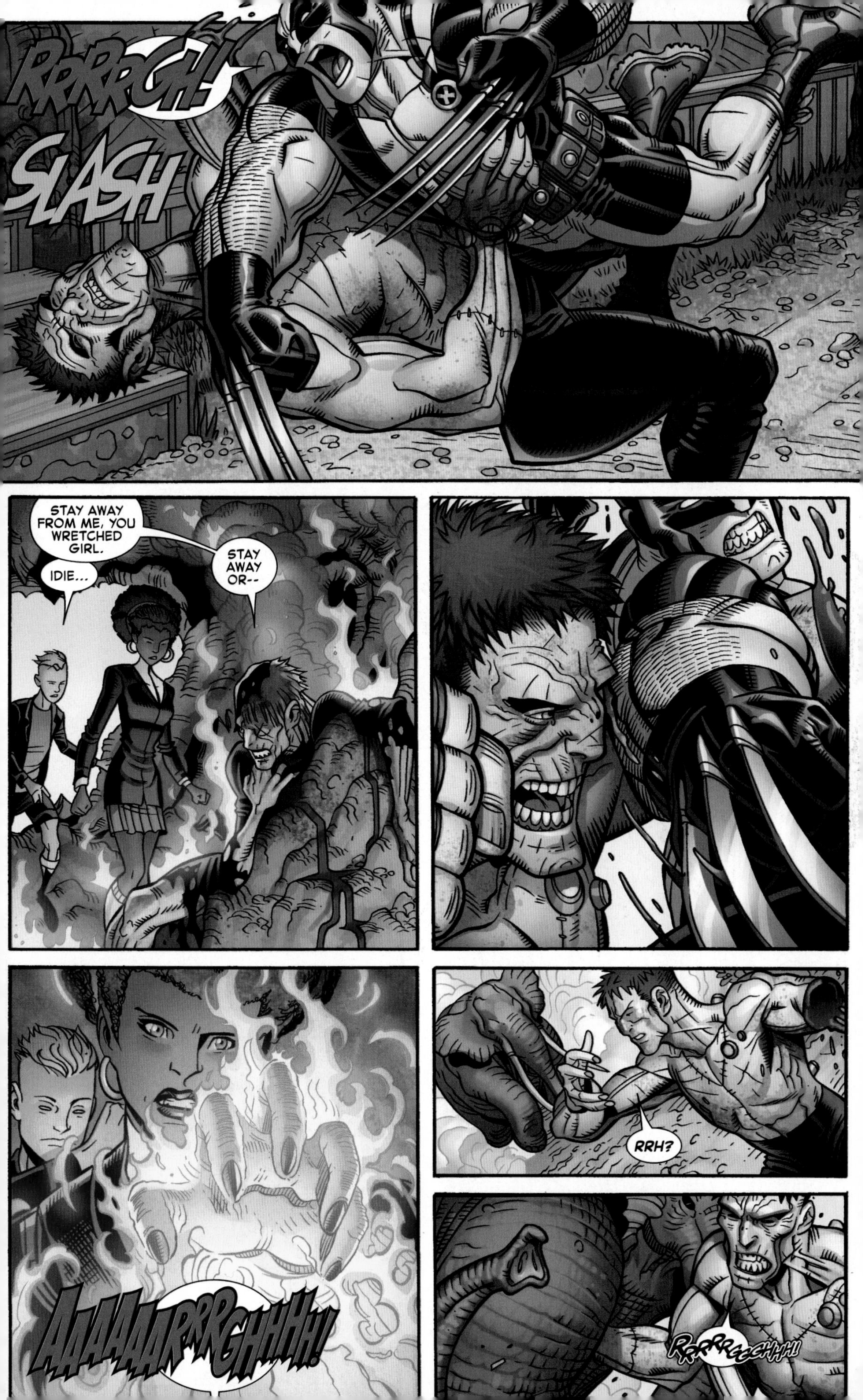
RRRRGH!
SLASH
STAY AWAY FROM ME, YOU WRETCHED GIRL.
IDIE...
STAY AWAY OR--
RRH?
AAAAAARRRGHHHH!
RRRRREECHHH!

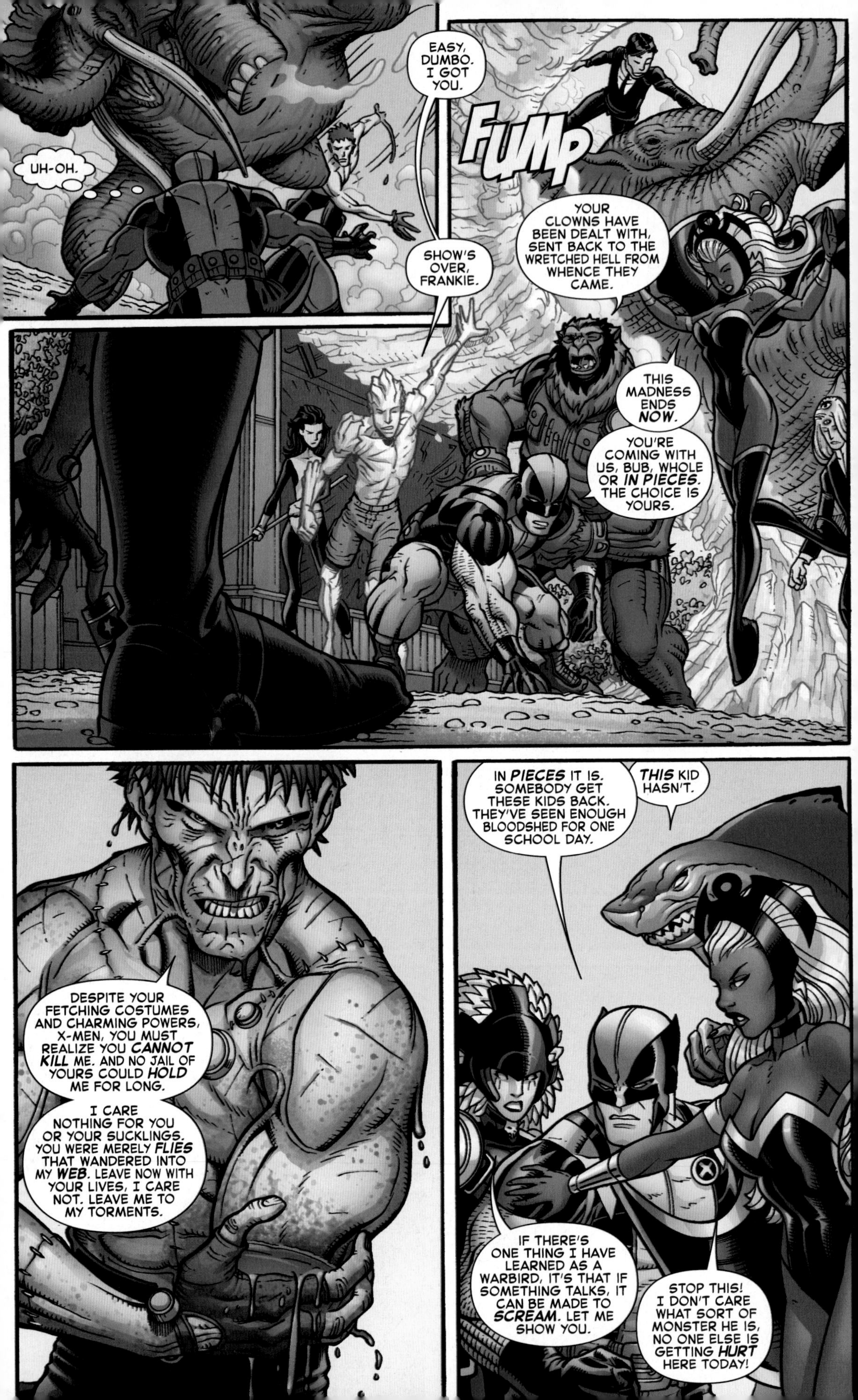
EASY, DUMBO. I GOT YOU.
UH-OH.
FUMP
SHOW'S OVER, FRANKIE.
YOUR CLOWNS HAVE BEEN DEALT WITH, SENT BACK TO THE WRETCHED HELL FROM WHENCE THEY CAME.
THIS MADNESS ENDS NOW.
YOU'RE COMING WITH US, BUB, WHOLE OR IN PIECES. THE CHOICE IS YOURS.
DESPITE YOUR FETCHING COSTUMES AND CHARMING POWERS, X-MEN, YOU MUST REALIZE YOU CANNOT KILL ME. AND NO JAIL OF YOURS COULD HOLD ME FOR LONG.
I CARE NOTHING FOR YOU OR YOUR SUCKLINGS. YOU WERE MERELY FLIES THAT WANDERED INTO MY WEB. LEAVE NOW WITH YOUR LIVES, I CARE NOT. LEAVE ME TO MY TORMENTS.
IN PIECES IT IS. SOMEBODY GET THESE KIDS BACK. THEY'VE SEEN ENOUGH BLOODSHED FOR ONE SCHOOL DAY.
THIS KID HASN'T.
IF THERE'S ONE THING I HAVE LEARNED AS A WARBIRD, IT'S THAT IF SOMETHING TALKS, IT CAN BE MADE TO SCREAM. LET ME SHOW YOU.
STOP THIS! I DON'T CARE WHAT SORT OF MONSTER HE IS, NO ONE ELSE IS GETTING HURT HERE TODAY!

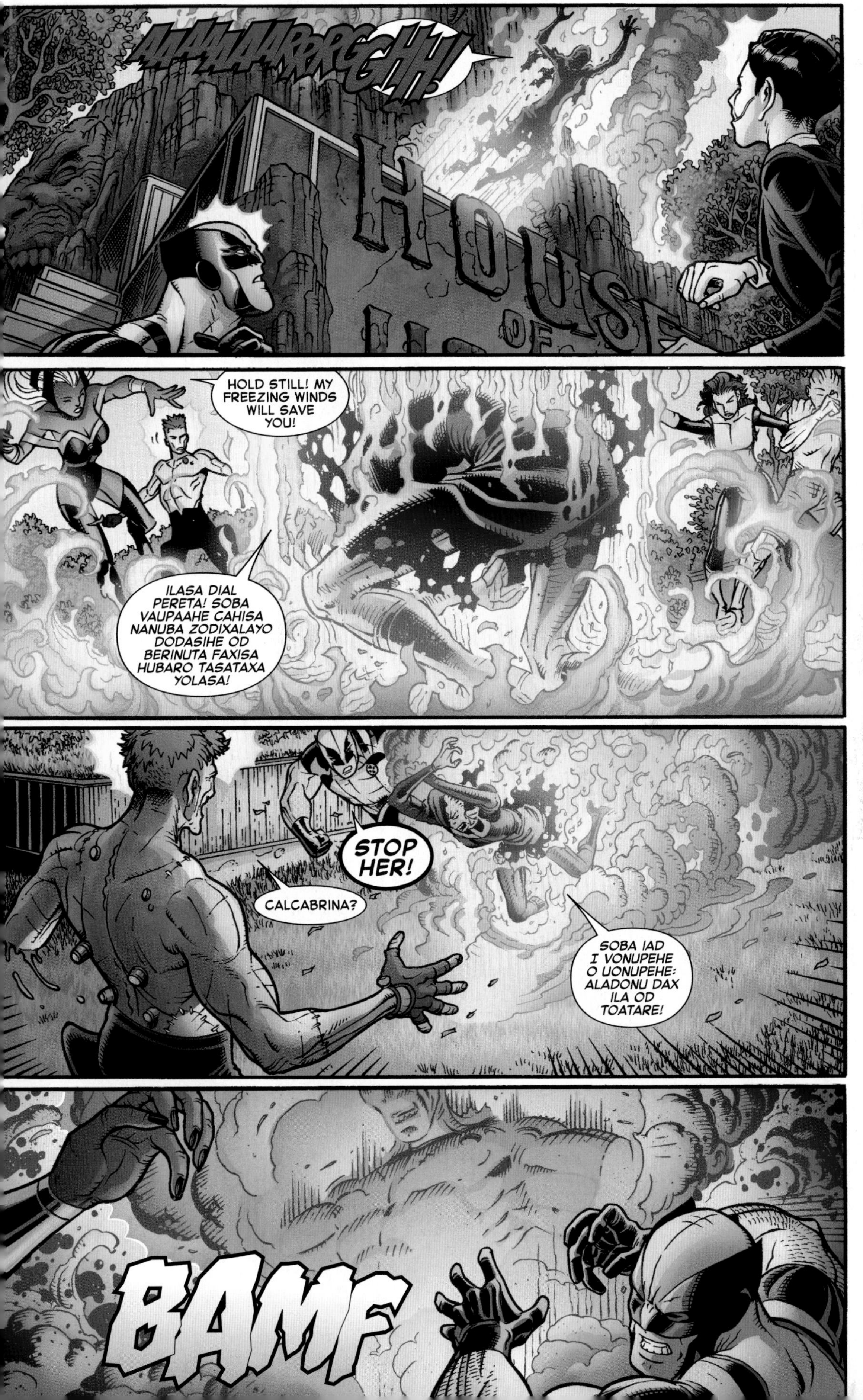
AAAAAAARRRGGHH!
HOLD STILL! MY FREEZING WINDS WILL SAVE YOU!
ILASA DIAL PERETA! SOBA VAUPAAHE CAHISA NANUBA ZODIXALAYO DODASIHE OD BERINUTA FAXISA HUBARO TASATAXA YOLASA!
STOP HER!
CALCABRINA?
SOBA IAD I VONUPEHE O UONUPEHE: ALADONU DAX ILA OD TOATARE!
BAMF

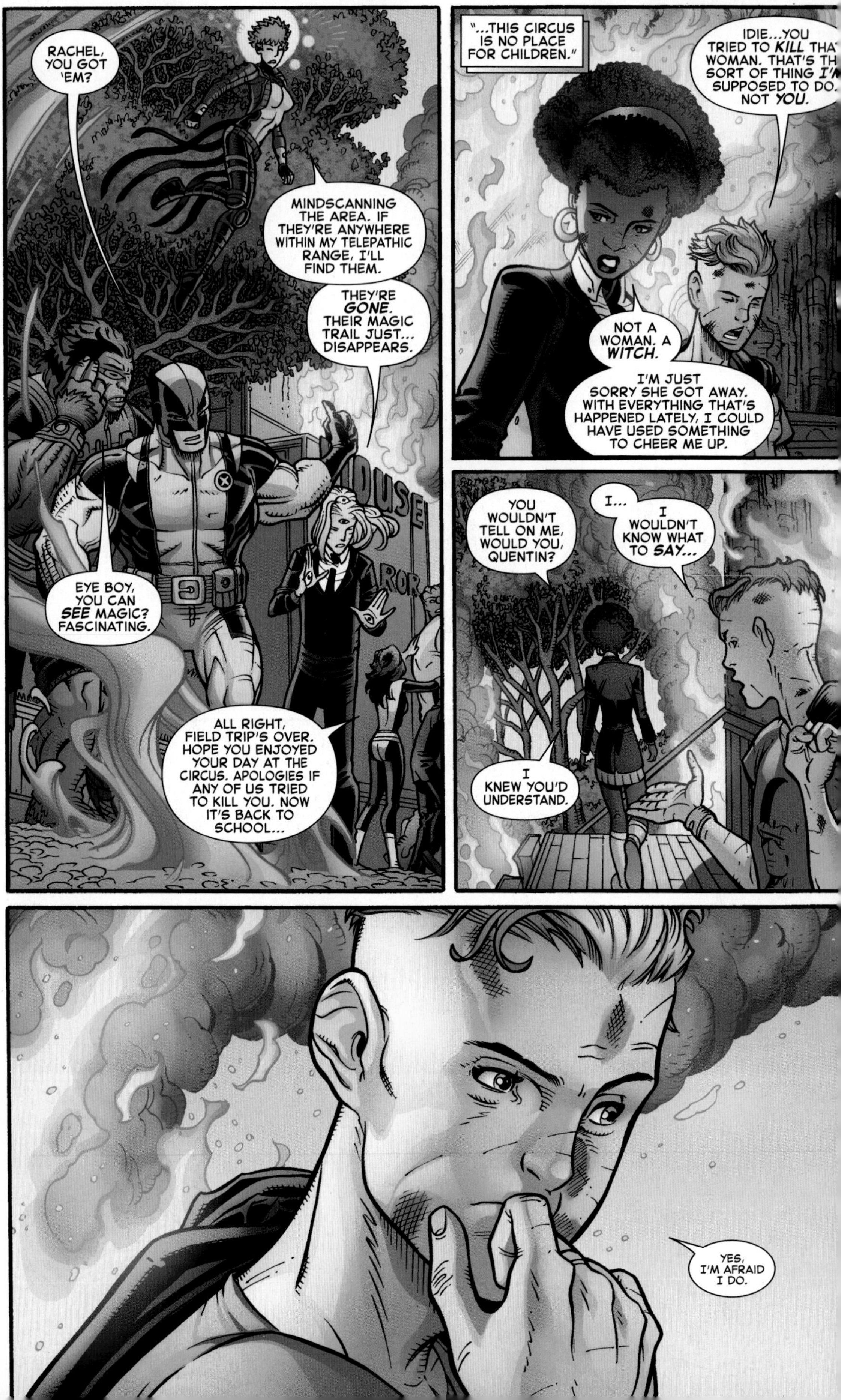
RACHEL, YOU GOT 'EM?
MINDSCANNING THE AREA. IF THEY'RE ANYWHERE WITHIN MY TELEPATHIC RANGE, I'LL FIND THEM.
THEY'RE GONE. THEIR MAGIC TRAIL JUST... DISAPPEARS.
EYE BOY, YOU CAN SEE MAGIC? FASCINATING.
ALL RIGHT, FIELD TRIP'S OVER. HOPE YOU ENJOYED YOUR DAY AT THE CIRCUS. APOLOGIES IF ANY OF US TRIED TO KILL YOU. NOW IT'S BACK TO SCHOOL...
"...THIS CIRCUS IS NO PLACE FOR CHILDREN."
IDIE...YOU TRIED TO KILL THAT WOMAN. THAT'S THE SORT OF THING I'M SUPPOSED TO DO. NOT YOU.
NOT A WOMAN. A WITCH.
I'M JUST SORRY SHE GOT AWAY. WITH EVERYTHING THAT'S HAPPENED LATELY, I COULD HAVE USED SOMETHING TO CHEER ME UP.
YOU WOULDN'T TELL ON ME, WOULD YOU, QUENTIN?
I... I WOULDN'T KNOW WHAT TO SAY...
I KNEW YOU'D UNDERSTAND.
YES, I'M AFRAID I DO.

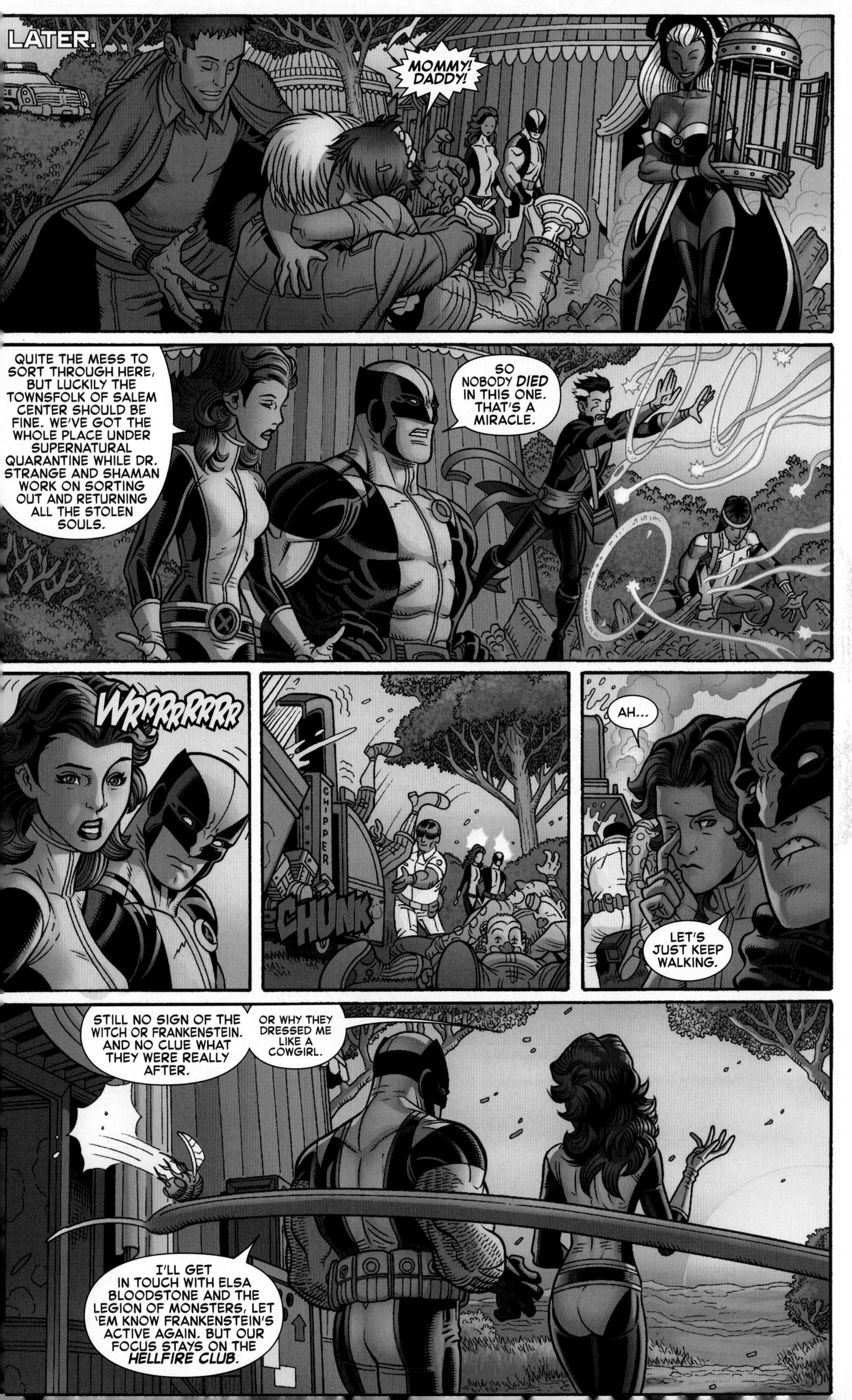
LATER.
MOMMY! DADDY!
QUITE THE MESS TO SORT THROUGH HERE, BUT LUCKILY THE TOWNSFOLK OF SALEM CENTER SHOULD BE FINE. WE'VE GOT THE WHOLE PLACE UNDER SUPERNATURAL QUARANTINE WHILE DR. STRANGE AND SHAMAN WORK ON SORTING OUT AND RETURNING ALL THE STOLEN SOULS.
SO NOBODY DIED IN THIS ONE. THAT'S A MIRACLE.
WRRRRRRRR
CHIPPER
CHUNK
AH...
LET'S JUST KEEP WALKING.
STILL NO SIGN OF THE WITCH OR FRANKENSTEIN. AND NO CLUE WHAT THEY WERE REALLY AFTER.
OR WHY THEY DRESSED ME LIKE A COWGIRL.
I'LL GET IN TOUCH WITH ELSA BLOODSTONE AND THE LEGION OF MONSTERS, LET 'EM KNOW FRANKENSTEIN'S ACTIVE AGAIN. BUT OUR FOCUS STAYS ON THE HELLFIRE CLUB.

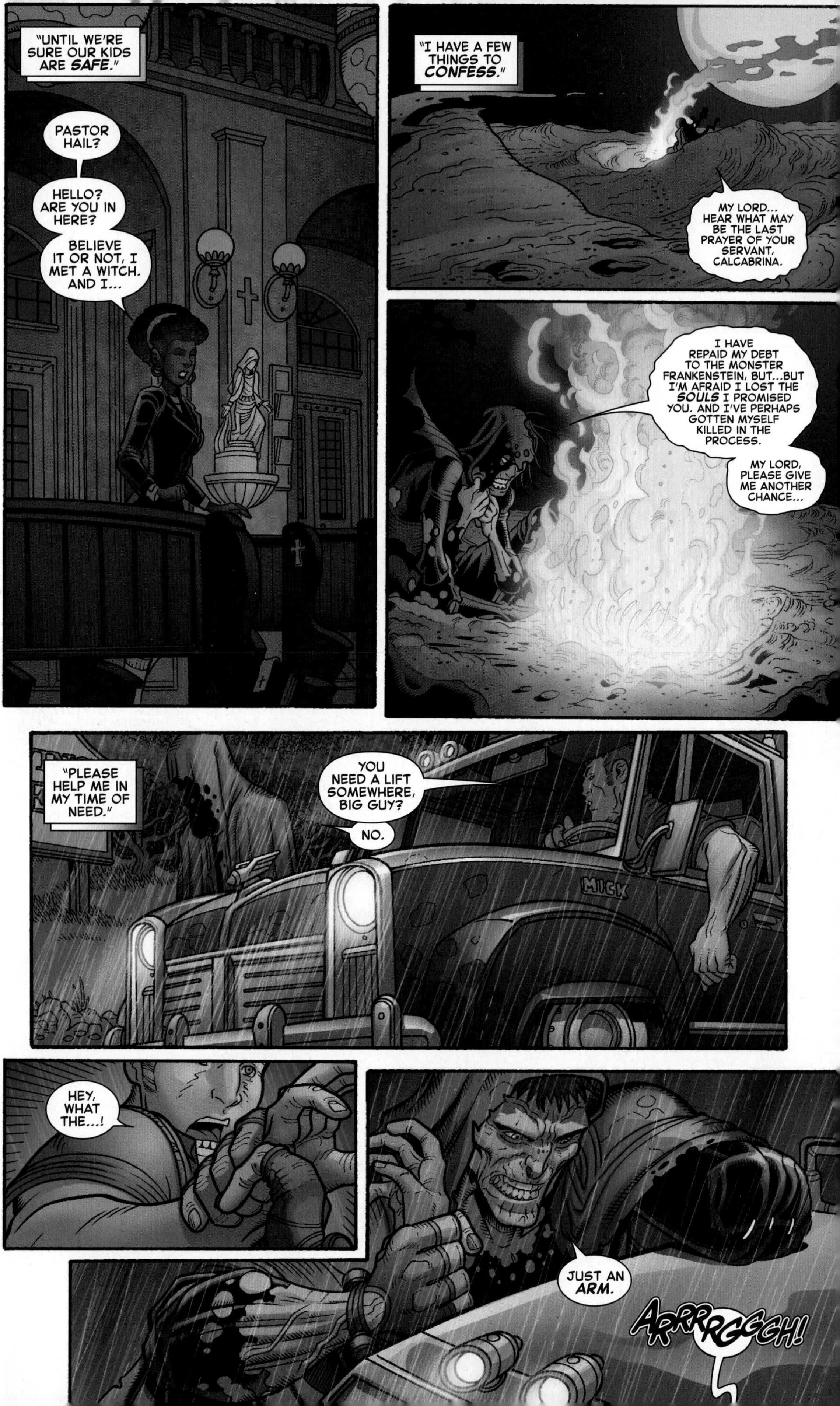
"UNTIL WE'RE SURE OUR KIDS ARE SAFE."
PASTOR HAIL?
HELLO? ARE YOU IN HERE?
BELIEVE IT OR NOT, I MET A WITCH. AND I...
"I HAVE A FEW THINGS TO CONFESS."
MY LORD... HEAR WHAT MAY BE THE LAST PRAYER OF YOUR SERVANT, CALCABRINA.
I HAVE REPAID MY DEBT TO THE MONSTER FRANKENSTEIN, BUT...BUT I'M AFRAID I LOST THE SOULS I PROMISED YOU. AND I'VE PERHAPS GOTTEN MYSELF KILLED IN THE PROCESS.
MY LORD, PLEASE GIVE ME ANOTHER CHANCE...
"PLEASE HELP ME IN MY TIME OF NEED."
YOU NEED A LIFT SOMEWHERE, BIG GUY?
NO.
MICK
HEY, WHAT THE...!
JUST AN ARM.
ARRRRGGGH!

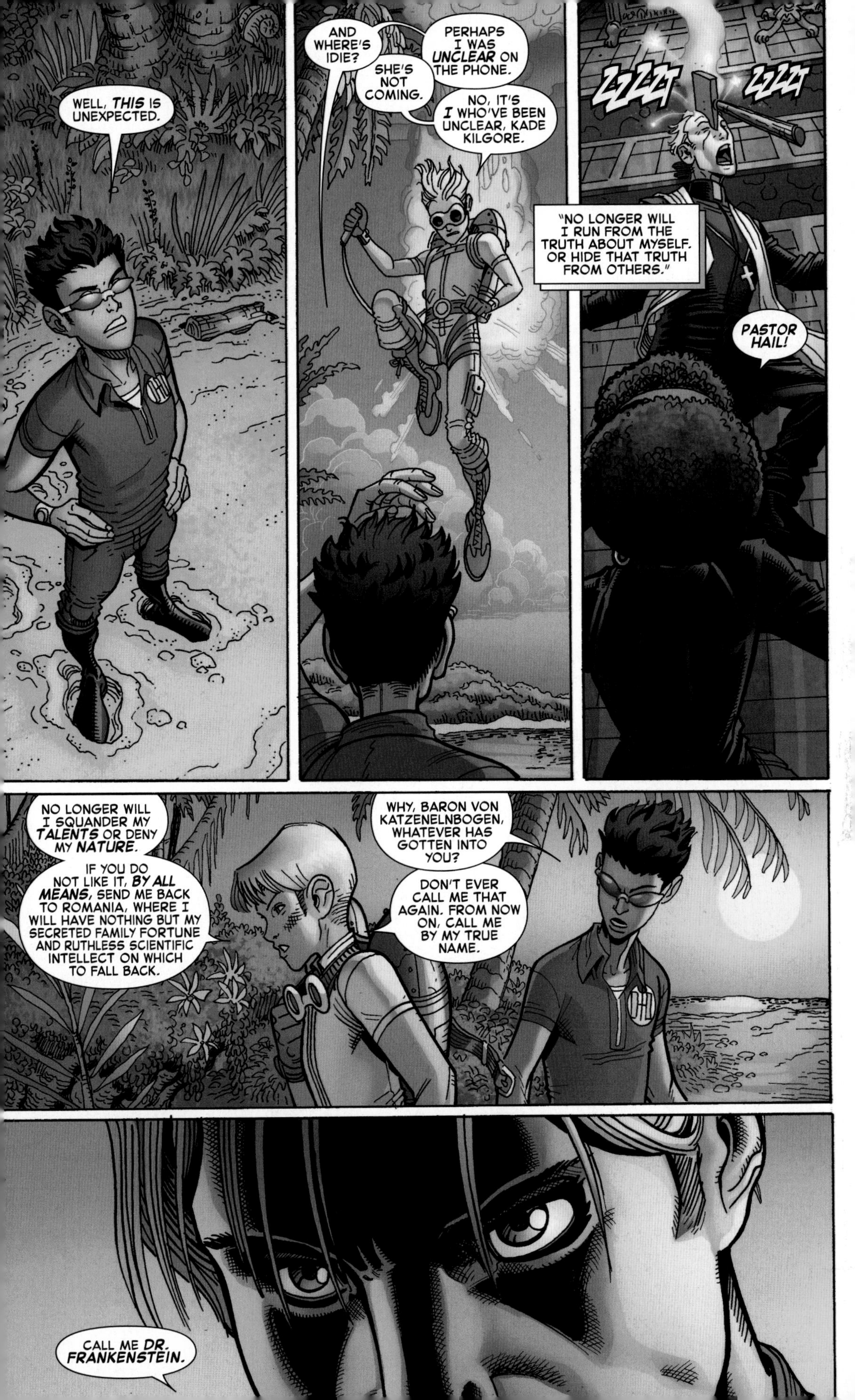
WELL, *THIS* IS UNEXPECTED.
AND WHERE'S IDIE?
PERHAPS I WAS *UNCLEAR* ON THE PHONE.
SHE'S NOT COMING.
NO, IT'S *I* WHO'VE BEEN UNCLEAR, KADE KILGORE.
ZZZZT
ZZZZT
"NO LONGER WILL I RUN FROM THE TRUTH ABOUT MYSELF. OR HIDE THAT TRUTH FROM OTHERS."
PASTOR HAIL!
NO LONGER WILL I SQUANDER MY *TALENTS* OR DENY MY *NATURE*.
IF YOU DO NOT LIKE IT, *BY ALL MEANS,* SEND ME BACK TO ROMANIA, WHERE I WILL HAVE NOTHING BUT MY SECRETED FAMILY FORTUNE AND RUTHLESS SCIENTIFIC INTELLECT ON WHICH TO FALL BACK.
WHY, BARON VON KATZENELNBOGEN, WHATEVER HAS GOTTEN INTO YOU?
DON'T EVER CALL ME THAT AGAIN. FROM NOW ON, CALL ME BY MY TRUE NAME.
CALL ME *DR. FRANKENSTEIN.*

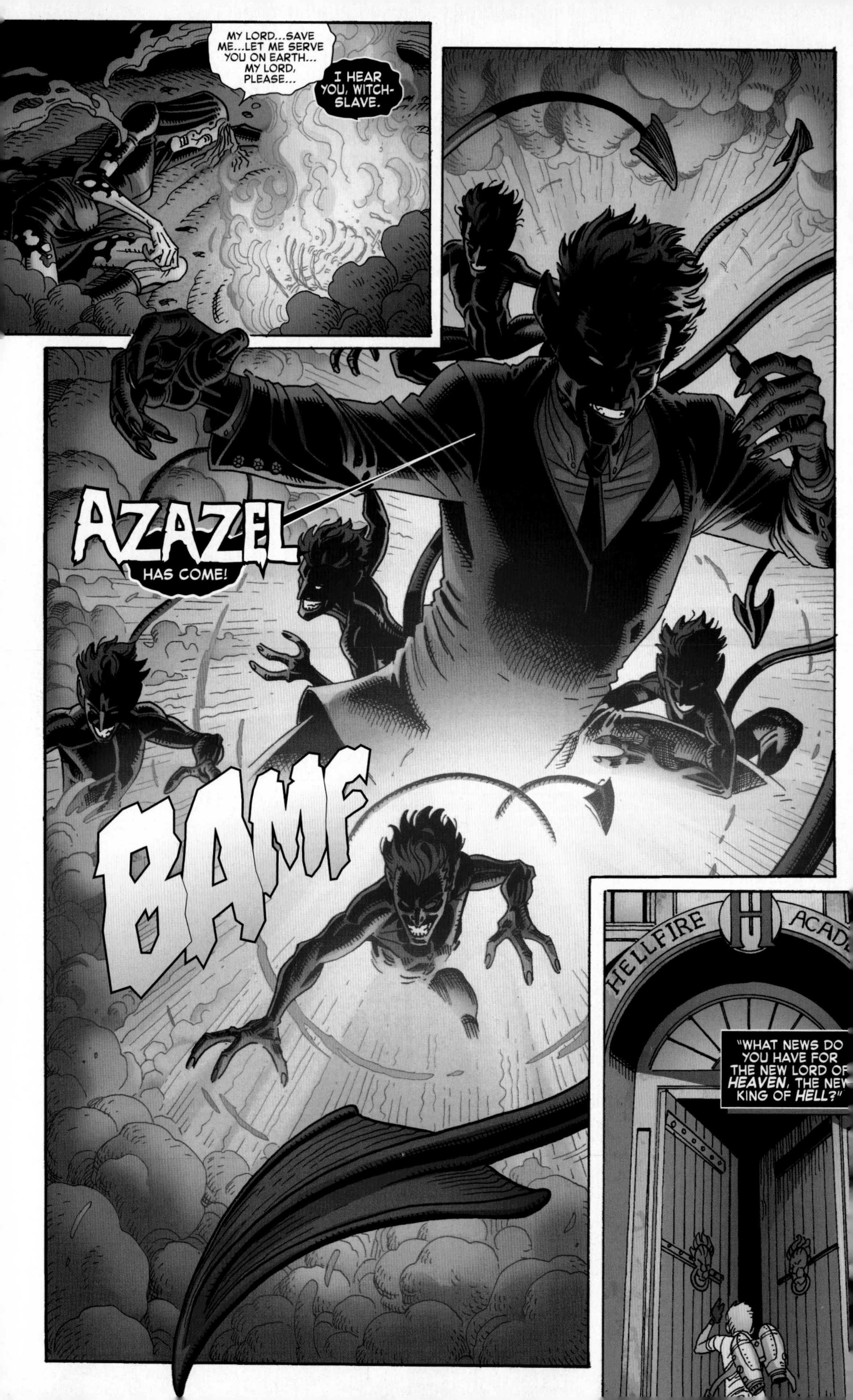
MY LORD...SAVE ME...LET ME SERVE YOU ON EARTH... MY LORD, PLEASE...
I HEAR YOU, WITCH-SLAVE.
AZAZEL HAS COME!
BAMF
HELLFIRE ACAD
"WHAT NEWS DO YOU HAVE FOR THE NEW LORD OF HEAVEN, THE NEW KING OF HELL?"

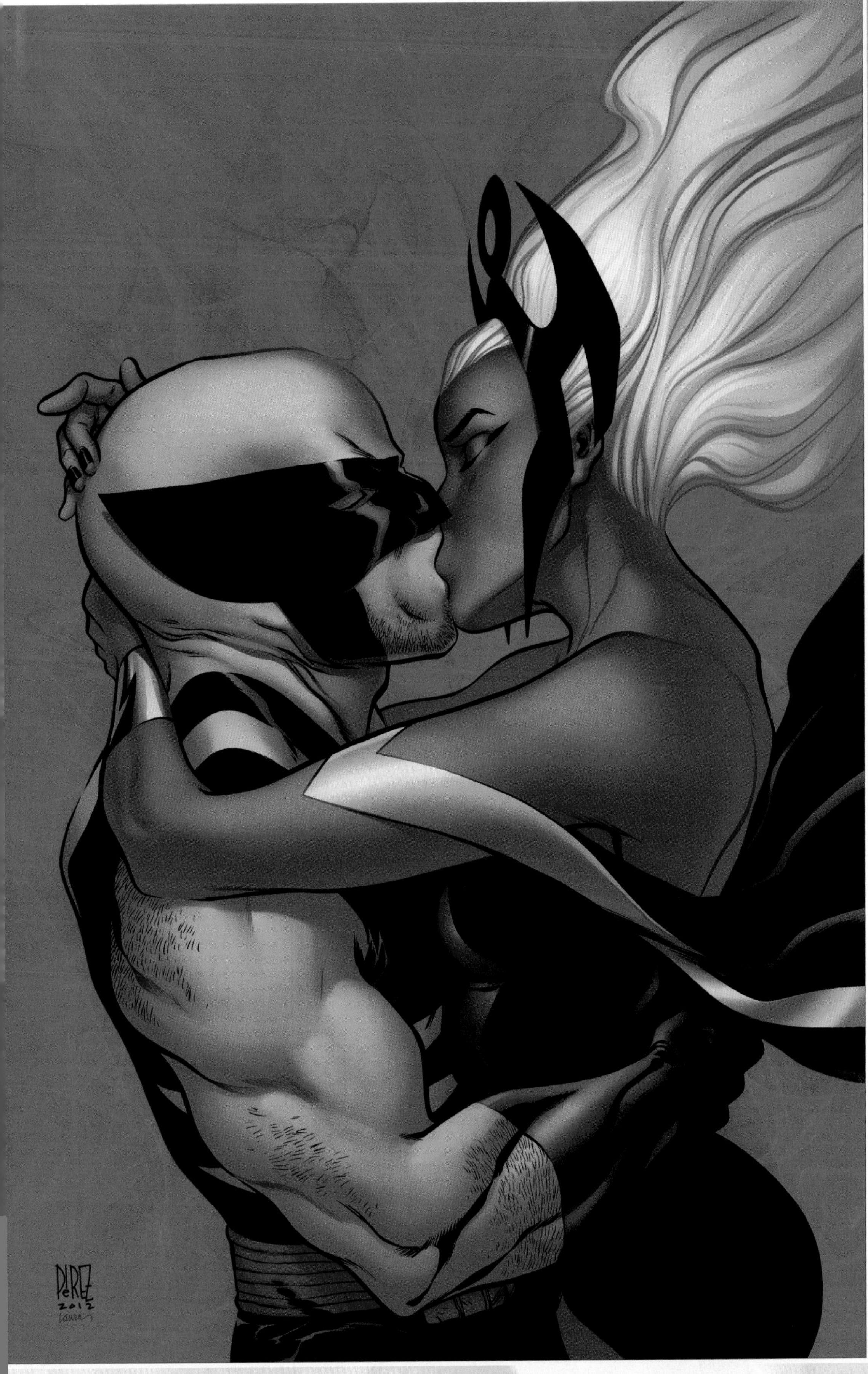

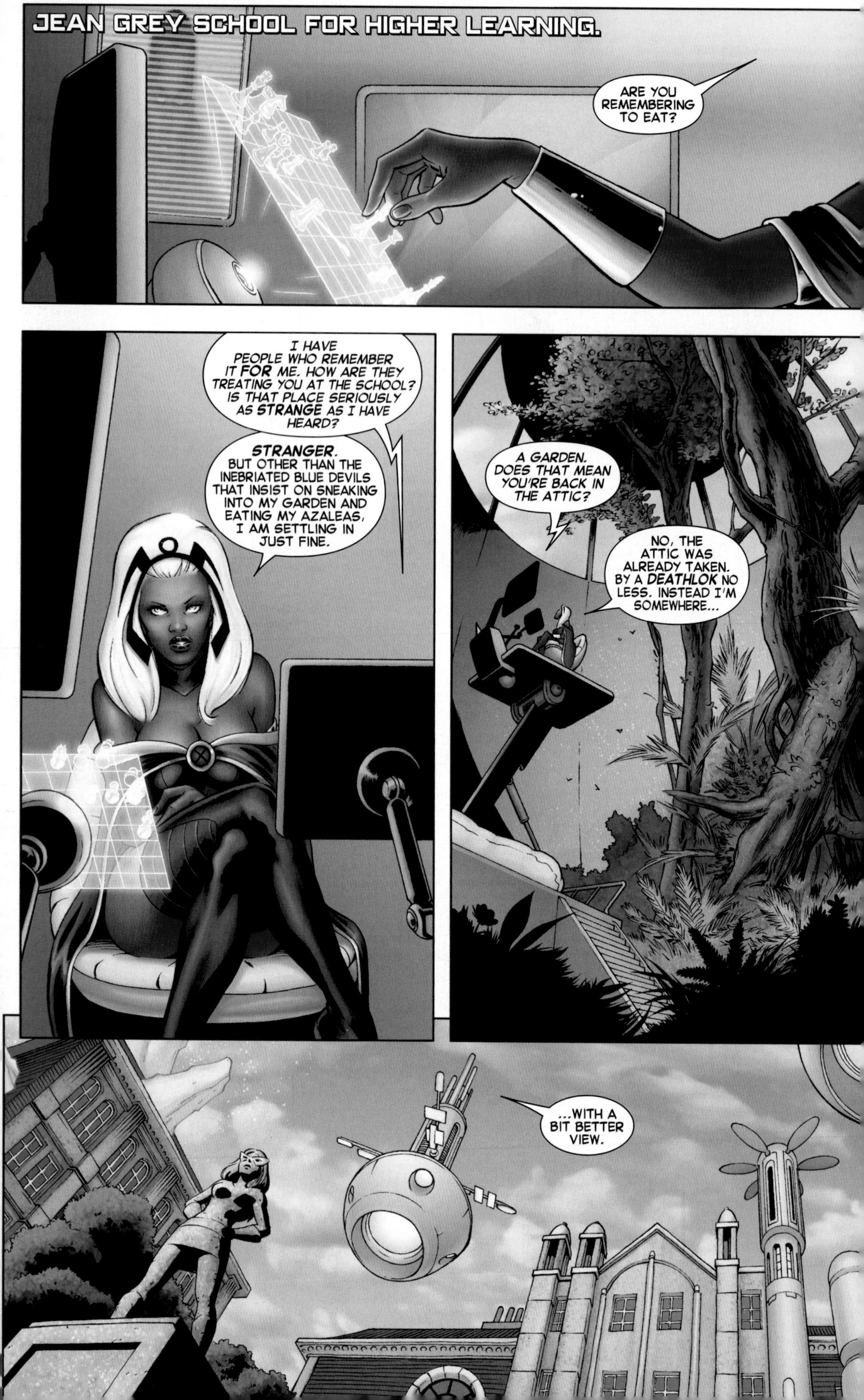
JEAN GREY SCHOOL FOR HIGHER LEARNING.
ARE YOU REMEMBERING TO EAT?
I HAVE PEOPLE WHO REMEMBER IT FOR ME. HOW ARE THEY TREATING YOU AT THE SCHOOL? IS THAT PLACE SERIOUSLY AS STRANGE AS I HAVE HEARD?
STRANGER. BUT OTHER THAN THE INEBRIATED BLUE DEVILS THAT INSIST ON SNEAKING INTO MY GARDEN AND EATING MY AZALEAS, I AM SETTLING IN JUST FINE.
A GARDEN. DOES THAT MEAN YOU'RE BACK IN THE ATTIC?
NO, THE ATTIC WAS ALREADY TAKEN. BY A DEATHLOK NO LESS. INSTEAD I'M SOMEWHERE...
...WITH A BIT BETTER VIEW.

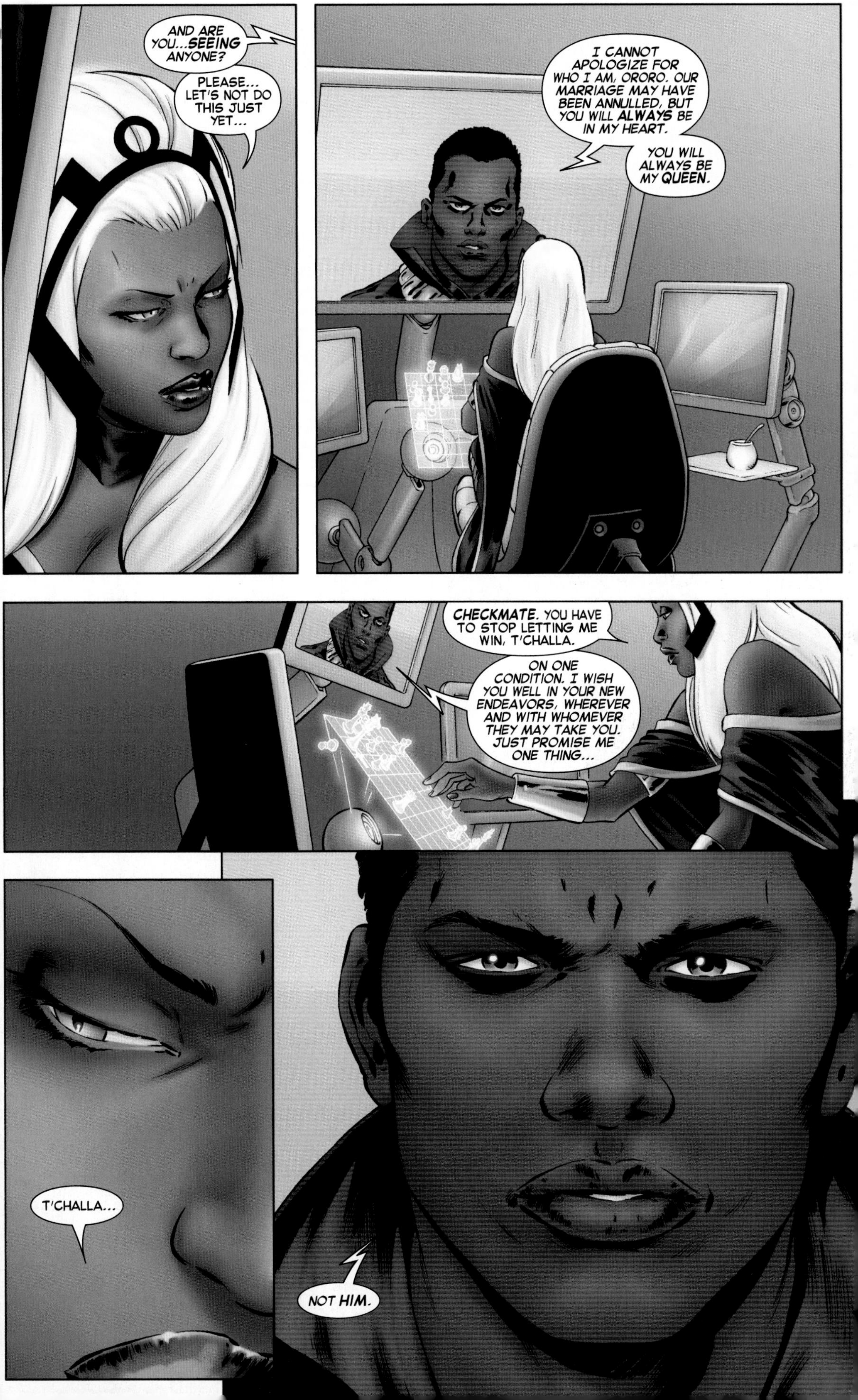
AND ARE YOU...SEEING ANYONE?
PLEASE... LET'S NOT DO THIS JUST YET...
I CANNOT APOLOGIZE FOR WHO I AM, ORORO. OUR MARRIAGE MAY HAVE BEEN ANNULLED, BUT YOU WILL ALWAYS BE IN MY HEART.
YOU WILL ALWAYS BE MY QUEEN.
CHECKMATE. YOU HAVE TO STOP LETTING ME WIN, T'CHALLA.
ON ONE CONDITION. I WISH YOU WELL IN YOUR NEW ENDEAVORS, WHEREVER AND WITH WHOMEVER THEY MAY TAKE YOU. JUST PROMISE ME ONE THING...
T'CHALLA...
NOT HIM.

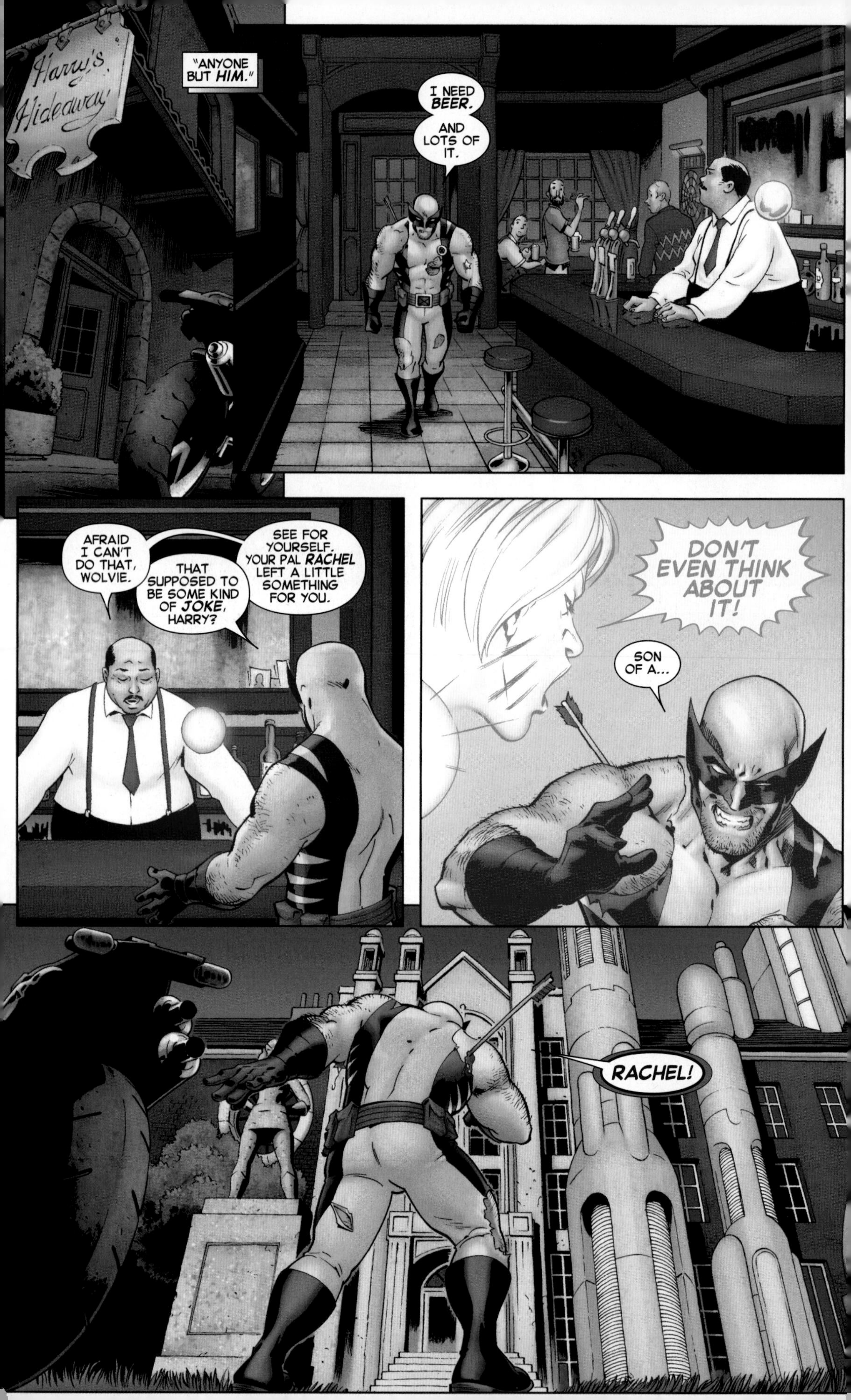
Harry's Hideaway
"ANYONE BUT HIM."
I NEED BEER.
AND LOTS OF IT.
AFRAID I CAN'T DO THAT, WOLVIE.
THAT SUPPOSED TO BE SOME KIND OF JOKE, HARRY?
SEE FOR YOURSELF. YOUR PAL RACHEL LEFT A LITTLE SOMETHING FOR YOU.
DON'T EVEN THINK ABOUT IT!
SON OF A...
RACHEL!

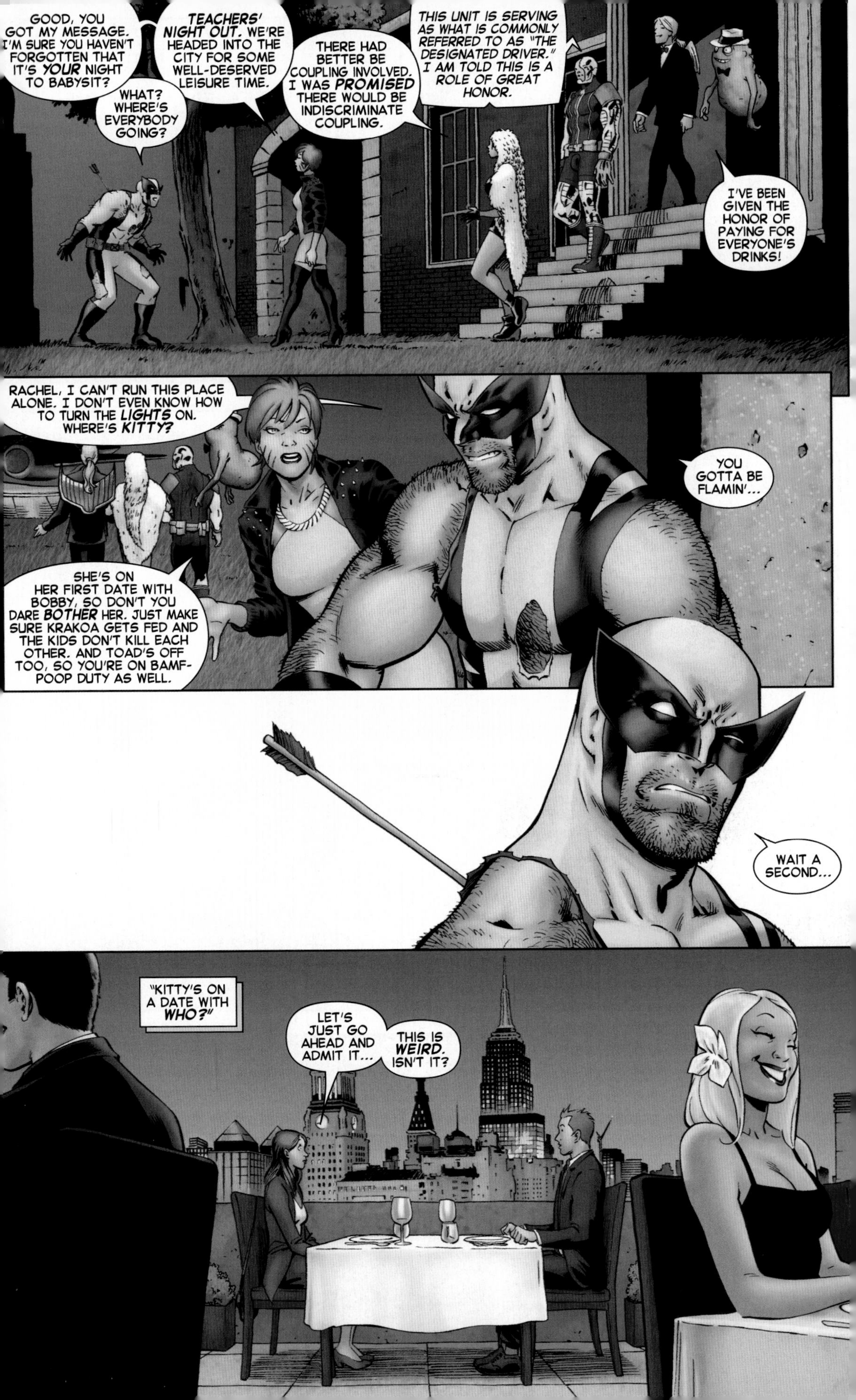
GOOD, YOU GOT MY MESSAGE. I'M SURE YOU HAVEN'T FORGOTTEN THAT IT'S YOUR NIGHT TO BABYSIT?
WHAT? WHERE'S EVERYBODY GOING?
TEACHERS' NIGHT OUT. WE'RE HEADED INTO THE CITY FOR SOME WELL-DESERVED LEISURE TIME.
THERE HAD BETTER BE COUPLING INVOLVED. I WAS PROMISED THERE WOULD BE INDISCRIMINATE COUPLING.
THIS UNIT IS SERVING AS WHAT IS COMMONLY REFERRED TO AS "THE DESIGNATED DRIVER." I AM TOLD THIS IS A ROLE OF GREAT HONOR.
I'VE BEEN GIVEN THE HONOR OF PAYING FOR EVERYONE'S DRINKS!
RACHEL, I CAN'T RUN THIS PLACE ALONE. I DON'T EVEN KNOW HOW TO TURN THE LIGHTS ON. WHERE'S KITTY?
SHE'S ON HER FIRST DATE WITH BOBBY, SO DON'T YOU DARE BOTHER HER. JUST MAKE SURE KRAKOA GETS FED AND THE KIDS DON'T KILL EACH OTHER. AND TOAD'S OFF TOO, SO YOU'RE ON BAMF-POOP DUTY AS WELL.
YOU GOTTA BE FLAMIN'...
WAIT A SECOND...
"KITTY'S ON A DATE WITH WHO?"
LET'S JUST GO AHEAD AND ADMIT IT...
THIS IS WEIRD. ISN'T IT?

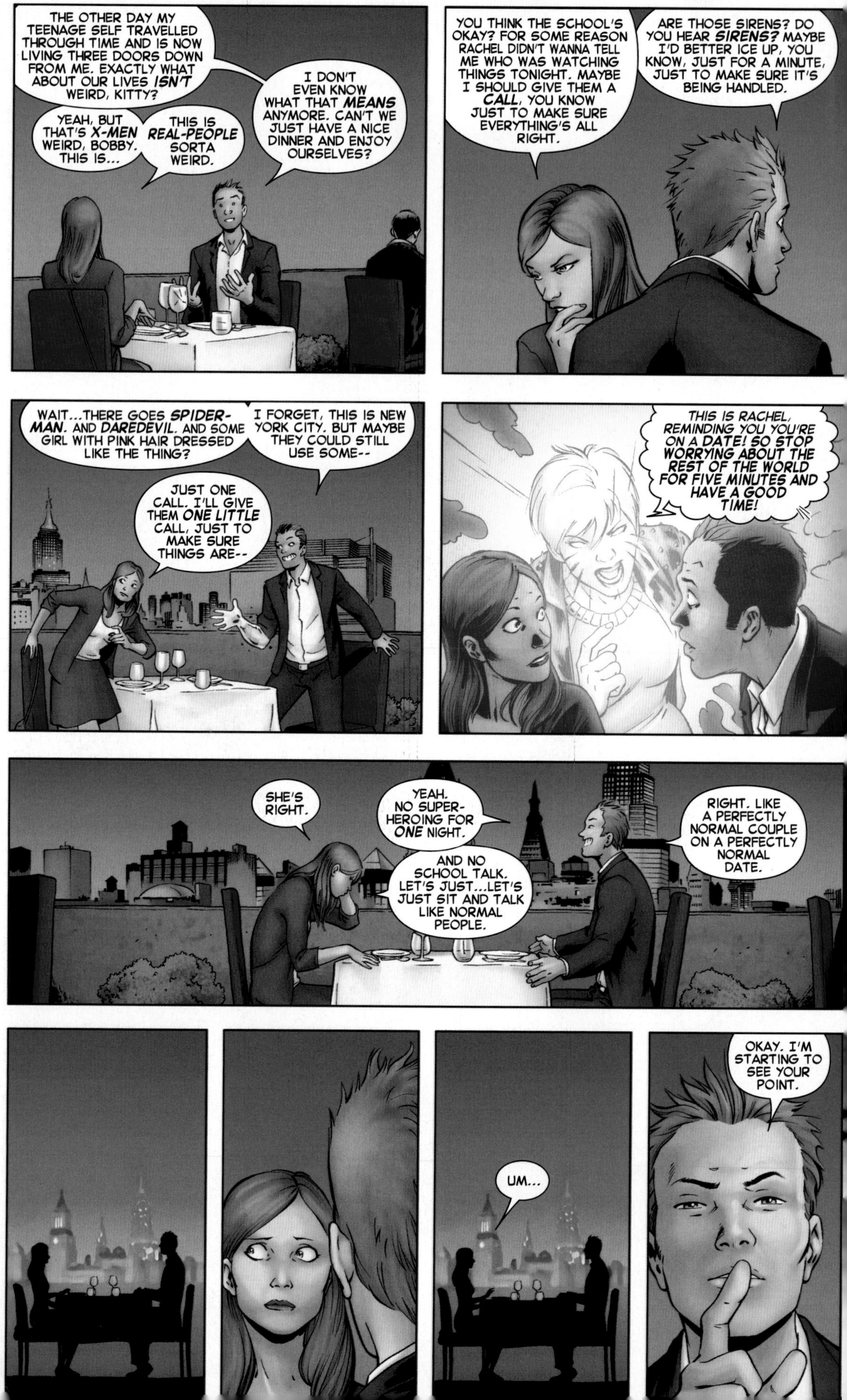
THE OTHER DAY MY TEENAGE SELF TRAVELLED THROUGH TIME AND IS NOW LIVING THREE DOORS DOWN FROM ME. EXACTLY WHAT ABOUT OUR LIVES ISN'T WEIRD, KITTY?
YEAH, BUT THAT'S X-MEN WEIRD, BOBBY. THIS IS...
THIS IS REAL-PEOPLE SORTA WEIRD.
I DON'T EVEN KNOW WHAT THAT MEANS ANYMORE. CAN'T WE JUST HAVE A NICE DINNER AND ENJOY OURSELVES?
YOU THINK THE SCHOOL'S OKAY? FOR SOME REASON RACHEL DIDN'T WANNA TELL ME WHO WAS WATCHING THINGS TONIGHT. MAYBE I SHOULD GIVE THEM A CALL, YOU KNOW JUST TO MAKE SURE EVERYTHING'S ALL RIGHT.
ARE THOSE SIRENS? DO YOU HEAR SIRENS? MAYBE I'D BETTER ICE UP, YOU KNOW, JUST FOR A MINUTE, JUST TO MAKE SURE IT'S BEING HANDLED.
WAIT...THERE GOES SPIDER-MAN. AND DAREDEVIL. AND SOME GIRL WITH PINK HAIR DRESSED LIKE THE THING?
I FORGET, THIS IS NEW YORK CITY. BUT MAYBE THEY COULD STILL USE SOME--
JUST ONE CALL. I'LL GIVE THEM ONE LITTLE CALL, JUST TO MAKE SURE THINGS ARE--
THIS IS RACHEL, REMINDING YOU YOU'RE ON A DATE! SO STOP WORRYING ABOUT THE REST OF THE WORLD FOR FIVE MINUTES AND HAVE A GOOD TIME!
SHE'S RIGHT.
YEAH. NO SUPER-HEROING FOR ONE NIGHT.
AND NO SCHOOL TALK. LET'S JUST...LET'S JUST SIT AND TALK LIKE NORMAL PEOPLE.
RIGHT. LIKE A PERFECTLY NORMAL COUPLE ON A PERFECTLY NORMAL DATE.
UM...
OKAY. I'M STARTING TO SEE YOUR POINT.

"THIS IS DEFINITELY WEIRD."

HELLO? IT'S IDIE.

WOULD YOU LIKE TO HAVE DINNER WITH ME?

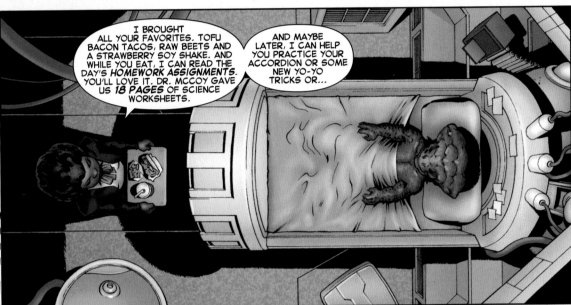

I BROUGHT ALL YOUR FAVORITES. TOFU BACON TACOS, RAW BEETS AND A STRAWBERRY SOY SHAKE. AND WHILE YOU EAT, I CAN READ THE DAY'S *HOMEWORK ASSIGNMENTS.* YOU'LL LOVE IT. DR. McCOY GAVE US *18 PAGES* OF SCIENCE WORKSHEETS.

AND MAYBE LATER, I CAN HELP YOU PRACTICE YOUR ACCORDION OR SOME NEW YO-YO TRICKS OR...

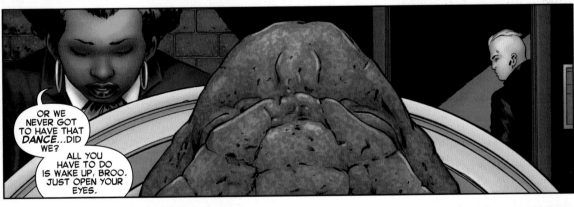

OR WE NEVER GOT TO HAVE THAT *DANCE*...DID WE?

ALL YOU HAVE TO DO IS WAKE UP, BROO. JUST OPEN YOUR EYES.

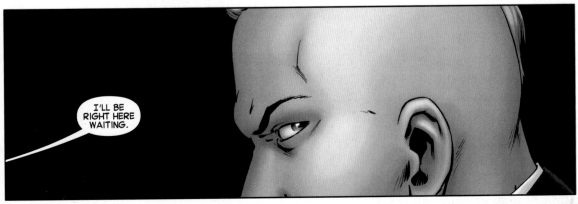

I'LL BE RIGHT HERE WAITING.

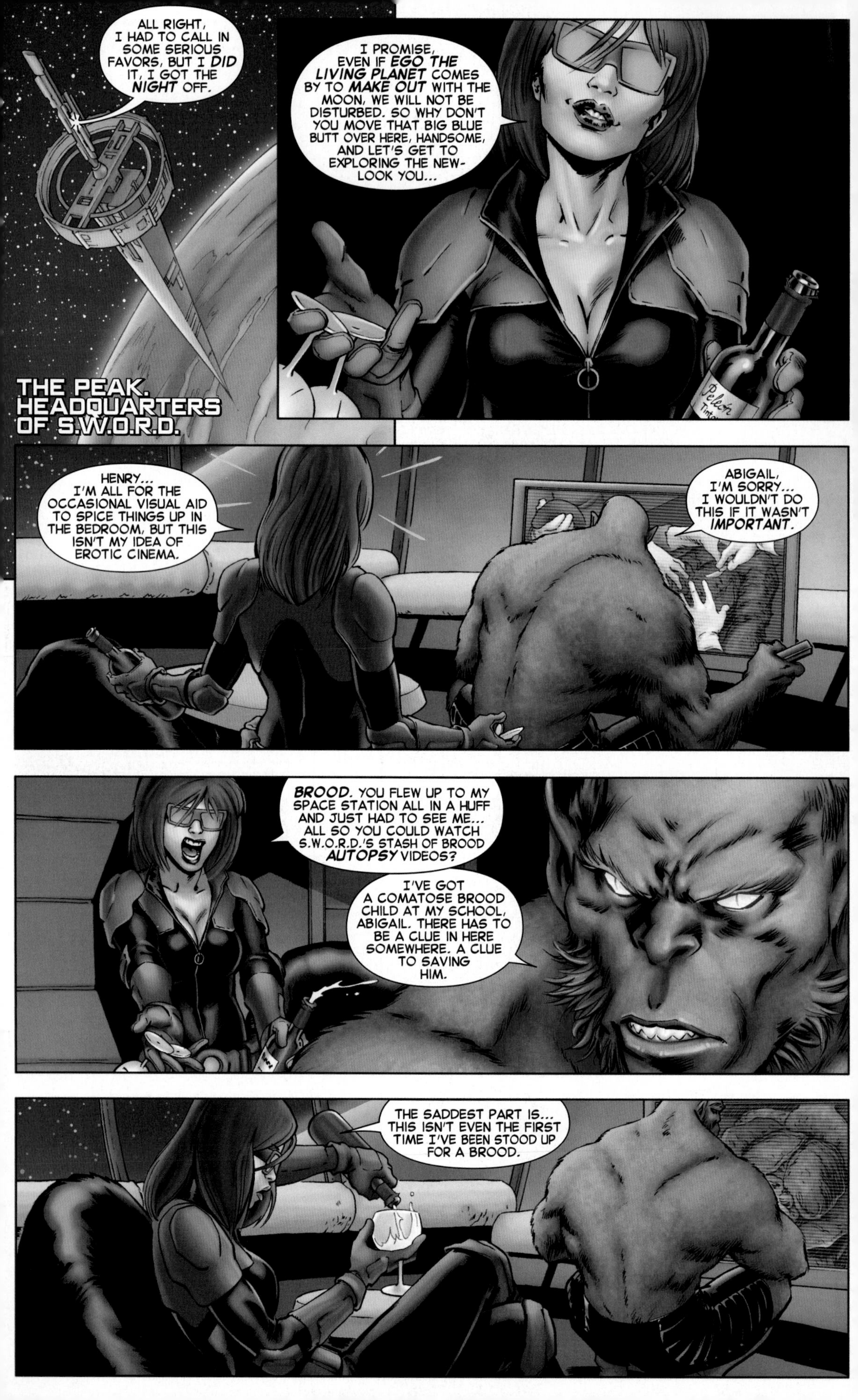
ALL RIGHT, I HAD TO CALL IN SOME SERIOUS FAVORS, BUT I DID IT, I GOT THE NIGHT OFF.
I PROMISE, EVEN IF EGO THE LIVING PLANET COMES BY TO MAKE OUT WITH THE MOON, WE WILL NOT BE DISTURBED. SO WHY DON'T YOU MOVE THAT BIG BLUE BUTT OVER HERE, HANDSOME, AND LET'S GET TO EXPLORING THE NEW-LOOK YOU...
THE PEAK. HEADQUARTERS OF S.W.O.R.D.
HENRY... I'M ALL FOR THE OCCASIONAL VISUAL AID TO SPICE THINGS UP IN THE BEDROOM, BUT THIS ISN'T MY IDEA OF EROTIC CINEMA.
ABIGAIL, I'M SORRY... I WOULDN'T DO THIS IF IT WASN'T IMPORTANT.
BROOD. YOU FLEW UP TO MY SPACE STATION ALL IN A HUFF AND JUST HAD TO SEE ME... ALL SO YOU COULD WATCH S.W.O.R.D.'S STASH OF BROOD AUTOPSY VIDEOS?
I'VE GOT A COMATOSE BROOD CHILD AT MY SCHOOL, ABIGAIL. THERE HAS TO BE A CLUE IN HERE SOMEWHERE. A CLUE TO SAVING HIM.
THE SADDEST PART IS... THIS ISN'T EVEN THE FIRST TIME I'VE BEEN STOOD UP FOR A BROOD.

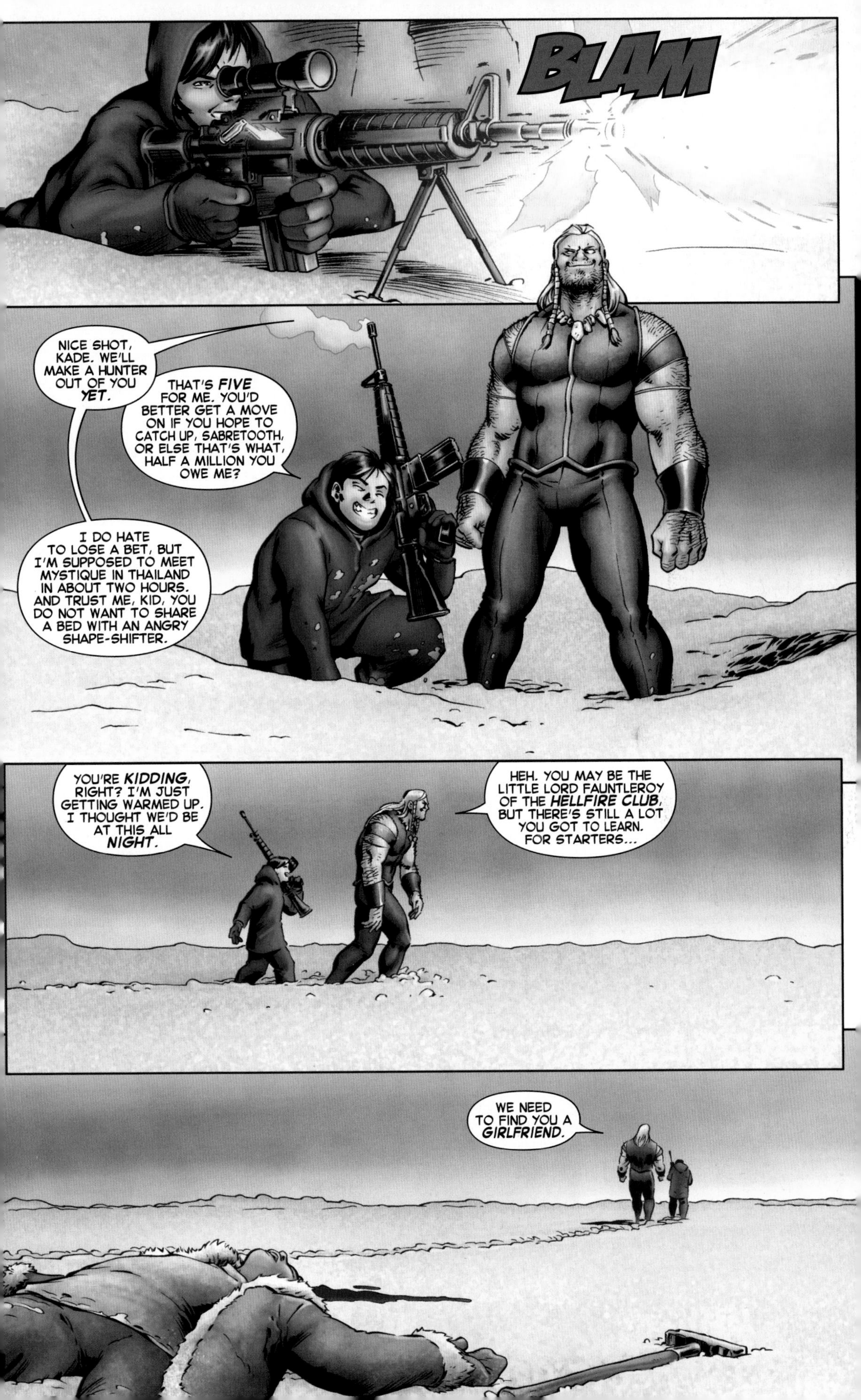
BLAM
NICE SHOT, KADE. WE'LL MAKE A HUNTER OUT OF YOU *YET*.
THAT'S *FIVE* FOR ME. YOU'D BETTER GET A MOVE ON IF YOU HOPE TO CATCH UP, SABRETOOTH, OR ELSE THAT'S WHAT, HALF A MILLION YOU OWE ME?
I DO HATE TO LOSE A BET, BUT I'M SUPPOSED TO MEET MYSTIQUE IN THAILAND IN ABOUT TWO HOURS. AND TRUST ME, KID, YOU DO NOT WANT TO SHARE A BED WITH AN ANGRY SHAPE-SHIFTER.
YOU'RE *KIDDING*, RIGHT? I'M JUST GETTING WARMED UP. I THOUGHT WE'D BE AT THIS ALL *NIGHT*.
HEH. YOU MAY BE THE LITTLE LORD FAUNTLEROY OF THE *HELLFIRE CLUB*, BUT THERE'S STILL A LOT YOU GOT TO LEARN. FOR STARTERS...
WE NEED TO FIND YOU A *GIRLFRIEND*.

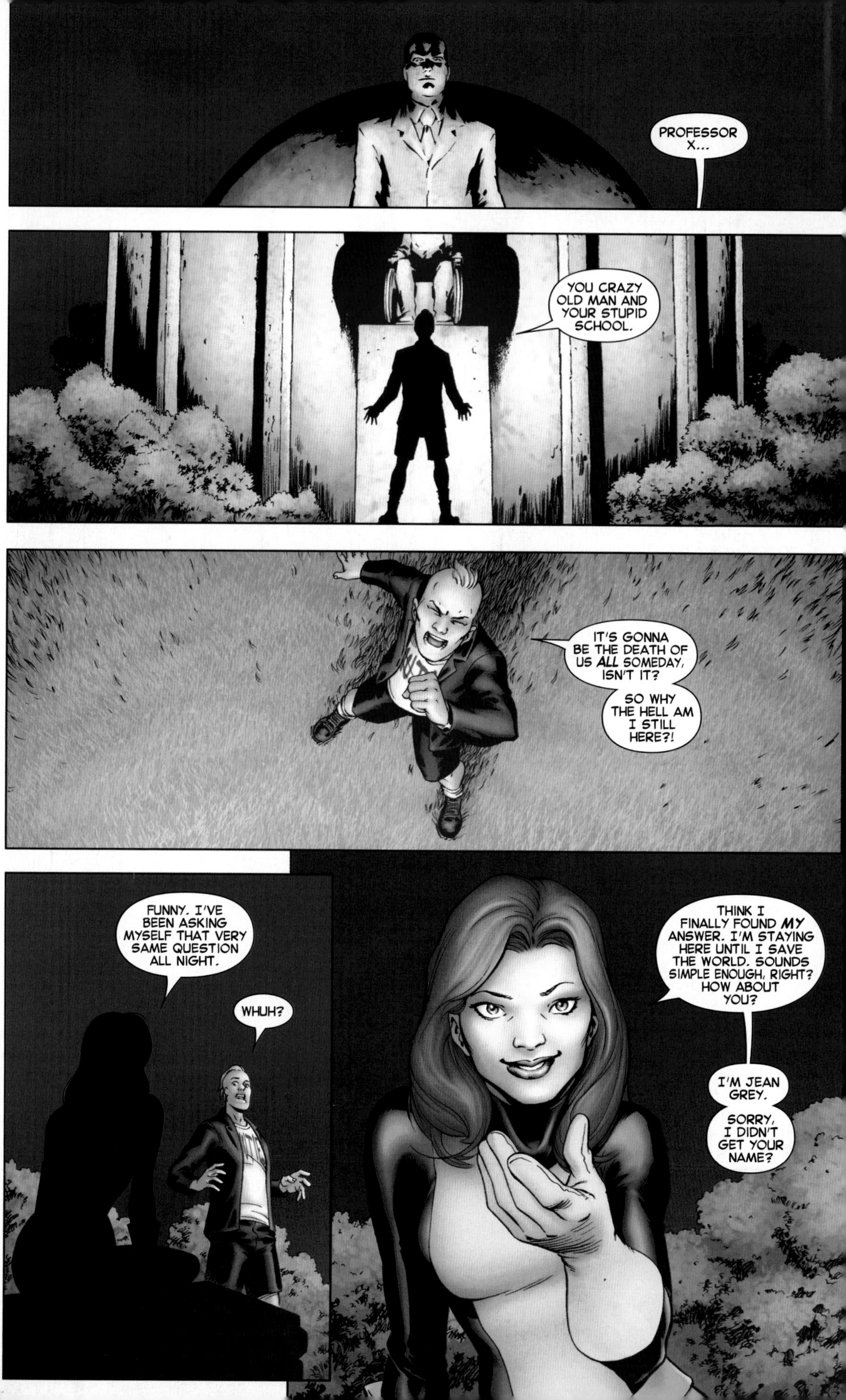
PROFESSOR X...
YOU CRAZY OLD MAN AND YOUR STUPID SCHOOL.
IT'S GONNA BE THE DEATH OF US ALL SOMEDAY, ISN'T IT?
SO WHY THE HELL AM I STILL HERE?!
FUNNY. I'VE BEEN ASKING MYSELF THAT VERY SAME QUESTION ALL NIGHT.
WHUH?
THINK I FINALLY FOUND MY ANSWER. I'M STAYING HERE UNTIL I SAVE THE WORLD. SOUNDS SIMPLE ENOUGH, RIGHT? HOW ABOUT YOU?
I'M JEAN GREY.
SORRY, I DIDN'T GET YOUR NAME?

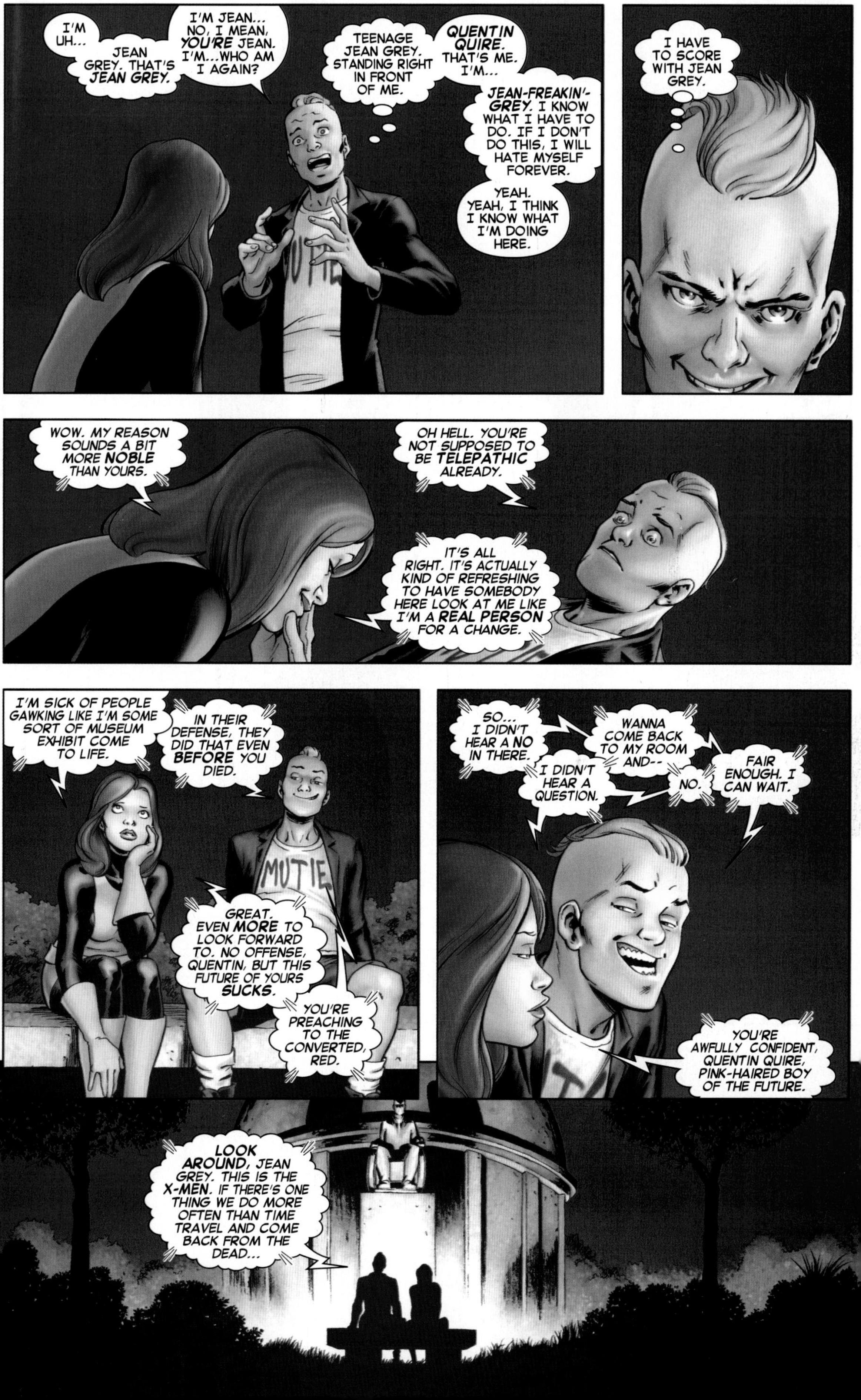

I'M UH...
JEAN GREY. THAT'S JEAN GREY.
I'M JEAN... NO, I MEAN, YOU'RE JEAN. I'M...WHO AM I AGAIN?
TEENAGE JEAN GREY. STANDING RIGHT IN FRONT OF ME.
QUENTIN QUIRE. THAT'S ME. I'M...
JEAN-FREAKIN'-GREY. I KNOW WHAT I HAVE TO DO. IF I DON'T DO THIS, I WILL HATE MYSELF FOREVER.
YEAH. YEAH, I THINK I KNOW WHAT I'M DOING HERE.
I HAVE TO SCORE WITH JEAN GREY.
WOW. MY REASON SOUNDS A BIT MORE NOBLE THAN YOURS.
OH HELL. YOU'RE NOT SUPPOSED TO BE TELEPATHIC ALREADY.
IT'S ALL RIGHT. IT'S ACTUALLY KIND OF REFRESHING TO HAVE SOMEBODY HERE LOOK AT ME LIKE I'M A REAL PERSON FOR A CHANGE.
I'M SICK OF PEOPLE GAWKING LIKE I'M SOME SORT OF MUSEUM EXHIBIT COME TO LIFE.
IN THEIR DEFENSE, THEY DID THAT EVEN BEFORE YOU DIED.
GREAT. EVEN MORE TO LOOK FORWARD TO. NO OFFENSE, QUENTIN, BUT THIS FUTURE OF YOURS SUCKS.
YOU'RE PREACHING TO THE CONVERTED, RED.
SO... I DIDN'T HEAR A NO IN THERE.
WANNA COME BACK TO MY ROOM AND--
I DIDN'T HEAR A QUESTION.
NO.
FAIR ENOUGH. I CAN WAIT.
YOU'RE AWFULLY CONFIDENT, QUENTIN QUIRE, PINK-HAIRED BOY OF THE FUTURE.
LOOK AROUND, JEAN GREY. THIS IS THE X-MEN. IF THERE'S ONE THING WE DO MORE OFTEN THAN TIME TRAVEL AND COME BACK FROM THE DEAD...

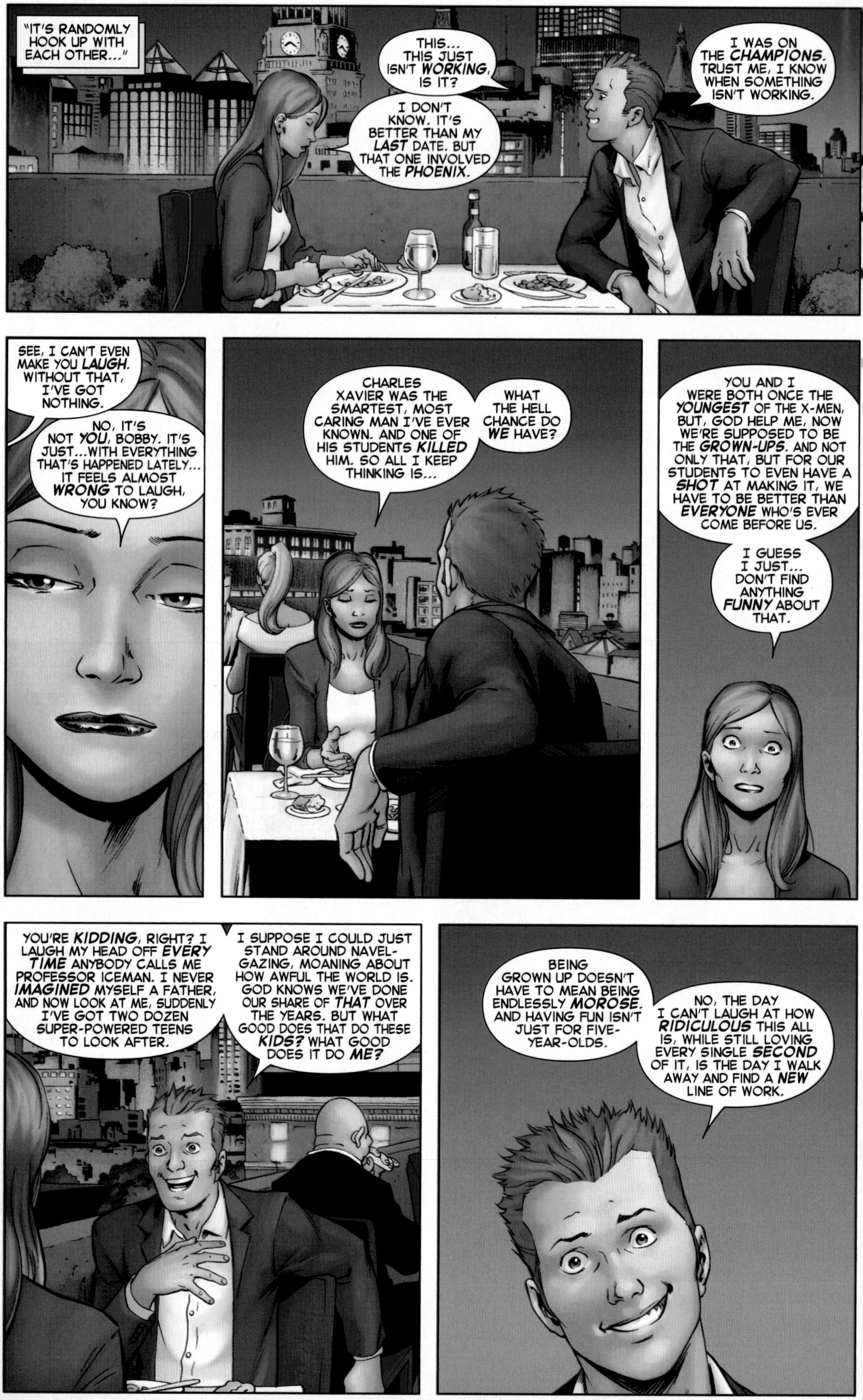
"IT'S RANDOMLY HOOK UP WITH EACH OTHER..."
THIS... THIS JUST ISN'T WORKING, IS IT?
I DON'T KNOW. IT'S BETTER THAN MY LAST DATE. BUT THAT ONE INVOLVED THE PHOENIX.
I WAS ON THE CHAMPIONS. TRUST ME, I KNOW WHEN SOMETHING ISN'T WORKING.
SEE, I CAN'T EVEN MAKE YOU LAUGH. WITHOUT THAT, I'VE GOT NOTHING.
NO, IT'S NOT YOU, BOBBY. IT'S JUST...WITH EVERYTHING THAT'S HAPPENED LATELY... IT FEELS ALMOST WRONG TO LAUGH, YOU KNOW?
CHARLES XAVIER WAS THE SMARTEST, MOST CARING MAN I'VE EVER KNOWN. AND ONE OF HIS STUDENTS KILLED HIM. SO ALL I KEEP THINKING IS...
WHAT THE HELL CHANCE DO WE HAVE?
YOU AND I WERE BOTH ONCE THE YOUNGEST OF THE X-MEN, BUT, GOD HELP ME, NOW WE'RE SUPPOSED TO BE THE GROWN-UPS. AND NOT ONLY THAT, BUT FOR OUR STUDENTS TO EVEN HAVE A SHOT AT MAKING IT, WE HAVE TO BE BETTER THAN EVERYONE WHO'S EVER COME BEFORE US.
I GUESS I JUST... DON'T FIND ANYTHING FUNNY ABOUT THAT.
YOU'RE KIDDING, RIGHT? I LAUGH MY HEAD OFF EVERY TIME ANYBODY CALLS ME PROFESSOR ICEMAN. I NEVER IMAGINED MYSELF A FATHER, AND NOW LOOK AT ME, SUDDENLY I'VE GOT TWO DOZEN SUPER-POWERED TEENS TO LOOK AFTER.
I SUPPOSE I COULD JUST STAND AROUND NAVEL-GAZING, MOANING ABOUT HOW AWFUL THE WORLD IS. GOD KNOWS WE'VE DONE OUR SHARE OF THAT OVER THE YEARS. BUT WHAT GOOD DOES THAT DO THESE KIDS? WHAT GOOD DOES IT DO ME?
BEING GROWN UP DOESN'T HAVE TO MEAN BEING ENDLESSLY MOROSE. AND HAVING FUN ISN'T JUST FOR FIVE-YEAR-OLDS.
NO, THE DAY I CAN'T LAUGH AT HOW RIDICULOUS THIS ALL IS, WHILE STILL LOVING EVERY SINGLE SECOND OF IT, IS THE DAY I WALK AWAY AND FIND A NEW LINE OF WORK.

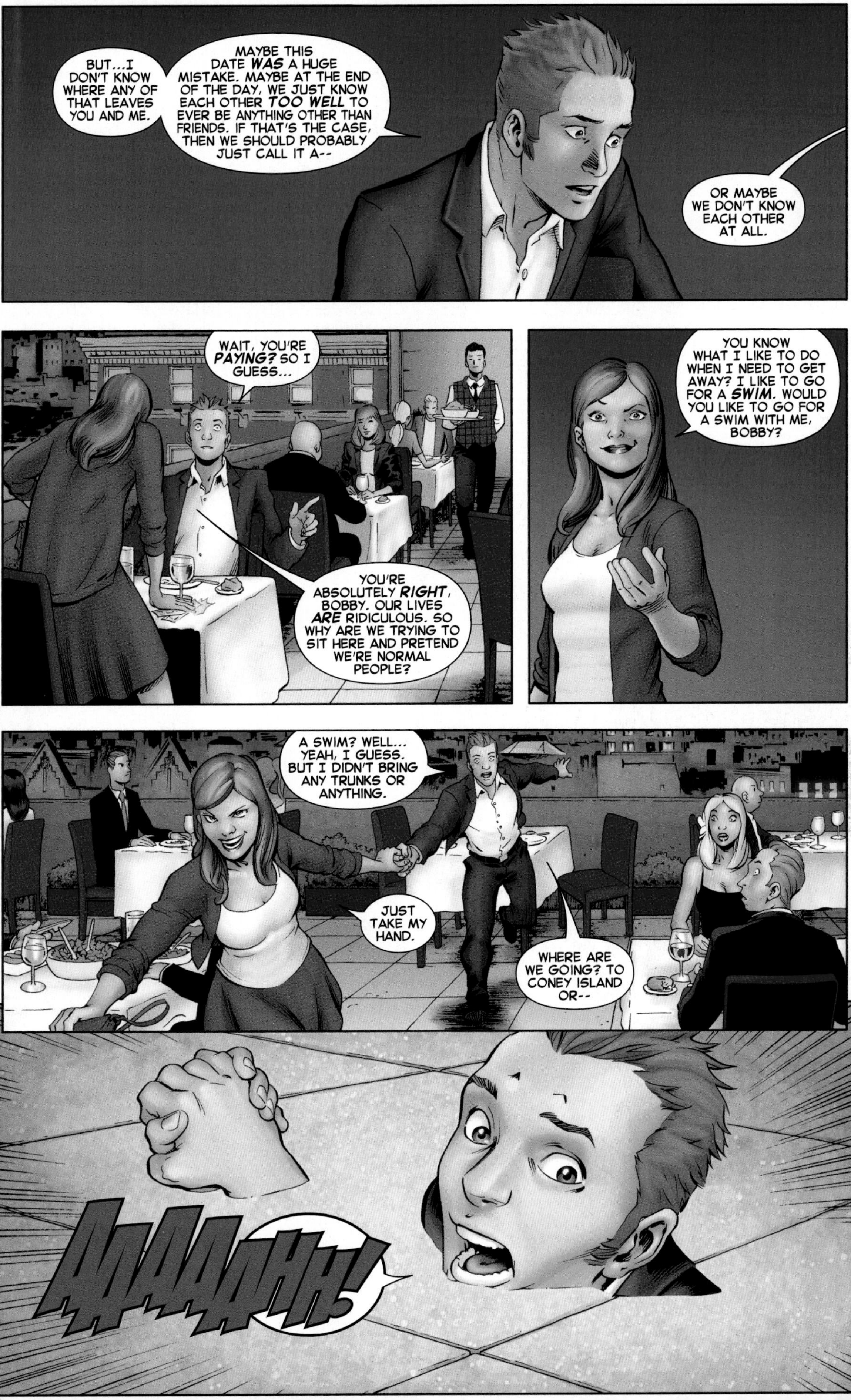
BUT...I DON'T KNOW WHERE ANY OF THAT LEAVES YOU AND ME.
MAYBE THIS DATE WAS A HUGE MISTAKE. MAYBE AT THE END OF THE DAY, WE JUST KNOW EACH OTHER TOO WELL TO EVER BE ANYTHING OTHER THAN FRIENDS. IF THAT'S THE CASE, THEN WE SHOULD PROBABLY JUST CALL IT A--
OR MAYBE WE DON'T KNOW EACH OTHER AT ALL.
WAIT, YOU'RE PAYING? SO I GUESS...
YOU'RE ABSOLUTELY RIGHT, BOBBY. OUR LIVES ARE RIDICULOUS. SO WHY ARE WE TRYING TO SIT HERE AND PRETEND WE'RE NORMAL PEOPLE?
YOU KNOW WHAT I LIKE TO DO WHEN I NEED TO GET AWAY? I LIKE TO GO FOR A SWIM. WOULD YOU LIKE TO GO FOR A SWIM WITH ME, BOBBY?
A SWIM? WELL... YEAH, I GUESS. BUT I DIDN'T BRING ANY TRUNKS OR ANYTHING.
JUST TAKE MY HAND.
WHERE ARE WE GOING? TO CONEY ISLAND OR--
AAAAAHH!

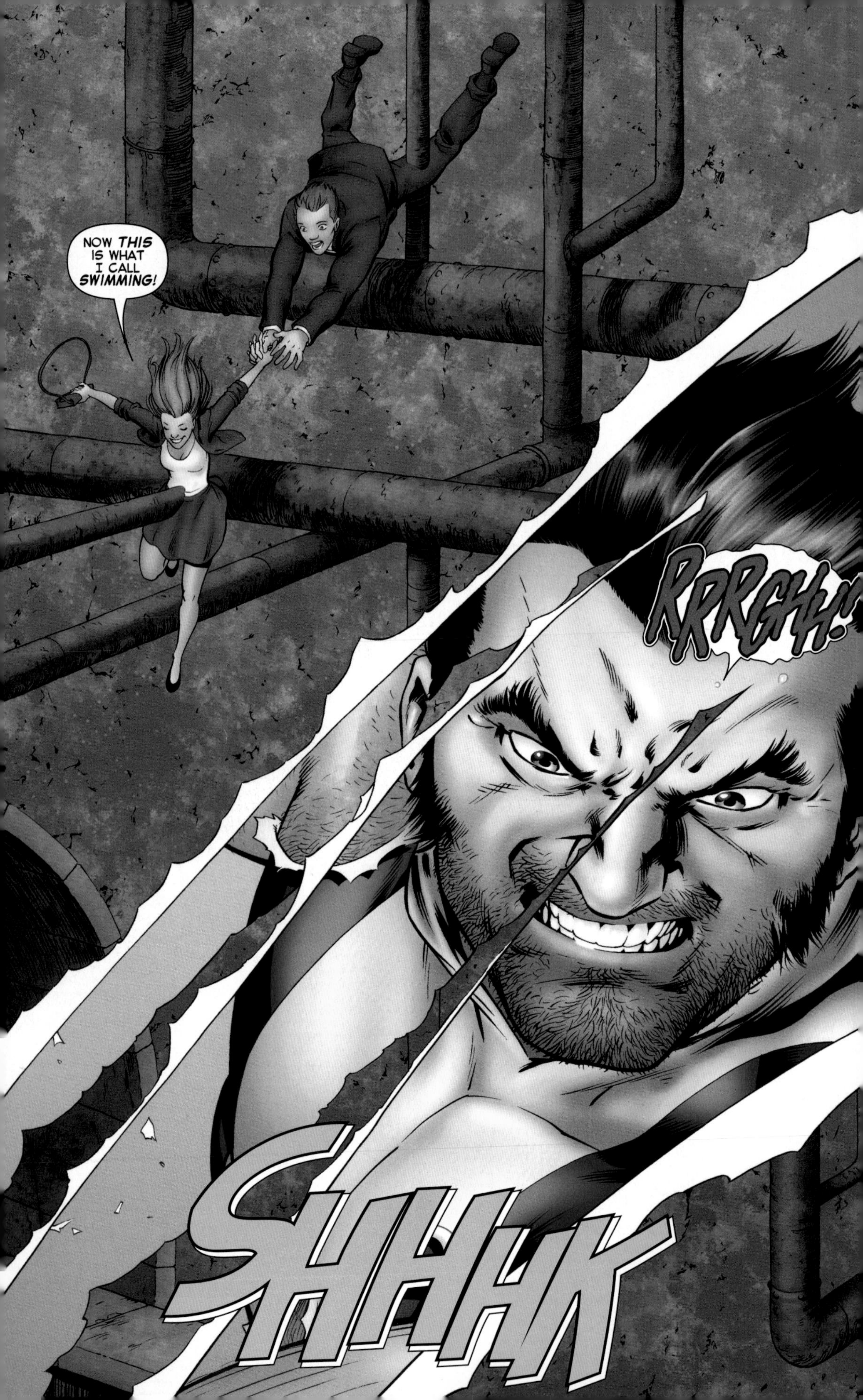
NOW THIS IS WHAT I CALL SWIMMING!
RRRGHH!
SHHK

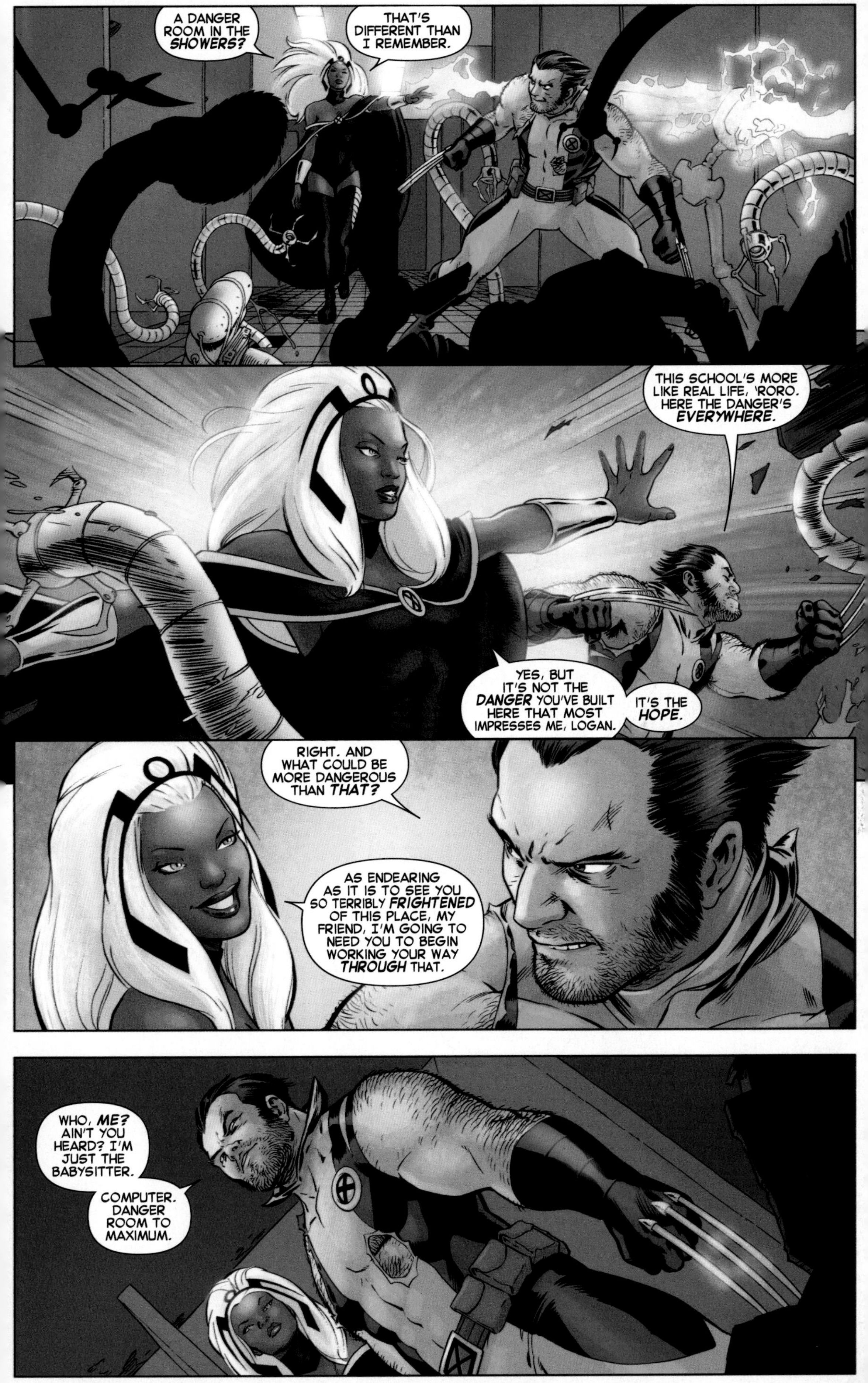

A DANGER ROOM IN THE SHOWERS?
THAT'S DIFFERENT THAN I REMEMBER.
THIS SCHOOL'S MORE LIKE REAL LIFE, 'RORO. HERE THE DANGER'S EVERYWHERE.
YES, BUT IT'S NOT THE DANGER YOU'VE BUILT HERE THAT MOST IMPRESSES ME, LOGAN.
IT'S THE HOPE.
RIGHT. AND WHAT COULD BE MORE DANGEROUS THAN THAT?
AS ENDEARING AS IT IS TO SEE YOU SO TERRIBLY FRIGHTENED OF THIS PLACE, MY FRIEND, I'M GOING TO NEED YOU TO BEGIN WORKING YOUR WAY THROUGH THAT.
WHO, ME? AIN'T YOU HEARD? I'M JUST THE BABYSITTER.
COMPUTER. DANGER ROOM TO MAXIMUM.

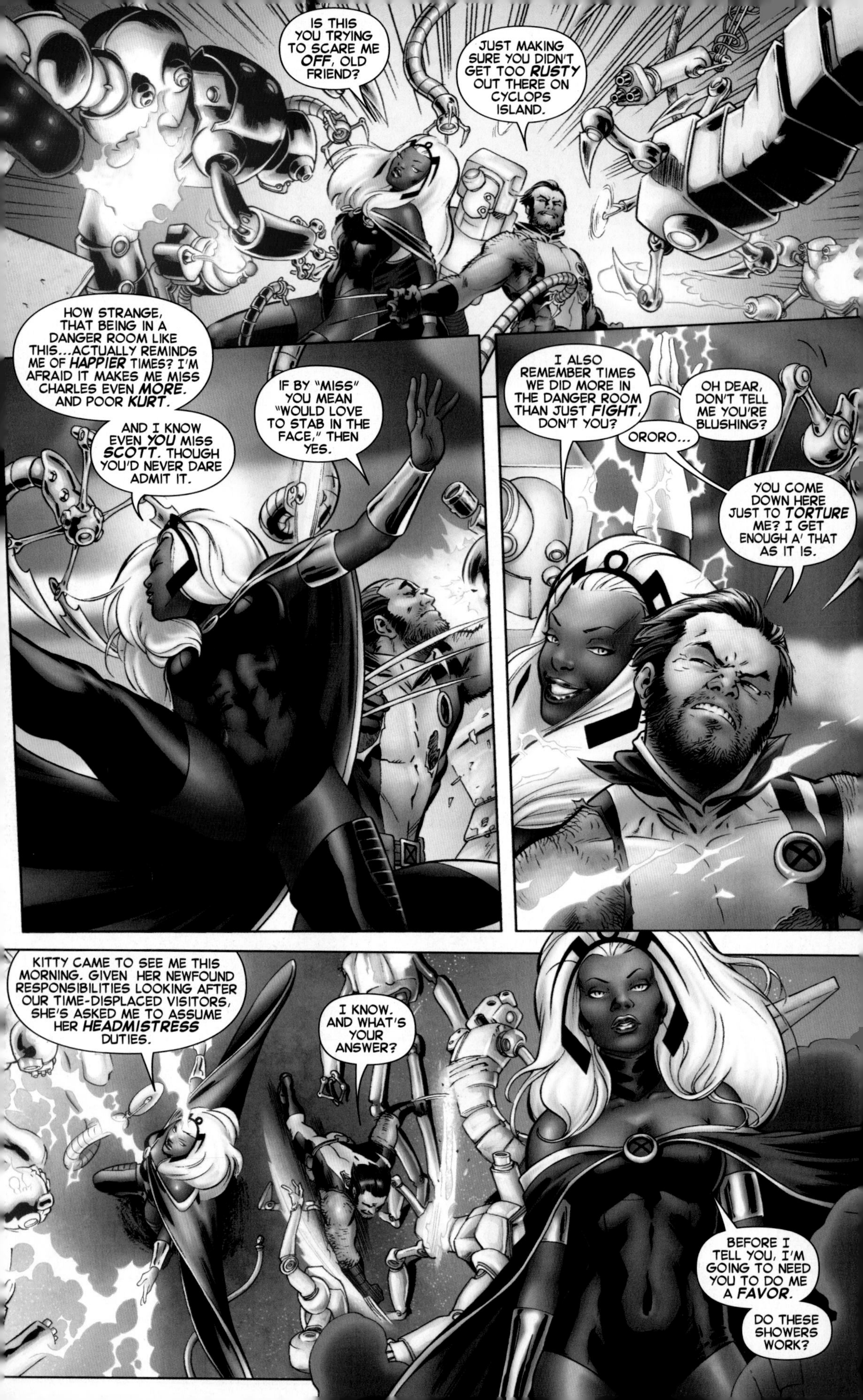

IS THIS YOU TRYING TO SCARE ME OFF, OLD FRIEND?
JUST MAKING SURE YOU DIDN'T GET TOO RUSTY OUT THERE ON CYCLOPS ISLAND.
HOW STRANGE, THAT BEING IN A DANGER ROOM LIKE THIS...ACTUALLY REMINDS ME OF HAPPIER TIMES? I'M AFRAID IT MAKES ME MISS CHARLES EVEN MORE. AND POOR KURT.
AND I KNOW EVEN YOU MISS SCOTT. THOUGH YOU'D NEVER DARE ADMIT IT.
IF BY "MISS" YOU MEAN "WOULD LOVE TO STAB IN THE FACE," THEN YES.
I ALSO REMEMBER TIMES WE DID MORE IN THE DANGER ROOM THAN JUST FIGHT, DON'T YOU?
ORORO...
OH DEAR, DON'T TELL ME YOU'RE BLUSHING?
YOU COME DOWN HERE JUST TO TORTURE ME? I GET ENOUGH A' THAT AS IT IS.
KITTY CAME TO SEE ME THIS MORNING. GIVEN HER NEWFOUND RESPONSIBILITIES LOOKING AFTER OUR TIME-DISPLACED VISITORS, SHE'S ASKED ME TO ASSUME HER HEADMISTRESS DUTIES.
I KNOW. AND WHAT'S YOUR ANSWER?
BEFORE I TELL YOU, I'M GOING TO NEED YOU TO DO ME A FAVOR.
DO THESE SHOWERS WORK?

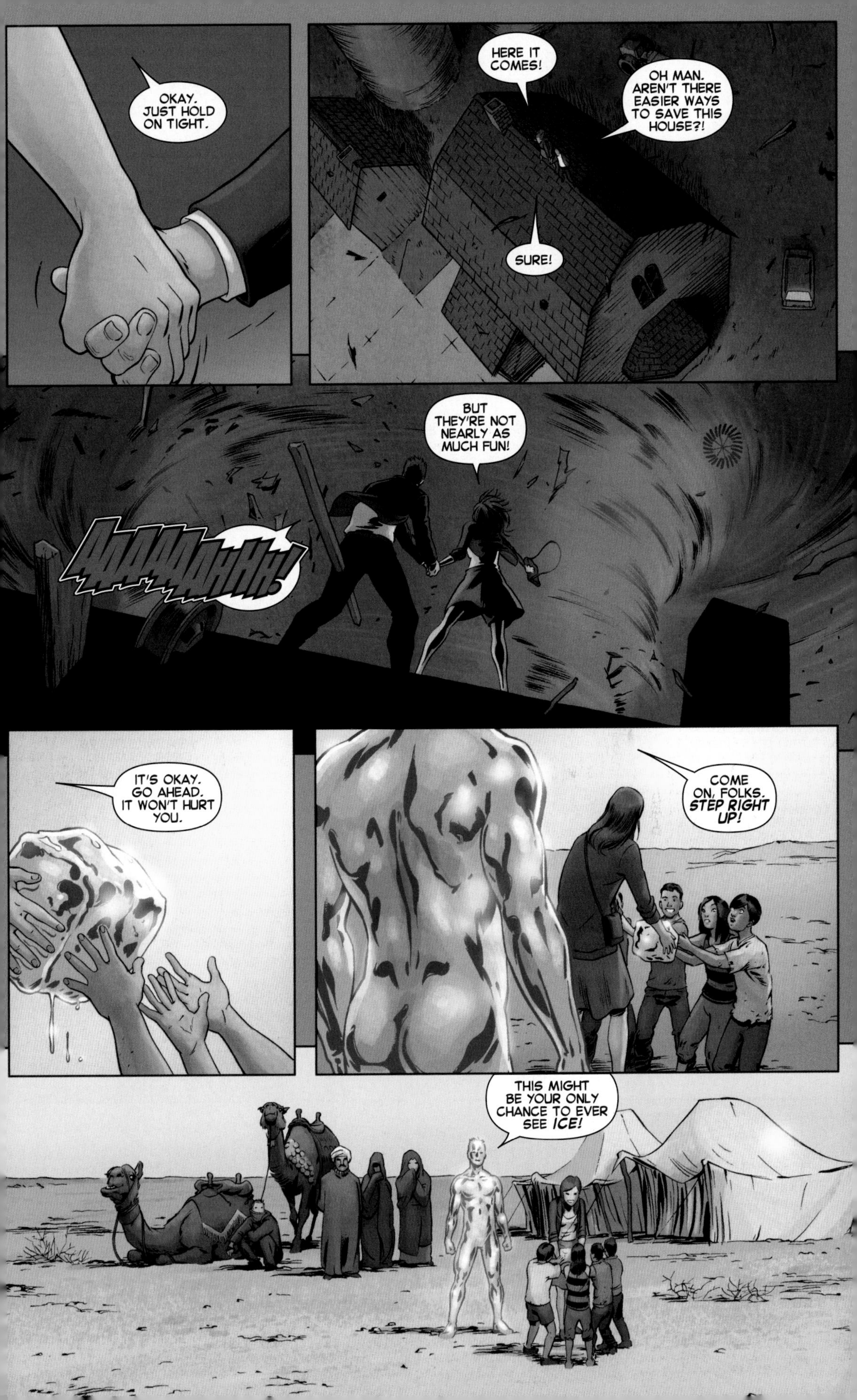
OKAY. JUST HOLD ON TIGHT.
HERE IT COMES!
OH MAN. AREN'T THERE EASIER WAYS TO SAVE THIS HOUSE?!
SURE!
BUT THEY'RE NOT NEARLY AS MUCH FUN!
AAAAAAHHH!
IT'S OKAY. GO AHEAD. IT WON'T HURT YOU.
COME ON, FOLKS. STEP RIGHT UP!
THIS MIGHT BE YOUR ONLY CHANCE TO EVER SEE ICE!

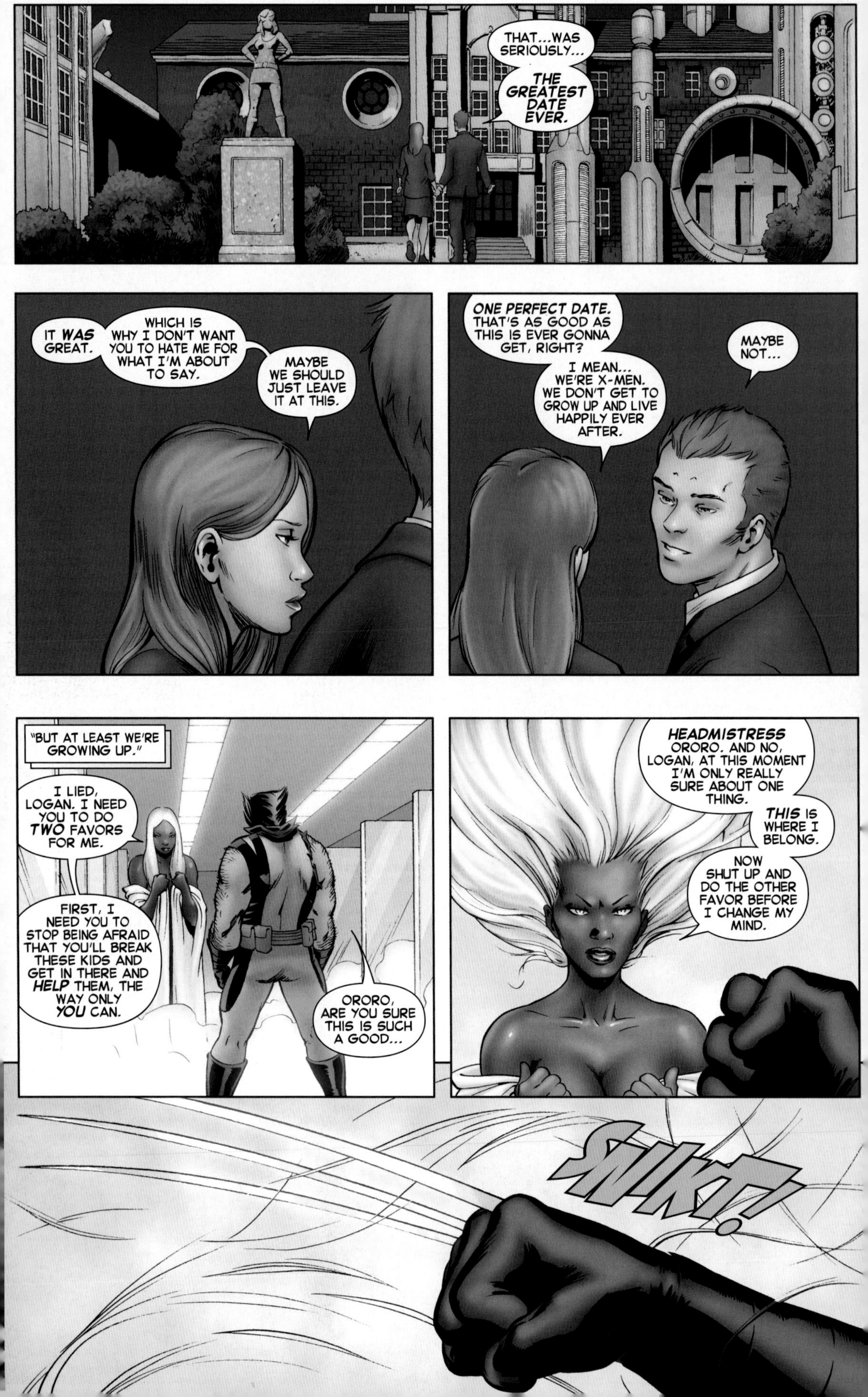
THAT...WAS SERIOUSLY...
THE GREATEST DATE EVER.
IT WAS GREAT.
WHICH IS WHY I DON'T WANT YOU TO HATE ME FOR WHAT I'M ABOUT TO SAY.
MAYBE WE SHOULD JUST LEAVE IT AT THIS.
ONE PERFECT DATE. THAT'S AS GOOD AS THIS IS EVER GONNA GET, RIGHT?
I MEAN... WE'RE X-MEN. WE DON'T GET TO GROW UP AND LIVE HAPPILY EVER AFTER.
MAYBE NOT...
"BUT AT LEAST WE'RE GROWING UP."
I LIED, LOGAN. I NEED YOU TO DO TWO FAVORS FOR ME.
FIRST, I NEED YOU TO STOP BEING AFRAID THAT YOU'LL BREAK THESE KIDS AND GET IN THERE AND HELP THEM, THE WAY ONLY YOU CAN.
ORORO, ARE YOU SURE THIS IS SUCH A GOOD...
HEADMISTRESS ORORO. AND NO, LOGAN, AT THIS MOMENT I'M ONLY REALLY SURE ABOUT ONE THING.
THIS IS WHERE I BELONG.
NOW SHUT UP AND DO THE OTHER FAVOR BEFORE I CHANGE MY MIND.
SNIKT!

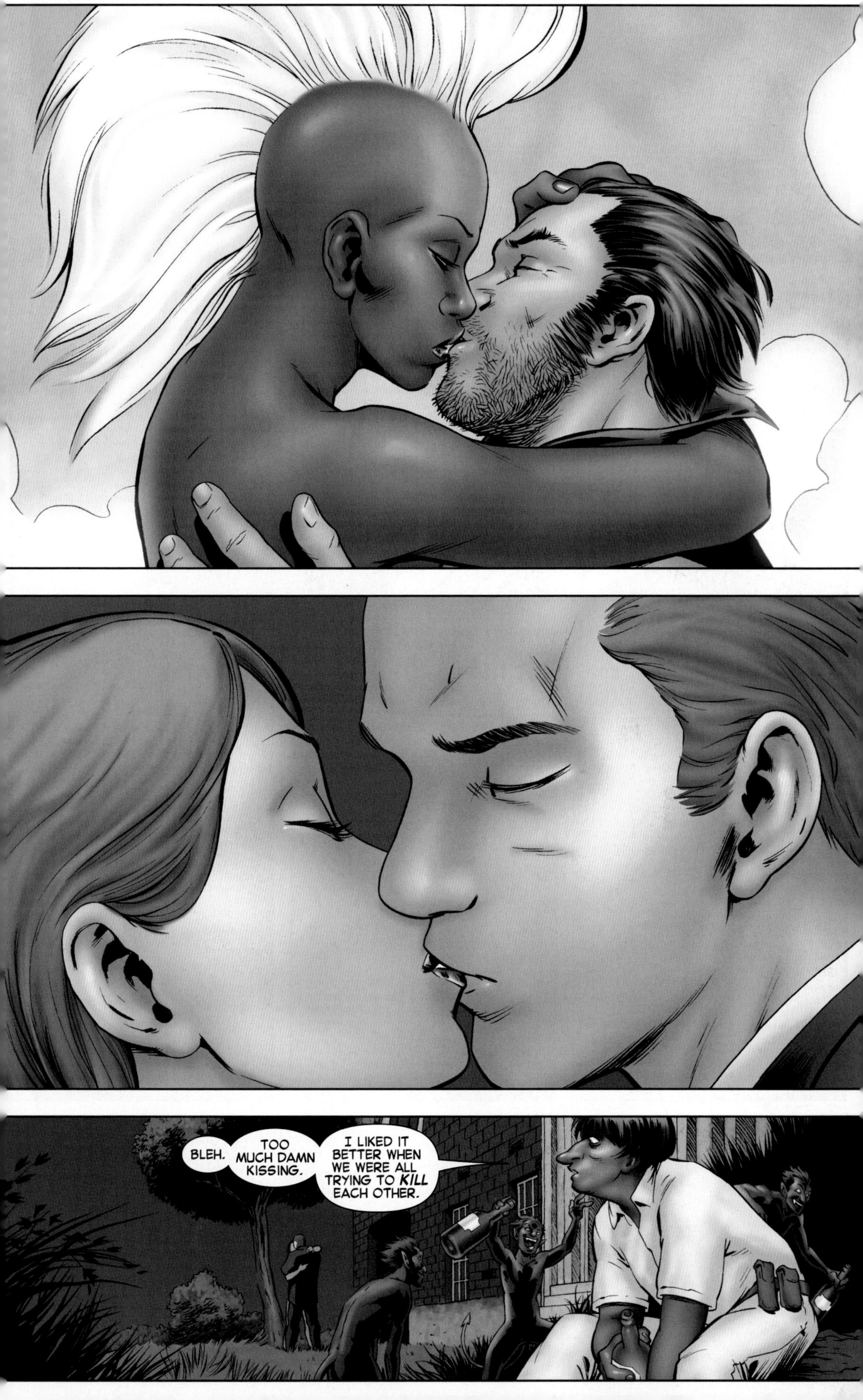
BLEH.
TOO MUCH DAMN KISSING.
I LIKED IT BETTER WHEN WE WERE ALL TRYING TO KILL EACH OTHER.

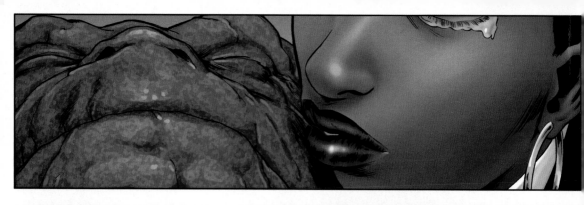

I MISS YOU, BROO. THIS PLACE JUST ISN'T THE SAME WITHOUT YOU.

PLEASE, COME BACK.

COME BACK AND MAKE IT ALL *FUN* AGAIN.

RRRR--?

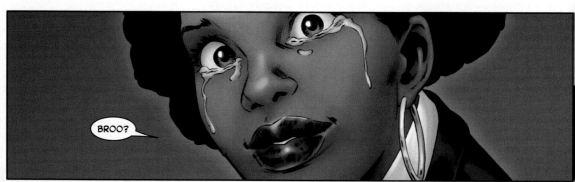

BROO?

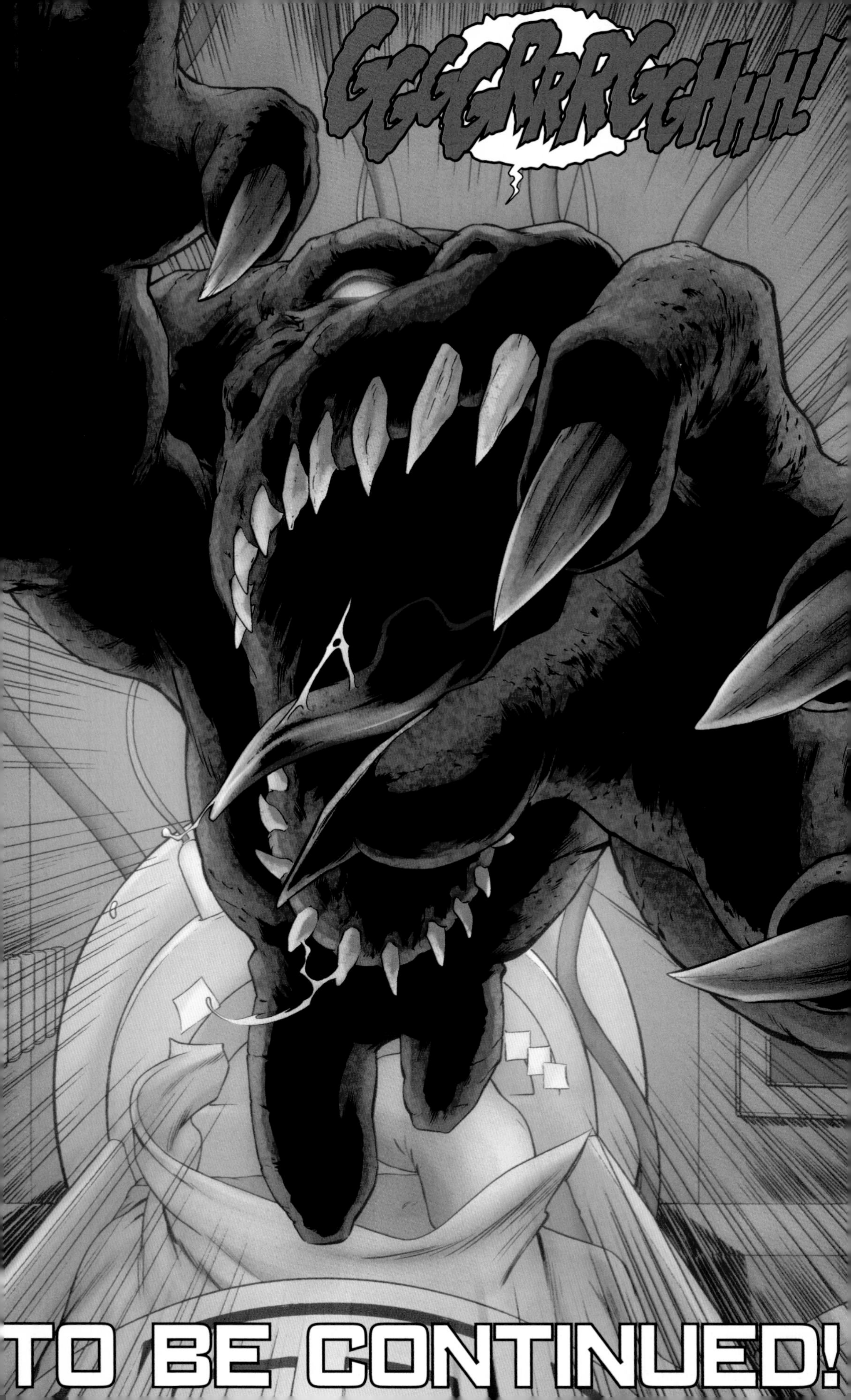
GGGRRRGGHHH!
TO BE CONTINUED!

ISSUE #19 LETTERS COLUMN

Hello there! It's great to be getting back to what passes for normal around here. I'm Headmistress Kitty Pryde and I've got the reins of the mailbag once more! First, the last response page wasn't an official Jean Grey School publication. Our state of the art systems (and I should know, I'm the certified computer genius who set them up) got hacked (see last parenthetical and imagine how peeved I am), but new security measures are in place that should stymie any troublemakers out there. Long story short, school is back in session, classes are on schedule and we're back to answering your letters.

Dear Aaron, Allred and Allred,

I just finished reading issue 17. My 3 year old son was looking at it as I read and commented on Doop: "Look at the big green pickle! He is an angry pickle! With a big mouth!".

I'm not sure what else I could possibly add except to say that it was a great issue... and that I hope Doop isn't insulted about the pickle comment.

Brad Reid
Surrey, British Columbia, Canada

Wait, a letter about Doop? All that guy does is sleep and fart and speak his ridiculous language. If someone can explain to me why he's here (Headmaster Logan refuses) I'd really appreciate it. I mean, I'm only the actual boss around here, right?

Dear X-People,

I can't help but write in and thank you for having Doop return to save Mutantkind. Want to stop the aftermath of the Avengers vs X-Men? Just put Doop in front of Scott Summers and Captain America. Doop will put those two posers in their places. I want a pet Doop to keep those dang stinkbugs outta my apartment!

Why is Kade Kilgore so intent on damaging the school? Doesn't he have anything better to do? Like most kids his age, he should be listening to Justin Bieber and ordering kids' meals. Personally, I think Toad and Doop could disarm him and stop this madness! Toad should dangle the dirty end of the mop on people's faces and call it "The Mop Treatment." Think about it, because that would rule.

Daniel Bellay
Fairmont WV

ANOTHER Doop letter? First of all, the only thing that green potato has ever saved is an entire collection of commemorative plates of the British Royal Family (that he shows off WAY too much). Second of all, you do not want a pet Doop. Get a dog, you'll enjoy picking up after him a lot more. As for Kade Kilgore, we'll think about the mop treatment, but first we have to find the little war-mongering brat.

Dear Jean Grey School,

I think I may be a telepath, and last time I was in New York, I was begging my family to take me to see the school! I originally was going to side with Cyclops, but he is now evil and wrong, and you are right. Keep it up, and I'll buy some sentinels to donate to a dump (which is where they belong). You rock!

Till I'm on Cerebra,
JJ Gluckman

Thanks for the letter, JJ. Next time you're in the area we can try to arrange a school visit and maybe you can shadow one of the students. I hate to use the "E" word about friends, so let's just stick to "misguided" to describe Scott Summers.

Dear X-Team and dear Faculty Members!

I would like to thank you for the most clever, funny, interesting comics I've read in a long time! WATX is magical for so many reasons - every character has his own unique personality and spirit, each bit of storytelling swallows the reader whole (and I'm not even looking at you, Krakoa!) and the art is simply stunning. And sometimes I laughed so hard I choked on my afternoon coffee. Please keep up the good work, you are literally making my life better! As for the parts I love the best:

The art, oh the art! There are no words! Every character breathes and lives... is that a good way to explain how much the art works for me?

I can't get enough of the inner workings of the school! Tell us more of how the school functions and its routine. So cool! I envy those kids!

The storytelling is filled with love of the characters. You give them voices and styles that are their own. So many of great characters become wallpaper nowadays, but not yours, dear team! Your Beast is just the somewhat eccentric gentleman he should be, your Kitty is strong, your Wolverine is grumpy but lovable. And don't make me start on Quentin! Wait a sec... Could you invite Emma Frost and make her joke around with Beast? This is a bromance, I swear to God.

The chemistry between the X-Men is so intriguing and lovely! I'm looking forward to the subtle romance between Kitty and Bobby - it's like I can feel the butterflies in the stomach, too. And please make Toad happy! You made him so lovable. Husk is such a nice person.

There is only one thing that would, for me personally, make WATX even more astonishing. If you could go into the stories of the students a little more, not just of the events that are happening! They are, after all, what the whole thing is about. I'd love to see X-23 join and rebuild her "relationship" with Hellion. Or Mercury, or Dust, just all of the old Academy team, I suppose. You've told so much already, and I'm still greedy for some good stories of the X-Kids.

Keep being amazing!
Katja S.

Fellow Katja! Sure, my "Katya" is spelled differently, but what the hey...I'm going to ignore your request to bring Emma Frost here. I'd be happy never to see her (surgically altered) face again. We went looking for X-23, but she disappeared from the Avengers Academy. It's very strange. Hope she's okay.

Dear Jean Grey School,

Everyone is referring to mutants as their own species, but a species is a group of organisms capable of producing fertile offspring. This would make humans and mutants the same species. If they were subspecies (which they aren't, since they aren't geographically separated), they would be Homo sapiens sapiens and Homo sapiens superior. In Namor's case, he would be a hybrid between the two subspecies Homo mermanus and Homo sapiens/superior, since Atlanteans are geographically separated from humans/mutants. I'm sure Beast is aware of these issues. Also, how does Magneto stop lead bullets, since only iron, cobalt, and nickel respond to magnetism?

Ben
Iowa City, IA

Look, Beast isn't the only brain here. First, mutant genetics are a whole other ball of wax. I had all these same questions about species and subspecies when I first came to the school and think my mutant biology classes are what led me to specialize in physics. As for Magneto, his powers have caused many many many scientists (including me) to scratch their heads. I wrote a paper back when I was at the Xavier school with several theories on how, exactly, Magneto's powers work (like when he freezes you in place and people say it's because of iron in blood which doesn't make scientific sense, trust me), but Professor X got kidnapped or something before he could properly grade it. Whoever was sitting in for him just gave me an "A" to shut me up, I think.

Dear Staff Member of the Month:

Thanks for using Avengers vs. X-Men to give Rachel Summers her richly deserved spotlight. I commented awhile back I found this book to be leaning toward its male cast, so it's nice to see some balance with story focusing in on Rachel. Here she is, thinking for herself, thinking hard about her future getting ever closer, and standing up to the newly almighty Cyclops himself. Heck, even Captain America was remembering what a major player she was in the Marvel Universe, just as she was in the comics of the late 1980's and early 1990's. I appreciated her perspective on having possessed the Phoenix Force...it's going to be interesting to see how/if this faculty is going to be able to come back together. Wolverine's stabbed Rachel before, and this was a harsh clash. Any thoughts toward the old theory that he's her real father?

Anyway, I'm hoping this book will keep powering through with this creative team, and get a little more offbeat once this AvX thing passes. You've done a great job so far: I feel like this issue really gave us clashes where the characters remembered and acted on the history they share. =)

Keep up the great work!
Ben Ebert
San Francisco, CA

Thanks for the thoughtful letter, Ben. First, Rach is the best and I can't tell you how happy I am to have her around. As for whether Wolverine is her father, this is the first I've heard of that theory. I never say never (if you know anything about the revelations that have come to light even just in my time with the X-Men) but I'd certainly be surprised. That's all the time I have, school to run and all. Thanks to everyone who wrote in and we'll see you soon!

SHARK GIRL DESIGNS BY STEVE SANDERS

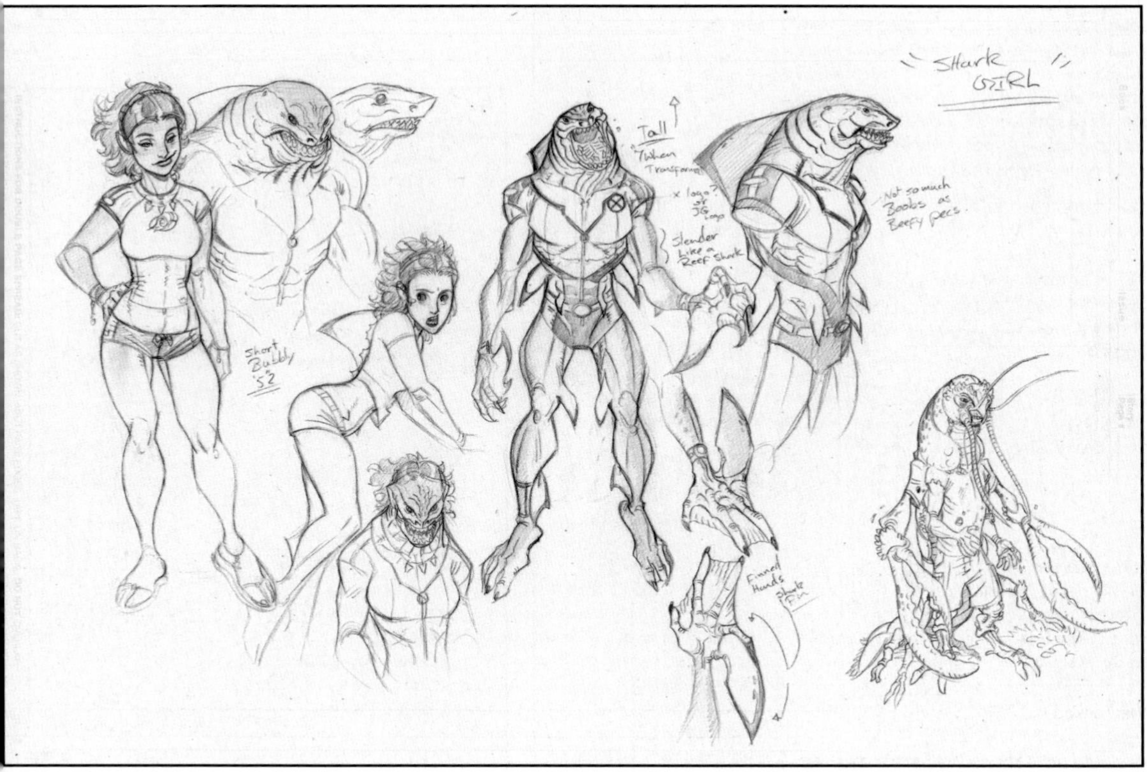

Shark GIRL
Short Bubbly 5'2"
Tall
When Transformed
x logo? or JG logo
Slender Like a Reef Shark
Not so much Boobs as Beefy pecs.
Finned Hands
Shark Fin

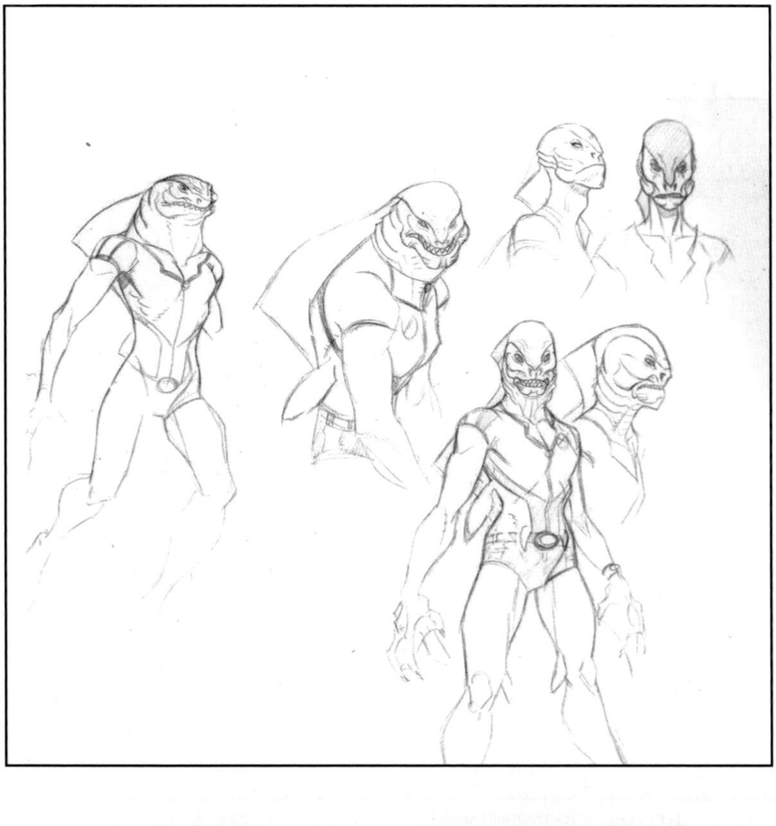

COVER SKETCHES BY NICK BRADSHAW

#19

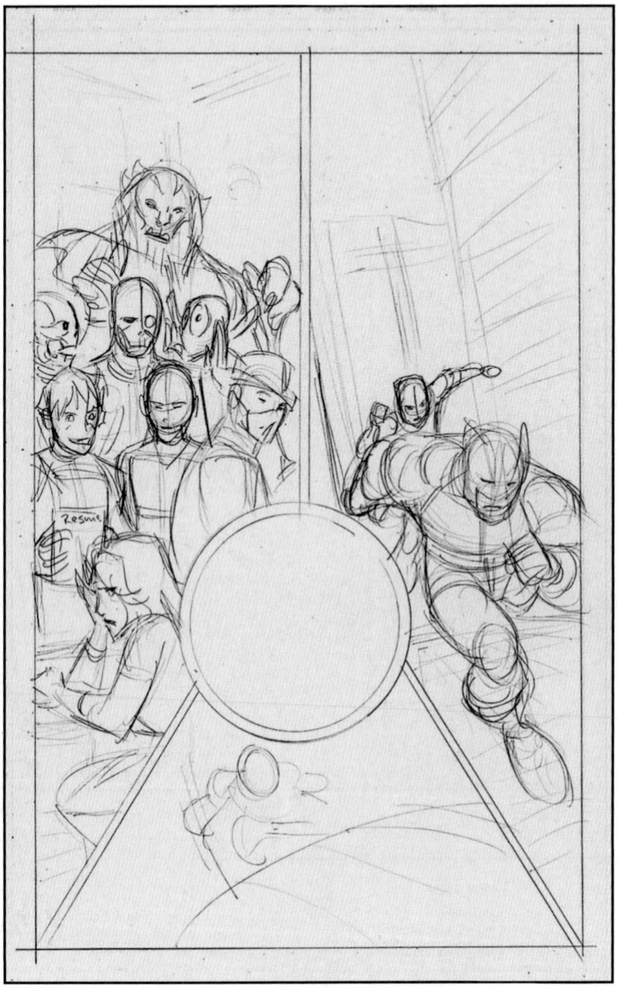
Resume

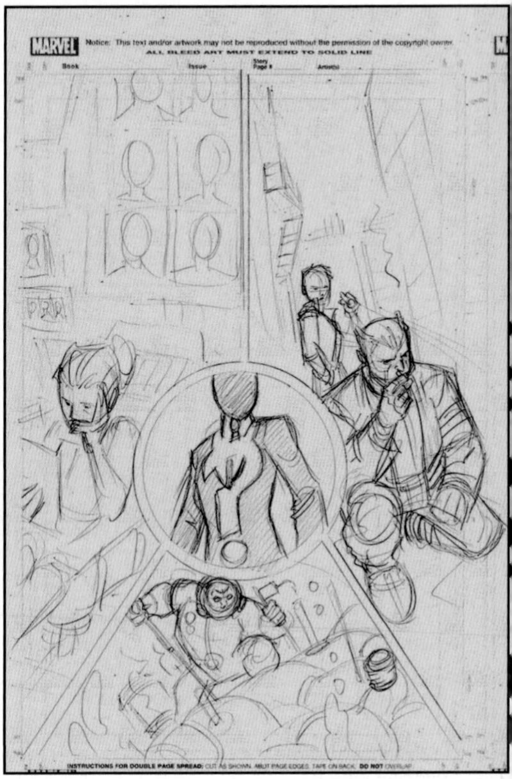
MARVEL
Notice: This text and/or artwork may not be reproduced without the permission of the copyright owner.
ALL BLEED ART MUST EXTEND TO SOLID LINE
Book
Issue
Story Page #
Artist(s)
INSTRUCTIONS FOR DOUBLE PAGE SPREAD: CUT AS SHOWN. ABUT PAGE EDGES. TAPE ON BACK. DO NOT OVERLAP

#20

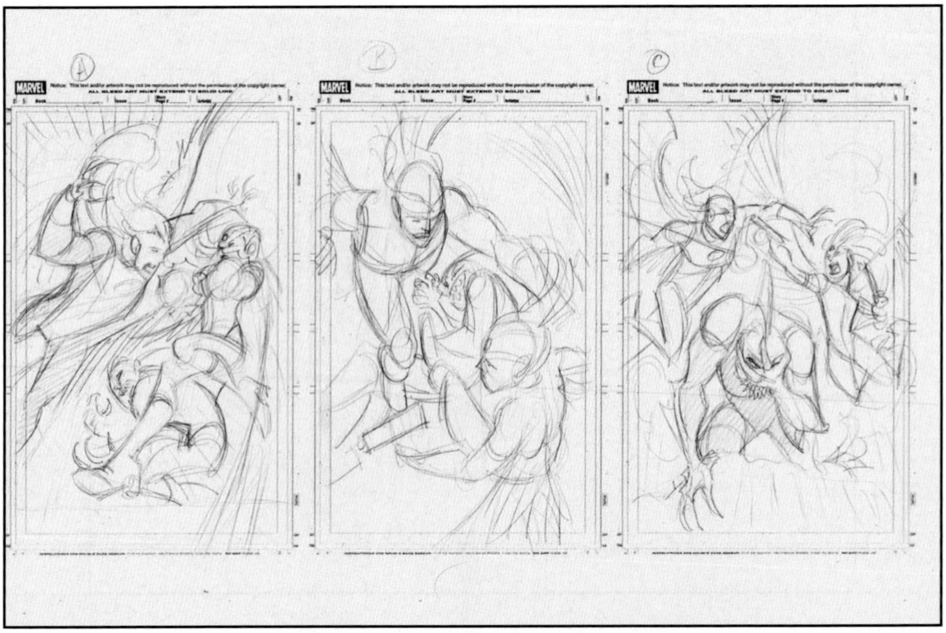
A
B
C

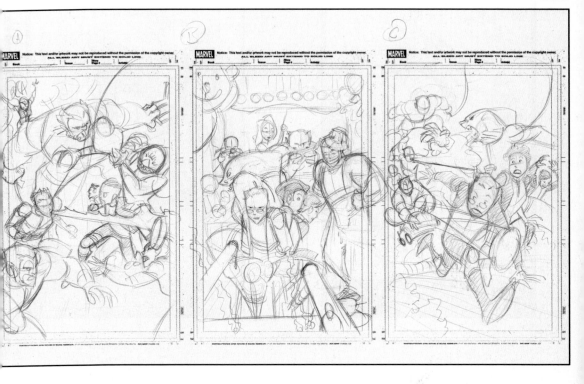

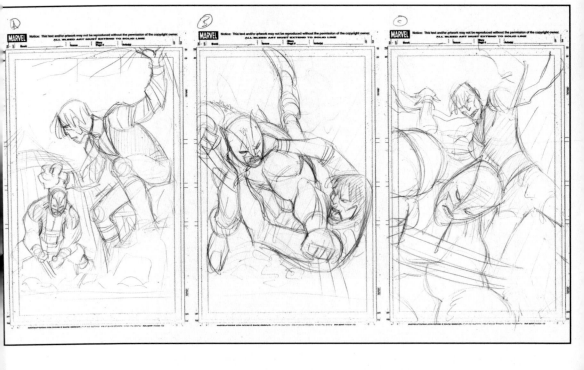

COVER SKETCHES BY RAMÓN PÉREZ

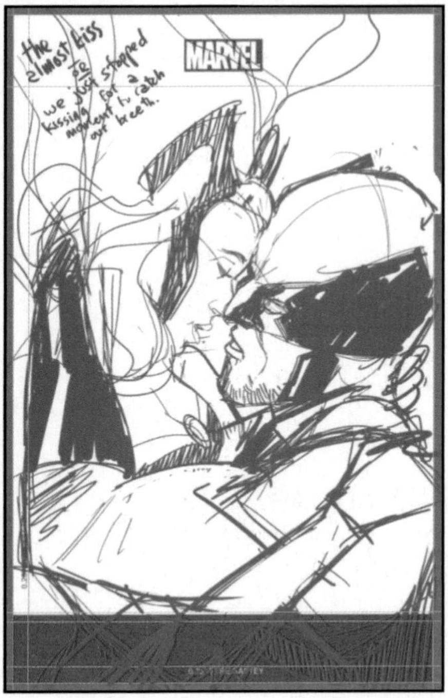
MARVEL
the almost kiss
or
we just stopped kissing for a moment to catch our breath.
0.25" TYPE SAFTEY

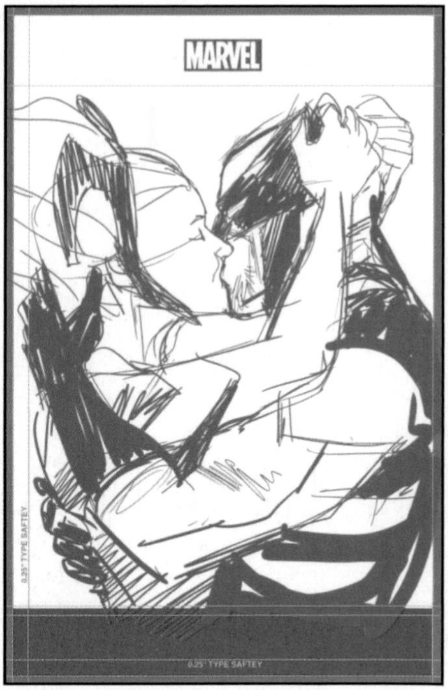
MARVEL
0.25" TYPE SAFTEY
0.25" TYPE SAFTEY

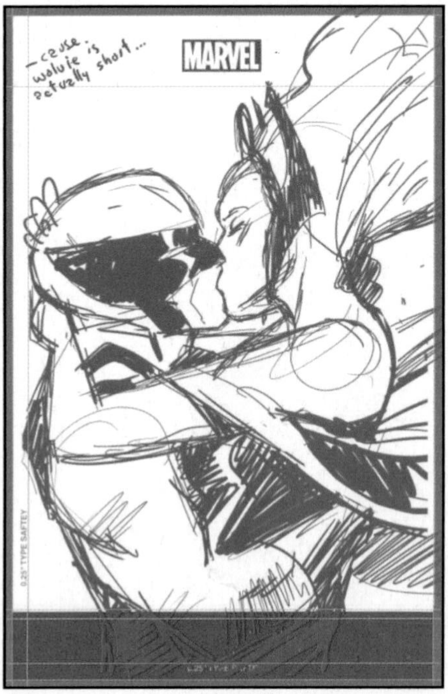
MARVEL
–cause wolvie is actually short...
0.25" TYPE SAFTEY